REVOLVER

●

REVOLVER

HOW THE BEATLES REIMAGINED
ROCK 'N' ROLL

ROBERT RODRIGUEZ

Backbeat
Books

AN IMPRINT OF HAL LEONARD CORPORATION

Published in 2012 by Backbeat Books
An Imprint of Hal Leonard Corporation
7777 West Bluemound Road
Milwaukee, WI 53213

Trade Book Division Editorial Offices
33 Plymouth Street, Montclair, NJ 07042

All images from the author's collection, except as follows: *Beatles '66* songbook courtesy of Garry Day; "Got to Get You into My Life" sheet music courtesy of Pete Nash from the British Beatles Fan Club; *Teen Life* cover courtesy of Guy Barbier. Thanks also to Robert Brundish and to Noah Fleischer / Heritage Auctions.

Every reasonable effort has been made to contact copyright holders and secure permissions. Omissions can be remedied in future editions.

Printed in United State of America

Book design by Michael Kellner

Library of Congress Cataloging-in-Publication Data
Rodriguez, Robert, 1961-
  Revolver : how the Beatles reimagined rock 'n' roll / Robert Rodriguez.
      p. cm.
  Includes bibliographical references and index.
  ISBN 978-1-61713-009-0
  1. Beatles. Revolver. 2. Beatles. 3. Rock music--1961-1970--History and criticism. I. Title.
  ML421.B4R64 2012
  782.42166092'2--dc23
                                    2011047486

www.backbeatbooks.com

To Klaus, who got it right . . .

CONTENTS

including and Eleanor Rigby

LET ME TELL YOU HOW IT WILL BE: A BRIEF INTRODUCTION

"Did you ever dream about a place you never really recall being to before?
A place that maybe only exists in your imagination? Some place far away,
half-remembered when you wake up. When you were there, though, you knew
the language, you knew your way around. That was the '60s. [Pause.] No,
it wasn't that either. It was just '66 and early '67. That's all it was."

—"Terry Valentine" (Peter Fonda) in *The Limey*, 1999

For too many years, assessments of the Beatles' recorded output have routinely placed their 1967 release, *Sgt. Pepper's Lonely Hearts Club Band*, atop the heap. The acclaim it received upon its arrival has echoed onward through the years as critics and a large segment of the fan population view it as the group's finest effort, an album that influenced everything that followed and set the standard against which all other acts would be measured.

Until perhaps the last decade or so, this was a common consensus. Other albums produced by the group might be better loved (*Abbey Road* comes to mind) or may have stirred more powerful feelings of personal nostalgia (Capitol's *Meet the Beatles!* was life-changing for the generation coming of age when it was new), while certain Beatles LPs ended up more respected than revered (e.g., 1968's sprawling "White Album" was seen by some as unfocused and self-indulgent in places: ". . . number nine, number nine . . ."). Yet it was *Sgt. Pepper* that seemed to live at the apex of the Beatles' creativity. Everything about it projected Importance, from its grandiose cover artwork to its apocalyptic ending chord—no rock album had ever seemed so much bigger than the sum of its tracks.

Currently, a dark horse within the Beatles' oeuvre has challenged—and in many instances, bested—that album for supremacy in lists assessing the group's finest work. Unlike *Sgt. Pepper*, the 1966 release of *Revolver* wasn't a major media event. There was no speculative buildup or public wondering about what the Beatles were about to unleash. Further, its issue came under a cloud: just as the band were preparing to undertake what became their final tour, a scandal prompting bannings and bonfires swept America, dwarfing their stunning achievement.

Knowledgeable fans noted too that what emerged in the U.S. was not even representative of the group's artistic intent, being an eleven-track condensation of what the rest of the world was getting to hear. (Three John Lennon compositions—"I'm Only Sleeping," "And Your Bird Can Sing," and "Doctor Robert"— were withheld from U.S. editions of *Revolver* while the sessions were in progress, and used as padding on an earlier stateside release to feed the insatiable demand for new product by Capitol, their American label.) Not only was the album overshadowed by collateral concerns, but—as presented in the world's biggest market—it didn't even represent fulfillment of the group's vision.

Revolver is the Beatles' artistic high-water mark. For a start, unlike *Pepper*, it was a true group collaboration. Their work would increasingly take on the appearance of a musical co-op, with three members supporting the fourth member's individual pursuits; but with *Revolver*, the music bears all the evidence of the group as a whole being fully vested in creating Beatle music.

For the first time, studio technology was deliberately incorporated into the conception of the recordings they made, rather than used merely as a tool to capture performances. Suddenly, the possibilities of what a rock band could aspire to create were not limited by what they were expected to reproduce onstage. Pushing the studio's technological limits, they now sought to capture sounds previously unheard and in their heads, conscious of their place in rock's hierarchy and driven by the need to stay ahead of the competition. With this, the concept of the "recording artist" was born.

Only an act on their level of success could demand—and get—almost unlimited studio time to pursue their artistic agenda. Enabling them were longtime producer George Martin and engineer Geoff Emerick, visionaries equal to the task of looking past what had been done and seeing what could be, fulfilling the Beatles' collective ambitions and inspiring them to reach for even greater heights. Their talents were as key to *Revolver*'s success as were the Beatles' own, resulting in a working relationship unique within their peer group.

Nineteen sixty-six was a year that saw major change in rock music as the dichotomy between pursuing chart success and aspiring to create something new forced many acts to choose sides. While the Beatles were able to stride both paths, seemingly with ease, others weren't so lucky. Perhaps the Beatles' closest artistic rival during this period, Brian Wilson of the Beach Boys, attempted to do both; but when *Pet Sounds*, his crowning achievement, failed to engage the masses, he was pressured by his bandmates and his label to abandon the pursuit of perfection and higher ideals, resulting in one of rock's most notorious breakdowns.

Sgt. Pepper, in contrast to its predecessor, is inextricably tied to its time: a pleasant period piece but a period piece nonetheless; not so *Revolver*, an album crackling with potent immediacy. It's been said that it sparked subgenres with every track, anticipating electronica ("Tomorrow Never Knows"); punk (the abrasive sneer of "Taxman"); Baroque rock ("For No One"); and world music ("Love You To"), among other subgroups—and all within the space of fourteen tracks. Its very eclecticism may have worked against it in the short run, making it difficult to pigeonhole, but today is seen by many as its most appealing quality.

The depth of the songcraft evident on *Revolver* is hard to better. While John and George broadened their horizons, addressing such subjects as politics, pill pushers, and the illusory nature of the material world, Paul reached the top of *his* game, offering up sharply etched portraits of romantic breakdowns and societal isolation, balanced with sunny optimism. One thing the Beatles didn't do on this album was shy away from dark themes. In contrast, much of *Sgt. Pepper* seems slight or self-indulgent now. Only the magnificent "A Day in the Life" marked genuine forward movement from *Revolver*'s achievements.

The Beatles are the most scrutinized and overanalyzed band

in rock history. It may be hard at this distance to grasp the innovation that marked their every release, so far removed from context is their music in the download era; but if seen alongside the work of other hit-makers of the day, one can appreciate the timelessness of their achievements all the better. The Beatles weren't the only rock group driven to advance their art in 1966—they were just the most successful at it.

One must recognize that they were far from alone in ambition. Perhaps one of the most satisfying aspects of researching this book was recognizing how many of their contemporaries shared a virtual creativity pool with the Beatles, swapping ideas, drawing inspiration, and challenging each other in (mostly) friendly rivalry. It's impossible to quantify what work the Beach Boys, the Rolling Stones, the Byrds, and even Bob Dylan might have created but not for the inescapable X factor that working alongside the Beatles meant. But it was a two-way street, and one can only guess what the Beatles would have sounded like without having such a rich environment from which to draw.

Reverberations of *Revolver*'s diversity and depth have only expanded since 1966. Not many acts attempt the feat of a holistic "concept" album à la *Pepper* these days; and those that do proceed at their own peril—but the model that *Revolver* set for effectively creating an eclectic collection of diverse songs lives on.

It is not my mission to tell people what should be their favorite Beatle album. Instead, I want to show how *Revolver* was their real game-changer—the work that signaled their intention of abandoning the lucrative live-performance side of their career in favor of creating soundscapes without limitations. *Revolver: How the Beatles Reimagined Rock 'n' Roll* tells the story of what they did, and how they did it.

—ROBERT RODRIGUEZ
Autumn 2011

PART I

●

SPINNING THE CHAMBER

Vox: it's what's happening

One of Brian Epstein's canniest moves was inking a deal with Vox in 1963. In exchange for the Beatles using Vox exclusively on stage, the musical-equipment company was allowed to use their image—a great deal for both parties.

1

AND THE BAND BEGINS TO PLAY: BEATLES '66

"What's going to come out of the next recording sessions?"
"Literally anything. Electronic music, jokes . . . one thing's for sure:
the next LP is going to be very different."

—JOHN LENNON, 1966

hough they did not yet know it, as the Beatles stepped out before some 10,000 screaming fans on that spring Sunday evening, it would be the last time that they would play before a paying audience in Great Britain. The date was May 1, 1966; the event was the *New Musical Express* Annual Poll-Winners All-Star Concert, held as always at London's Empire Pool, Wembley. The legions that had been waiting to see them through nearly twenty other acts didn't know it either, but as they witnessed the largely inaudible spectacle before them, an era was ending. The Beatles' participation in this annual event had become practically routine since 1963, but with this, their fourth appearance, they were happy to dispense with the ceremony once and for all.

Clad in black, and with John sporting dark glasses throughout, the Beatles offered an anticlimactic finish to this particular tradition. They were already agitated before taking the stage, locked in a battle against their comrades, the Rolling Stones, over who would close the show. At issue was who would appear last; though the set-enders would garner all the prestige as Britain's top rock act, they would also miss out on the television broadcast due to unresolved issues with the BBC. Therefore, the *second*-to-last act would get the coveted TV exposure.

This was what Brian Epstein and Andrew Loog Oldham (the

NEW MUSICAL EXPRESS POLL-WINNERS PROGRAMME

ALPHABETICAL ORDER OF ARTISTS TAKING PART IN THIS CONCERT

BEATLES
John Lennon, Paul McCartney, George Harrison, Ringo Starr

SPENCER DAVIS GROUP
Spencer Davis, Stevie Winwood, Muff Winwood, Pete York

DAVE DEE, DOZY, BEAKY, MICK AND TICH
Dave Dee, Trevor Davis, John Dymond, Mick Wilson, Ian Amey

FORTUNES
Rod Allen, Dave Carr, Glen Dale, Andy Brown, Barry Pritchard

HERMAN'S HERMITS
Herman, Karl Green, Keith Hopwood, Lek Leckenby, Barry Whitwam

ROY ORBISON
Backed by the Barry Booth Orchestra

OVERLANDERS
Terry Widlake, Paul Arnold, Laurie Mason, David Walsh, Peter Bartholomew

ALAN PRICE SET
Alan Price, John Walters, Boots Slade, Clive Burrows, Steve Gregory, Roy Mills

CLIFF RICHARD
Accompanied by The Shadows

ROLLING STONES
Brian Jones, Mick Jagger, Keith Richard, Charlie Watts, Bill Wyman

SEEKERS
Judith Durham, Keith Potger, Bruce Woodley, Athol Guy

SHADOWS
Brian Bennett, Hank Marvin, John Rostill, Bruce Welch

SMALL FACES
Steve Marriott, Kenny Jones, Ronnie "Plonk" Lane, Ian MacLagan

SOUNDS INCORPORATED
Griff West, Barrie Cameron, John St. John, Alan Holmes, Wes Hunter, Tony Newman

DUSTY SPRINGFIELD
(with her backing group, The Echoes)

CRISPIAN ST. PETERS

WALKER BROTHERS
Gary Leeds, John Maus, Scott Engel

WHO
John Entwistle, Keith Moon, Roger Daltrey, Pete Townshend

YARDBIRDS
Paul Samwell-Smith, Chris Dreja, Keith Relf, Jim McCarty, Jeff Beck

THE ARTISTS WILL BE INTRODUCED BY

PETER MURRAY

JIMMY SAVILE

The 1966 NME *Poll-Winners concert was probably the high-water mark of this annual event. The following year saw Cream, the Beach Boys, the Small Faces, the Move, and Cat Stevens—but no Stones or Yardbirds.*

Stones' manager and Epstein's former employee) were battling over. Apparently both bands were secure enough in their status to take a pass on the honor of closing; but in the end, the Stones prevailed and went on *first.* As it happened, neither band's set was filmed—which is probably for the better. By now viewing such occasions as a chore, the Beatles phoned in their performance, even opening with the same 1964 hit—"I Feel Fine"—that they'd played at the same event a year earlier. To those in attendance the Beatles could do no wrong, but on this evening they seemed under-rehearsed, and looked as if they didn't want to be there.

By then the Beatles were one month into crafting *Revolver,* the follow-up to *Rubber Soul*—which, upon its December 1965 release, had been seen as a major breakthrough beyond the Merseybeat sounds of their previous five LPs. Their ambitions to move beyond their peers were manifest, as Paul's "Yesterday" from the *Help!* album had proved in late summer. Issued as a single in the

U.S., the string-laden ballad went to number one, proving that their fan base was willing to accept something new and different from the Beatles.

The song's arrangement, layering a classical string quartet atop Paul's solo acoustic guitar, had been the inspiration of their producer, George Martin, and not the Beatles themselves. But as their artistry began to bloom in late 1965 and their innate ambition to stay ahead of the competition asserted itself, *Rubber Soul* emerged as a triumph that hinted at grander ambitions, perhaps ones that the existing rock paradigm could not contain. The album contained some of the most transcendent Lennon–McCartney originals yet: John's "Norwegian Wood," "Girl," and "In My Life" being chief among them. Paul's way with a hook was as strong as ever, evidenced by "Drive My Car" and "You Won't See Me." A tune originally conceived during their Liverpool days as a send-up of French art students was dusted off and reinvented as "Michelle," stirring dozens of covers as well as a Grammy Award for Song of the Year. And George Harrison too kept pace, weighing in with a pair of his most sophisticated offerings yet. One, the ambiguous "If I Needed Someone," would provide the Hollies with their next single. In short, the Beatles were on a roll.

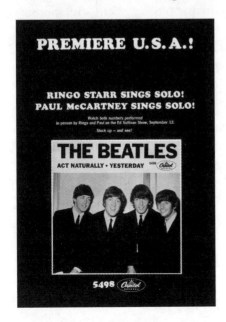

It must have struck the group as a complete waste of time to disrupt their focus as they worked on an album that already showed the promise of eclipsing even *Rubber Soul* just to perform a mini-set at Wembley before a crowd determined not to listen. Ostensibly showcasing recent fan favorites, the Beatles plowed

Two tracks originally appearing on U.K. editions of the **Help!** *album saw issue in the states as a single in September 1965, featuring the two most popular Beatles on vocals.*

through "I Feel Fine"; a pair of *Rubber Soul* cuts, "Nowhere Man" and "If I Needed Someone" (the only Harrison composition the Beatles would ever perform live); the A-side of their most recent single, "Day Tripper"; and "I'm Down," the Little Richard retread that had replaced "Long Tall Sally" as set closer in 1965.

Their new single, "Paperback Writer" / "Rain," was already in the can and would drop in the U.K. in six weeks. To contemporary readers, it must seem unfathomable that the Beatles would squander the opportunity of such a high-profile gig to preview their next release. Their approach to the *NME* Poll-Winners gig serves as a perfect illustration of the schizophrenic nature that their career path had taken on. Conventional wisdom of the day held that a pop act could not survive purely as a recording entity; live appearances were essential to sustain one's career, not only as a means to stay fresh in the public's mind within a very competitive business, but also for monetary reasons.

The deal that the Beatles signed with EMI in 1962 was particularly punitive, paying one cent per single sold (which was then split four ways) and *half that* on overseas sales, which was the bulk of their business. (Album sales paid them two shillings per, which again was split four ways.) Lennon–McCartney's deal with Dick James Music was equally draconian, paying them the *minimum* of the time, fifty percent, which was then split 20-20 between John and Paul, with ten percent to Brian. Dick James received the other fifty percent.

Not until January 1967 did the group re-sign with EMI, agreeing to a nine-year deal that gave them a substantial raise; if not what they deserved, it was at least more in line with fairness than existed previously. They received a $2 million signing bonus, plus a royalty increase to ten percent. (Most importantly to the group, the contract stipulated that Capitol was no longer allowed to reshape their albums.)

But until them, the bulk of the Beatles' income had been derived from live appearances. On the high end of things, their famed appearance at Shea Stadium in August 1965 gave them a $160,000 payday (almost $1 million today); Chicago's White Sox Park gig paid nearly as much, $155,000, while other dates paid in the $80–90,000 range. Sweetening the deal was the fact that they did not pay U.S. tax on their earnings, only U.K. tax, which, though high, at least made their typical thirty-minute-maximum sets worth the effort. The Beatles thus viewed touring as a necessary evil, though one that stirred increasing disenchantment as time went on.

By the time the Beatles took the stage at Wembley, they'd already completed or started work on "I'm Only Sleeping," "Got to Get You into My Life," "Love You To," "Doctor Robert," "Taxman," "And Your Bird Can Sing," "Eleanor Rigby," and—with the greatest leap into the future the band had yet undertaken—"Tomorrow Never Knows." Yet here they were, cranking out a set not too far advanced from what they'd been playing at the Cavern only three years prior. The situation demonstrated the dichotomy between fulfilling duties out of financial need (and fan demand), and pursuing their artistic destiny in the studio, where their creative heart lie. As far as they were concerned, the latter course was the way of the future.

How *Revolver* came together was a matter of circumstance as much as design. Nineteen sixty-six was originally mapped out to be an echo of the preceding two years: a film, a soundtrack album, tour dates, another album. But the plan was thrown into disarray when they found they could not agree on a script for their third film, on which they were due to begin work in April. Brian Epstein had blocked out three months to accommodate a shooting schedule that did not materialize; once it became evident that plans would be postponed, the group suddenly found themselves with some unexpected downtime for the first period since Epstein had entered their lives.

In February 1965, it had been announced in *NME* that the Beatles had selected *A Talent for Loving*, written by Richard Condon (*The Manchurian Candidate*), to be the basis of their third collaboration with producer Walter Shenson and director Dick Lester. A Western satire—à la *Cat Ballou*—it would have, for the first time, given the four the opportunity to play actual characters, and not versions of themselves. But without a decent script (as well as enough fittingly themed songs to fill up the soundtrack), it was announced in *Billboard* in December that the launch had been scrubbed. (It eventually emerged in 1969, directed by Richard Quine and starring Richard Widmark and Cesar Romero.) This unplanned bounty of free time proved to be a creative catalyst. In the meantime, Brian scrambled to put together a tour to fill the unexpected opening in their schedule.

The year had begun with the group tying up some loose ends: a film of their 1965 Shea Stadium concert was being prepared for television broadcast (in America, the film would not be televised until January 1967, just as a very different group was at work crafting *Sgt. Pepper*). Before it could be completed, though, some audio shortcomings had to be patched up. On January 5, the Beatles duly arrived at London's CTS Studio to lay down retakes of some of their set; most of the issues centered on a complete lack of bottom end or inaudible drums on the recording.

A detailed account of the session exists in a letter written by the project's overseer, production manager M. Clay Adams, to his teenage son. Adams was a seasoned professional with many years in the business, notably on the 1950s *Victory at Sea* series, but also *Sgt. Bilko*, and, most importantly, *The Ed Sullivan Show*. It was Sullivan's production company that was producing the film (in collaboration with NEMS Enterprises, Brian Epstein's company), hence Adams's involvement. His son Michael was a certifiable Beatlemaniac, and had been from the beginning. Adams's work accorded him the privilege of proximity, and he made the most of it, making sure that he got his son a ticket not only for the Beatles' 1964 *Sullivan Show* debut, but even access to their dress rehearsal as well.

The elder Adams's account offers a rare glimpse from a non-insider into the group's work habits and individual personalities. Of the four Beatles, it was Paul that arrived first. Granted, he lived the closest, but he also seemed keen on making the most of the time, quickly knocking out all the songs that he alone was needed on ("I'm Down," "Dizzy Miss Lizzie," "Can't Buy Me Love," and "Baby's in Black"). Describing him as "full of fun," Adams also opined that Paul was the most inherently musical, sitting down at the piano between takes and compulsively pounding out improvised melodies.

The others arrived at 10:30—exactly one hour late—having carpooled together. This didn't seem to concern them, nor did the fact that their guitars hadn't yet arrived. Ringo was sporting a full beard, glasses, and a Civil War–type cap, while John was prepared to give Adams a hard time. Reminding John that, without the instruments, there'd be no point in being there, Adams was told, "Well, at least they didn't get here all smashed. They wouldn't be any good to us if they arrived smashed, would they, now?" The producer quickly realized that he was being subjected to the Beatles' brand of Scouse humor, and with that, the ice was broken.

Once their gear showed up, the group proved themselves to be quick and disciplined performers, listening attentively to the

directions issued by George Martin and following them to the letter. Several songs were tweaked in part only, or "fortified," as Adams phrased it. The word seemed to amuse Paul, who kept asking after each take, "How are we doing, Clay—did we fortify that one okay?" "Ticket to Ride" and "Help!" were re-cut in their entirety. Running short on time, they elected to substitute the live Hollywood Bowl recording of "Twist and Shout" for the Shea Stadium one, while Ringo's "Act Naturally" was repaired by simply dropping in the studio recording wholesale.

Adams noted the musical telepathy between the four Beatles. If John or Paul began trying out a musical idea, the rest of the group would quickly fall in, "no matter how complex the arrangement." There was also a lot of instrument swapping going on, with George demonstrating some drum patterns behind Ringo's kit, while the latter doodled around on guitar or piano. Also evident was their high regard for George Martin, whom Adams described as "thoughtful, cooperative, and very 'giving' of himself." Before Adams returned to New York, Martin graciously gifted him a copy of the U.K. edition of *Rubber Soul,* plus *Beatles for Sale* and a pile of British musical magazines to give to his son.

Whatever regard they'd once had for the material they were trotting out on tour had since been diminished by the passage of time and the freshness of what they now aspired to create. John told *Melody Maker,* "I can't stand listening to most of our early stuff . . . songs like 'Eight Days A Week' and 'She Loves You' sound like big drags to me now." If the necessity of revisiting their back catalog for their stage set wasn't enough to weary him, the stifling effects of fame more than made up for it.

In the May 1966 issue of *Flip,* a youth-oriented journal that contained surprisingly insightful interviews, John confided, "If I thought I'd [have] to go through the rest of my life being pointed and stared at, I'd give up the Beatles now. It's only the thought that one day it will all come to an end which keeps me going." Remarks like this were one element that prompted a continual cycle of rumors throughout the year that the group was breaking up. Seen within a wider context, what they really revealed was a restlessness within John that somehow, all the fame, adulation, and success had so far failed to satisfy.

This chronic emptiness had been amplified within the pages of London's *Evening Standard* back in March, when John, along with his bandmates, were each profiled by journalist Maureen Cleave, a friend of the group's. During an multiple-hour visit to Kenwood, the Lennons' home in Weybridge (the "stockbroker belt" outside of London), Cleave succeeded in getting John to reveal his belief that being a Beatle wasn't his life's mission. "You see, there's something else I'm going to do, something I must do, only I don't know what it is. That's why I go 'round painting and taping and drawing and writing and [all] that, because it may be one of them. All I know is, this isn't it for me."

This was an astonishingly frank admission for someone in his position to make. Rather than the standard "it's lonely at the top" confessional seen from time to time in show business, John was musing aloud that everything the Beatles had worked for and achieved left him feeling dissatisfied. It was, to be sure, a trait that would follow him the rest of his life, but readers in 1966 must have been incredulous. It underscored his perception that he was an artist that performed, not a performer (or "entertainer") with an artistic bent.

For most of their recorded output to this point, it had been John more or less in the driver's seat. His dominant, assertive personality and need to be the first spurred the band's boldness. For example, opening "I Feel Fine" with feedback had been his idea; and to his credit, George Martin happily fulfilled the request without simply dismissing it out of hand, as another producer might have. It was John that suggested George use his sitar on "Norwegian Wood," and came up with the bright intake of air as an element of the refrain on "Girl" (reminding some listeners of the sound of taking a hit on a joint). His loud dissatisfaction with double-tracking his vocals led to engineer Ken Townsend's invention of ADT—Automatic Double Tracking—a technique that would be used almost relentlessly not only on this record, but would eventually become a common studio trick in all of pop music.

Not every idea panned out. During the session for "Tomorrow Never Knows," he opined that the distant vocal sound he was after might best be achieved by swinging him upside down from a rope in the studio and capturing his singing into the microphone as he swung to and fro. This was one idea that George Martin was unwilling to test out, but it did indicate John's eagerness to do what hadn't been tried before.

Conversely, though, the dominant Beatle was easily distracted, and if it took some extra discipline to achieve greatness, he'd just as soon not bother. Membership in the Beatles placed him in the ideal situation, however, for whenever his interests flagged, Paul was there to keep things focused, while George possessed a sin-gular never-say-die attitude that would see an idea through to completion, no matter how long it took to master. Paul's biggest

The year they first came to America, the Beatles enjoyed an unprecedented level of success, including two Grammys. For 1965, they were nominated for ten more, spread between "Yesterday" and the Help! soundtrack, but they won none, beaten in more than one category by Frank Sinatra.

contributions to this point mostly focused on the high level of musicianship he provided, be it on bass, vocals, piano, or—on occasion—lead guitar. He also provided an unerring ear for detail, suggesting Ringo's drum pattern in "Ticket to Ride," for instance, or the sustained violin note heard in "Yesterday" during the start of the last verse.

Though artistry is something that cannot be quantified, it is a fairly accepted notion that John and Paul were, through 1966, on

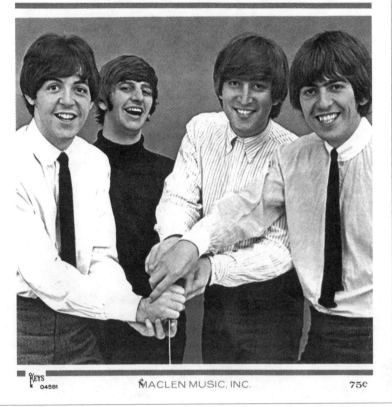

Held back in the U.S. from December 1965's Rubber Soul *release, "Nowhere Man" was released as a single by Capitol in early 1966. The song revealed John's deeper exploration into more introspective subjects, in this case his own ennui.*

fairly equal footing, possessing complementary talents that, more often than not, canceled out each other's weaknesses. In very general terms, John led Paul further outside existing boundaries than he was usually inclined to go, while Paul tended to rein in John's excesses. The result was music that represented each man's optimum talents. John's deep-rooted insecurities were masked by outward aggression, leading to his domineering presence within the group. His bandmates were, for the most part, happy to let

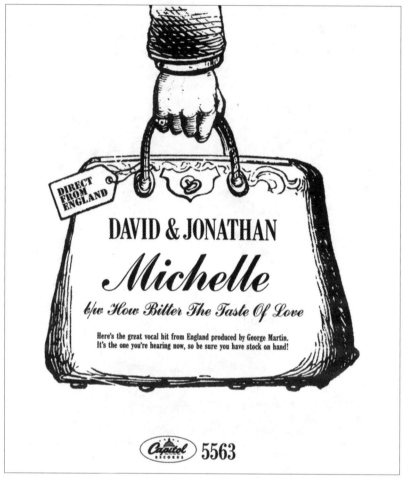

At the same time John's worldview was turning inward, Paul was hitting his stride as a writer of standards. Rubber Soul's "Michelle" drew a raft of covers by other artists, including this "sanctioned" one by David and Jonathan (the nom de plume of songwriters Roger Greenway and Roger Cook). Produced by George Martin, it peaked at number eighteen in the U.S.

him take the lead. It was no coincidence that his vocals had been featured most prominently on the majority of their singles to this point, or that it was he that sang lead on four of six album openers and five of six album closers.

But 1966 marked the point where things began to shift. Paul's creative renaissance came just as John's point of engagement started to wane. Every one of the Beatles' big concepts after this year came from Paul: *Sgt. Pepper*; *Magical Mystery Tour*; the formation of Apple as a clothes shop, record label, and film company; the *Get Back* project; and *Abbey Road*. The biggest single the group would ever record, "Hey Jude," would be written by Paul with virtually no input from John. *Revolver* marked the exact midpoint in the shift between dominance of the two top-tier Beatles.

Maureen Cleave's profile of John was equal parts provocative bluster ("Famous and loaded as I am," he told her, "I *still* have to

As George developed as a songwriter, he gravitated toward the sitar as a means of distinguishing his sound. It stirred no little resentment in John when the Rolling Stones picked up the exotic embellishment three months later and used it to take "Paint It Black" to number one on both sides of the Atlantic.

meet soft people") and confessional. It was also the forum where, in a tangent on religion, he offered the following: "Christianity will go. It will vanish and shrink. I needn't argue about that; I'm right and I will be proved right. We're more popular than Jesus now. I don't know which will go first: rock 'n' roll or Christianity. Jesus was all right, but his disciples were thick and ordinary. It's them twisting it that ruins it for me."

His remarks drew comparatively small notice at the time: in England, a few readers noted his arrogance—but in a land where Lennon's intemperate mouth was well known, most ignored it. In America, a brief mention of John's remarks ran in a March issue of *Newsweek*, but only as an aside within an otherwise complimentary article about their music. Otherwise, no one much noticed. For now.

Living nearby Kenwood was Ringo, in a home called Sunny Heights. Having grown up an only child in impoverished conditions, the Beatles and their success gave him much that he never expected to experience, including three "brothers." The years between 1963 and 1966 enforced closeness due to the demands of being a Beatle, but even in their downtime, members of the group stayed tight. "John comes to my house one day; I go to his the next. I find it's better to go to his house because he's got all the toys there, tape recorders and things, which we like playing about with."

Ringo noted that experiences no one else would ever be able to fully understand bonded them. The four of them lived, he said, "like Siamese quads, eating out of the same bowl." Cleave called him "less complicated and more mature than the others," despite the goofy image that some members of the public attached to him as the least sophisticated of the four. It couldn't have helped that his persona was then being caricatured in the states on the Saturday-morning cartoon version of the Beatles, which presented "Ringo" as little more than a juvenile half-wit and butt of all the jokes—although others saw him possessing considerable charm and charisma that translated well to the silver screen. Whatever the Beatles' future held, it was widely assumed that their drummer's star power would sustain him in whatever he chose to do.

Public image notwithstanding, Cleave found George to be far from a "quiet one." At the time of the interview, George was a newlywed, having tied the knot with model Pattie Boyd on January 21. Cleave found him full of conversation on subjects ranging from life with his new bride to current events like Vietnam and politics. Like John, he too had strong opinions on religion, which he wasn't particularly shy about voicing. "If Christianity's as good as they say it is, it should stand up to a bit of discussion."

Though not terribly attentive during his school years, George possessed a curious, analytical mind, and was keen to learn about the world on his own terms. *Revolver* would place him as first among the Beatles to address topical concerns in song with "Taxman." (His "a plague on both your houses" sentiments came through when he invoked both incumbent Labour Party Prime Minister Harold Wilson and Conservative Party leader Edward Heath by name.) But bigger obsessions, ones that would consume him the rest of his life, were on the horizon: Indian culture and Eastern philosophy.

Once he began a serious study of the latter, its outlook that the material world is nothing but an illusion would heavily influence his worldview and musicality, as well as his attitude toward the phenomenon of being a Beatle. In June, he told *Melody Maker*, "I've changed a lot over the past two years. I've realized that the Beatle bit is only a small part of myself, and I try to keep it in perspective." While not wishing that he could walk away from the whole thing, he did note, "I am fed up with all the trivial things that go with it." Indeed, three years of Beatlemania had notice-ably transformed him into the most easily irritated of the four, and the one least willing to play the game as expected of him.

While George's attitude toward fame was closely aligned with John's, it couldn't have been more at odds with Paul's. The latter was depicted in Cleave's article as John's opposite: self-effacing, engaged with his peers, and bereft of ambiguities. "I don't want to live in Weybridge," he told her. "I love the *look* of London," he added, reminding readers that despite the band's whirlwind existence, he was at heart still a Liverpool kid, very much in awe of the city he'd read about his whole life. Whereas John saw the

Beatles as a vehicle for personal expression, Paul looked at it as a livelihood, and therefore approached it like an artisan. Very early on in their recording career, he began taking piano lessons; at the same time, George Martin attempted to learn guitar in order to best bridge the gulf between their respective disciplines. But Paul's progress was so rapid that Martin soon recognized the futility of further study.

Paul's receptivity was heightened during this time by proximity to and immersion in London's thriving cultural community. In 1966, he told *New Musical Express*, "I find life is an education. I go to plays and I am interested in the arts, but it's only because I keep my eyes open and I see what's going on around me. Anyone can learn if they look." Paul's absorption of ideas would manifest itself, but slowly, in his music. Mostly, as a member of the team setting up and running Indica Gallery, the London counterculture's hub, Paul was too busy nurturing the burgeoning scene to directly plug what was happening around him into Beatle product. (Tellingly, Ms. Cleave observed, "He is half Beatle and half not.")

While the creative side of him was flourishing and would soon blossom to a higher level, Paul's love of performing tended to put him at odds with the others. Though logistically challenging matters did sometimes arise while on the road, the actual performances tended to invigorate him. Paul was the band's sparkplug onstage, making the announcements and engaging the crowds effortlessly. Still, he was beginning to recognize the straitjacket that fan expectations were exerting upon them by demanding live appearances that had little to do with music.

His tipping point arrived weeks after the others, when, after performing a gig in the rain in St. Louis on August 21 that year, the pointlessness of it all sank in. As told to Barry Miles in *Many Years from Now*, "We did the show and piled into the back of one of these chrome-lined panel trucks; they were always empty . . . on this tour, which had become spiritually rather empty, and this empty playing. And on that one occasion, I said, 'okay,' and I let off a bit of steam, swore a bit, and said, 'Oh, well, I really fucking agree with you. I've fucking had it up to here, too!' The others responded with a 'What took you so long?'"

The decision to quit the road for good had not yet been arrived at by the time the group commenced work on *Revolver*, but certainly the way that things were moving in the studio made such a decision inevitable. One of the greatest perks of their success, as George Martin noted to *Melody Maker* in 1971, was that if they wanted to indulge themselves for the odd experimental track or two, that was their prerogative: ". . . by this time we were so established that we could afford to take risks . . . if people didn't like it, hard luck. It was . . . an indulgence, if you like, and we thought it was worthwhile."

The bulk of George Martin's non-Beatle production duties in those days were largely pure pop—Cilla Black, David and Jonathan—as well as novelties like Rolf Harris ("Tie Me Kangaroo Down, Sport") and the occasional stage production (Lionel Bart's disastrous *Twang!*, for example). Martin also found an outlet in producing instrumental recordings under his own name with an ensemble of studio musicians he dubbed the "George Martin Orchestra." (Following the *Revolver* sessions, he issued his own "concept album": *George Martin Instrumentally Salutes the Beatle Girls*, a collection of songs loosely connected by girls' names or female motifs. The title was a misnomer, as his take on "Eleanor Rigby" had vocals, while the presence of "Yellow Submarine" remains unexplained.) It therefore represented an exciting opportunity to break new ground when his top-tiered clients indicated an interest in using the studio itself as an instrument. Whether their fans wanted to follow or not was another issue.

By spring 1966, it became evident that the Beatles were no longer interested in playing the game: previously the decision to indulge photographer Robert Whitaker in a bizarre photo shoot that ended up producing the infamous "butcher cover" would have been unimaginable. Whitaker was an Australian who'd relocated to London after meeting the Beatles during their 1964 tour. He shared photography duties for the group with Robert Freeman; one of his first assignments was the "four seasons" series used for the cover of the *Beatles '65* album released by Capitol in late 1964. (These photos depicted the group holding umbrellas, springs, et cetera.)

The Beatles' feelings toward their producer's extracurricular excursions can only be imagined. During his off-hours, Martin issued a series of mostly instrumental albums, typically but not always featuring new arrangements of Beatle material, seemingly aimed at the easy-listening crowd.

On the afternoon of Friday, March 25, the Beatles convened at Whitaker's Chelsea studio. Before his shoot got underway, the group was photographed in a traditional fashion by Nigel Dickson for *The Beatles Monthly*. One frame from this series found use as their official 1966 group photo. After the boys did an interview with Radio Caroline deejay Tom Lodge for a giveaway flexi disc, Whitaker began the session. In preparation, he had secured a supply of plastic baby dolls, as well as white butcher's smocks, cuts of pork and sausage links from the local butcher, and a supply of false teeth and eyes. Whitaker's intent was to create a triptych: a three-part landscape piece he called "A Somnambulant Adventure." The concept had come to him in a dream, he said—hence the title—and was intended as a commentary on the Beatles' fame and iconic status.

If the idea seems wooly-headed now, it did then too, despite its in-vogue Pop Art context among London's creative elite. Whitaker's numerous explanations of the concept through the years haven't made things any clearer; among the other photos shot that day were ones depicting the four Beatles connected to a young woman via a sausage umbilical cord; and ones of George pounding massive nails into John's head, as well as Ringo's head in a box labeled "2,000,000." The most famous sequence shot was, of course, the one depicting the group wearing the smocks and surrounded by various pieces of raw meat and doll parts.

The so-called butcher photo was inspired by the work of a pair of German surrealists: Hans Bellmer, who in 1937 published a book, *Die Puppe* (The Doll), that featured a series of photos depicting dismembered dolls; and Méret Oppenheim, whose Object (*Le déjeuner en fourrure*, or "Lunch Fur"), a tea setting covered in fur, caused a stir in 1936 by eroticizing everyday nonsexual objects. John, who didn't need to be asked twice to embrace the surreal, was especially gung ho on the concept, as was Paul. Ringo accepted their lead that this was a good thing, while George found it all disgusting, and said so.

Though John and Paul later asserted that the photo was meant as a commentary on war generally and Vietnam specifically, this appears to be after-the-fact revisionism, for Whitaker intended nothing more topical than to offer that the Beatles' popularity was misplaced: "All over the world I'd watched people worshipping like idols, like gods, four Beatles. To me they were just stock, standard, normal people. . . . My own thought was: How the hell do you show that they've been born out of a woman the same as anybody else?"

Following the photo's issuance—and then swift recall—by Capitol after it had been used to grace the cover of the U.S.-only "*Yesterday*" . . . *and Today* album, many (including Ringo) came to believe that it had been intended as a commentary on how the Beatles' music was routinely "butchered" in America to create more product to sell, despite the group's intentions presentation-wise. This is incorrect, for the photo was never even intended to be used as an album cover in the first place. (Ironically, the banal photo used to replace it, showing the Beatles grouped around a trunk, was also shot by Whitaker, but without any thought whatsoever given to how it would be used.)

The first public display of a photo from the session came in the June 3 issue of *NME*, accompanying an ad for their "Paperback Writer" / "Rain" single. The same display ran in other music mags soon after; but then a week later, *Disc and Music Echo* upped the ante, running an alternate shot (reversed for some reason) in full color on the cover. This one, featuring some of the eyeballs

Robert Whitaker's conceptual centerpiece image was never intended for an album cover, much less an advertisement. But its appearance in the pages of NME *gave it the opportunity to gauge U.K. opinion, at least.*

and teeth, was, if anything, even more gruesome than the one actually used on the *"Yesterday" . . . and Today* cover. The weekly realized they had something hot and therefore ran quotes from Whitaker and the Beatles beneath the headline WHAT A CARVE-UP!

Said Whitaker to *Disc* magazine, "I wanted to do a real experiment—people will jump to wrong conclusions about it being sick. But the whole thing is based on simplicity—linking four very real people with something real." "Very tasty meat," Paul was quoted as saying. Ringo only stated the obvious with, "We haven't done pictures like *this* before . . ." George, meanwhile, smoldered. "We won't come to any more of your sick picture sessions," he warned, while John attempted to downplay the dissent with, "Oh, we don't mind doing anything."

Capitol issued a call to England for a cover image sometime in early May. While the "butcher" shot was sent over, so too was the trunk shot. Evidence suggests that a variant of what became the replacement cover had actually been prepared *before* the "butcher" one, and nearly became *the* cover. (A photo taken at the May 20 "Paperback Writer" promo shoot at Chiswick House shows Brian Epstein examining what appears to be a mockup of the trunk cover, weeks before the "butcher" one shipped.) But it was the "butcher" shot that became approved (on May 17) and was ultimately printed up—an estimated 750,000 copies thereof. Why Capitol went with a cover about which they had reservations instead of the more conventional one they already had in hand was probably due to pressure from the Beatles themselves. (Years later, Capitol president Alan Livingston recalled *Paul* as being especially forceful.)

Capitol's art department loved the bizarre imagery, and their designers prepared it to look like it had been printed on canvas, like a painting. (Whitaker's original intent was to apply gilt to the background and halos around the Beatles' heads, to take on the air of Russian iconic art, but he never got the chance to complete his work.) The work was approved, and went off to their pressing plants. The first week of June, advance copies were shipped to retailers (for in-store play) and radio stations, while full shipments were sent to distributor warehouses around the country.

The negative response was immediate and universal. Alarmed at the prospect of not having a salable product on store shelves in time for the announced June 15 release date, the label went into a full state of emergency.

"Operation Retrieve" was announced on June 10. A letter signed by Capitol Press and Information Manager Ron Tepper informed everyone who'd been sent a copy that it had all been an ill-conceived mistake: in the words of Livingston (quoted in the letter) with considerable understatement, "A sampling of public opinion in the United States indicates that the cover design is subject to misinterpretation." He asked for the earlier copies to be shipped back on Capitol's dime, with a replacement forthcoming. Meanwhile, Capitol's employees were summoned to work on the weekend as pressing plants went into overdrive destroying stock on hand as well as returned shipments. But as the task seemed impossibly big to fulfill within such a tight window, someone had the bright idea of simply stripping the shrinkwrap off the returns and pasting the replacement slick on top, thereby saving a step— and considerable expense.

An indeterminate number of paste-overs were then reshipped, and made it to retailers. (Meanwhile, a precious few independent distributors fulfilled orders with the original cover; a handful of people actually bought a "butcher" cover off the rack before they were reclaimed.) The cost of the entire episode was an estimated quarter-million dollars for Capitol. (Said a Capitol exec: "That wipes out the profit.")

That the album existed at all was something of a sore point with the Beatles, who were becoming increasingly galled that collections they crafted with care were subject to arbitrary de-construction across the Atlantic by Capitol Records. Nowadays, in the post-CD era, Beatle fans in America have become accus-tomed to the group's sanctioned composition of their recorded output, getting acquainted with albums that did not exist here back in the '60s, like *Beatles for Sale*. But back when the music was new, their U.S. label took full advantage of the Beatles' gener-ous recording habits (much to their chagrin), taking the fourteen-track LPs issued alongside two non-album songs on a single—as well as any four-track EPs in between—and cobbling together twelve-track albums for U.S. consumption.

By shrewd repackaging of their recorded output, the dawn of 1966 saw eight "official" U.S. Beatle albums in existence, as compared to six in Britain. (Of the stateside releases, each was typically built around tracks found on one side of a U.K. long-player and then augmented by whatever contemporaneous singles were about.) *"Yesterday"* . . . *and Today* would add a ninth to the mix before *Revolver* was even issued, making the score U.S. nine, U.K. six. To add insult to injury, many of the mixes prepared by George Martin and EMI's engineering staff were judged to be deficient for AM airplay, and so became subjected to applications of echo and reverb. In their haste to bring new product to the market, Capitol sometimes used "Duophonic" mixes in place of true stereo ones. These were produced by taking mono mixes and splitting the left and right channels to filter high end one way, low end the other, offering an illusion of separation. The crassness with which their music was being treated in the world's largest market annoyed the Beatles, Brian, and George Martin to no end, but at this point in time they were powerless to stop it.

Capitol was accustomed to at least three new Beatle albums per year; with nothing new forecast until midsummer, they were getting nervous. In early May, the label let Brian Epstein know that they were planning on issuing a new collection in late spring. Using tracks they had siphoned off of the British editions of *Help!* and *Rubber Soul*, plus the "Day Tripper" / "We Can Work It Out" single, gave them nine songs with which to work; this was still too short for a complete album, even by Capitol's less-than-value-added standards. By the time they contacted Epstein to see what three tracks from the current project could be lopped off (in *advance* of their official release, for once), the Beatles had completed six songs: "Tomorrow Never Knows," "Love You To," "Doctor Robert," "Taxman," "And Your Bird Can Sing," and "I'm Only Sleeping." As it happened, the majority of them were John's.

It was George Martin's unenviable task to choose which songs to throw onto the cobbled-together *"Yesterday"* . . . *and Today*, thus warping the integrity of *Revolver* (in America, at least). He elected to hold onto George's two tunes, perhaps recognizing at this juncture the suitability of "Taxman" to lead off the new album and the complete unsuitability of "Love You To" to sit beside "What Goes On" or "Yesterday." "Tomorrow Never Knows" was definitely out of the question for the same reasons, so that left "Doctor Robert," "And Your Bird Can Sing," and "I'm Only Sleeping"—the only choices possible under the circumstances— to be excised from the American *Revolver*.

For all of the effort exerted into putting things right with the potential audience of the compilation, this U.S.-only abomination was a hot seller, validating the decision to go to all the trouble of burying the offending cover art. *"Yesterday"* . . . *and Today* hit number one by the end of July, staying there until bumped by *Revolver* in September for a total of five straight weeks at the top. Still, for the Beatles, its success wasn't terribly meaningful. They'd lost the battle for their chosen cover; but more importantly, a mishmash of material without any aesthetic cohesion went out with their name on it. The feeling that they were being treated like pawns did not sit well with them, increasing their determination to control their own destiny on all future projects.

Another observation to be made regarding the *"Yesterday"* . . . *and Today* debacle was that where the Beatles, and Brian Epstein especially, had been quite protective of their image to this point, there seemed to be a certain amount of deliberate provocation in evidence. By demanding something so clearly outside of the heretofore talented but "cute and harmless mop-top" personas, they were offering a glimpse of what they actually were to the public: outré, anti-Establishment artists existing on an entirely different aesthetic plane than most of the contemporaries with whom fan magazines routinely lumped them. They'd been clawing at the box they'd been put into for some time, along with Brian's edict not to publicly comment on anything controversial. (Brian had completely misread how John's Christianity remarks to Maureen Cleave would play in America's Bible Belt; otherwise he certainly would have had them suppressed well before they were reprinted months later.)

John announced in advance of their 1966 tour dates that he,

for one, was not going to shy away from political questions anymore. At the various press conferences held at each stop of their tour dates that year, he would indeed hold forth with abandon, as did the others, with varying degrees of candor. Increasingly, they saw no upside in suffering fools. Things came to a head in West Germany in June when they arrived at what they expected to be a nostalgic homecoming. Instead, exhausted from rushing to complete *Revolver* up to the eleventh hour, and facing a particularly clueless press corps, they openly snapped at their inquisitors.

After a round of inanities ranging from "How many girls have you had here in Hamburg?" to "What do you think about the anti-baby (birth-control) pill?" (to which John rather tactlessly remarked, "I wish they'd had it a few years ago"), the quality of the queries rapidly deteriorated.

Replacing the "butcher cover" was this clean (if bland) design, recalling similar artwork used by lesser acts of the day.

Ringo was asked if his one-year-old son Zak would be accompanying him to Japan, to which John interjected, "What kind of questions are these? . . . Are there any members of the press here?" Undeterred, the journalists pressed on.

"What do you dream of when you sleep?" the group was asked.

Paul, less annoyed than John, played along. "The same as anyone else dreams of—standing in your underpants."

Though prompting some mirth, which may have been the intent, John was having none of it. "What do you think we are? What do *you* dream of?" Then, under his breath, but audibly, he sighed, "Fucking hell!"

Ringo quickly stepped over it and remarked, "I just dream of everything like you do, you know. It's all the same."

John then spit, "We're only the same as you, man, only we're rich."

At long last, this mutual antagonism prompted a female reporter to burst out, "Why are you all so horrid and snobby?"

"We're not," Paul returned.

"Only in your mind, we are," George offered.

"Is it because we're not flattering you?" John retorted.

Taking a breath, Paul explained, "Y'know, you expect sort of nice answers to *all* the questions. But if the questions aren't nice questions, they don't have to have nice answers. And if we don't give nice answers, it doesn't mean we're snobby. It just means we're natural." His efforts to calm the waters were met with an outburst of applause from the assembled media.

The gathering ended with an uncharacteristically meaningful exchange. When asked if, after years of success, the band was growing weary, Paul leapt in: "No . . . if we were tired, then we'd stop, because there's no need to. We started out wanting money like everybody else. But when you get money, you don't *have* to go on, you know. We only go on 'cause we enjoy it. We enjoy making records and we enjoy singing, and things. That's the only reason. And having money as well, but the other one is the main reason."

2

I WANT YOU TO HEAR ME: THE BEATLES AND THEIR PEERS

*"Paul McCartney was one of the most competitive people I've ever met.
Lennon wasn't. He just thought everyone else was shit."*

—RAY DAVIES

When the Beatles topped the bill at the 1966 *NME* Poll-Winners concert, they headed a lineup that concentrated an unheard of amount of talent on one stage. The two British acts that they considered to be their closest peers were there: the Rolling Stones and the Who. Also appearing: Dusty Springfield, the Yardbirds, the Small Faces, and the Spencer Davis Group—acts that would live on well past their chart life. Hit-makers of the day like Herman's Hermits, the Fortunes, the Walker Brothers, the Seekers, and Crispian St. Peters were also present; and each of them had scored hits in America as part of the "British Invasion."

Upon their bursting into American consciousness in 1964, the Beatles and the acts that followed them out of England were initially painted with a broad brush, as if musically indistinguishable. Familiarity quickly changed that perception, but among the acts following in their wake, it was the Rolling Stones that became the Beatles' closest "rivals." Arriving on the scene in 1963, it took a long time for the Stones to find their groove as a band worthy of comparisons, even though those groups were frequently played against each other. Like so many other British Invasion acts, they had begun as a band steeped in American blues and R&B. Singer Mick Jagger conspicuously modeled his singing style after American artists, while guitarist Keith Richards's musical vocabulary was firmly rooted in Chuck Berry's lead / rhythm riffing.

Brian Jones, a charismatic, multitalented musician who, nonetheless, could not write a song to save his life, had formed the band in 1962. Though a phenomenally quick study on an array on instruments, Jones's position as leader of the group was severely undermined with the ascension of the Jagger–Richards songwriting team. Seeing what he viewed as the foundation of his personal stardom slipping from his hands, he deteriorated over time, sublimating the damage to his prestige with copious drug use and increasingly erratic behavior that would eventually cost him membership in the band he'd started. But all of that was in the future; and as of 1966, his band role as facilitator-in-chief was still nominally present.

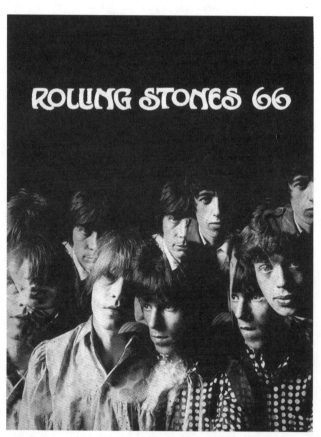

The Rolling Stones nearly crossed paths with the Beatles in America in the summer of '66, finishing up their tour just before the latter's August arrival. Unlike the Fabs, the Stones frequently recorded in the states.

Keith had followed a familiar academic pattern in England: students thought to have few future prospects were shuffled off to art school, while Mick had attended the London School of Economics. Those facts speak volumes about the musicians' respective approaches to their work. But in the beginning, it was their manager, Andrew Loog Oldham, who had set them on their course as writers. Unlike Lennon–McCartney, who from day one had set out to be superlative songwriters—"the Goffin and King of England"—the Stones harbored no ambitions to write; they were merely white urban *interpreters* of African-American music.

But Oldham, who'd worked for Brian Epstein for six months and saw what stardom looked like up close, realized that: 1) the

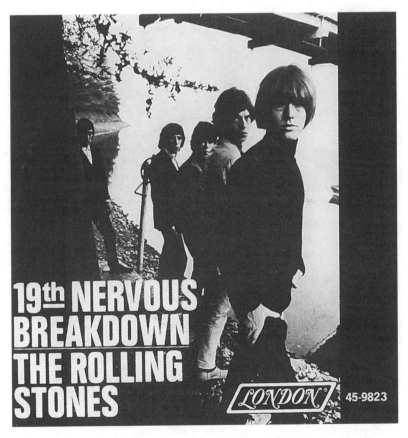

Based on a riff boosted from the Bo Diddley song "Diddley Daddy," "19th Nervous Breakdown" was the Stones' third straight killer single, peaking at number two on both sides of the Atlantic.

Beatles had set the bar high, and anyone aspiring to operate on their level had better be prepared to figure out songwriting; and 2) with so many drawing from the same well (the Animals, the Yardbirds, the Who, et cetera), a finite number of decent songs meant that sooner or later they'd be stepping on each other. Also, Oldham—ever the hustler—knew that songwriting publishing was where the real revenue stream lay. To that end, he literally locked Jagger and Richards in a room and set them to work.

As Jagger–Richards endeavored to master that reality, the Stones sustained themselves with shrewdly selected covers, starting with the minor Chuck Berry song "Come On." It just missed landing in the Top Twenty in the summer of '63, at the same time the Beatles owned the charts with "She Loves You," which was quickly becoming the bestselling British single of all time (which it would remain for another fifteen years, until displaced by a Scottish-sounding campfire sing-along, "Mull of Kintyre," recorded by a 1970s band called Wings). Oldham decided to ask a favor and see if his former employers had a spare tune lying about.

By this time, the Beatles were already onto the Stones, having caught their act at London's Crawdaddy club. (Word was that the Stones secured their recording contract with Decca after George Harrison, in a characteristic act of largesse, tipped off Dick Rowe—the A&R man who had turned down the Beatles—that the Stones should be his next signing.) No fools they, John and Paul offered that they had something in their style, the R&B-flavored "I Wanna Be Your Man," though privately they knew full well that they weren't about to give up any "A" material.

Jagger and Richards watched as John and Paul finished off the "song," which consisted of little more than a lick and a verse, *before their very eyes*. So *this* was how songwriting was done! The Stones were much obliged by the favor; they then took the Lennon–McCartney tune and de-Beatlized it, making it their own by adding an authentically bluesy slide-guitar motif and a pumping bass line. The Rolling Stones' second single peaked at number twelve in the U.K. charts, while the Beatles took the same song and handed it off to Ringo to help round out their second number-one British album, *With the Beatles*.

Though a large segment of the pop world had been bowled over by the Beatles by 1964, Decca was not ready to crown the Stones as their creative runners-up just yet, not without their proving that they'd mastered Songwriting 101. Before committing to the release of a full album, they accorded the group a four-song EP in January 1964, followed by a new single. All the new recordings were comprised of covers, with artists ranging from Chuck Berry (naturally) to R&B singer Arthur Alexander. Selected for release as a single was a Buddy Holly number, "Not Fade Away"; this third record proved the charm, peaking at three in the U.K., while the EP hit the top slot. It probably helped that the Stones had toured relentlessly throughout Britain between the fall of 1963 and March 1964, consolidating their fan base. More importantly, Oldham had hit upon the perfect marketing strategy for the Stones.

Beatlemania was inescapable during this time, with the group enjoying a string of number-one singles in the U.K., the most recent of which, "I Want to Hold Your Hand," became their first American chart-topper—a much-coveted prize. Coming off a period which saw the Beatles play before the Royal Family as well as appear on a number of popular mainstream television shows in Britain and America, their success across all demographics was secure, fueled by their blend of cheeky charisma and showbiz style. (Brian Epstein's instruction to bow in unison was a touch designed to soften resistance from older generations.)

Given such a clean-cut image for the Fabs (though their reality was considerably less pristine), Oldham saw an opening: the Rolling Stones could be the "bad boys" to the Beatles' "good boys." It wouldn't take that much doing: the same year (1965) that saw the Beatles receive their MBEs from the Queen, the Stones were arrested for urinating on a gas-station wall. The difference between the two acts was summed up best by Tom Wolfe: "The Beatles want to hold your hand, but the Stones want to burn your town."

Oldham's marketing campaign, "Would you let your daughter marry a Rolling Stone?" was perfect, giving the group an outlaw image that it would take them years to actually earn. Also taking years was their mastery of songwriting, which had the misfortune of being carried out in public. Their first efforts, produced as a group, were self-consciously credited to "Nanker Phelge," a pseudonym perhaps contrived to cover the embarrassment of material that might not match the level of their myriad covers. (Their self-titled debut album finally emerged in April 1964, containing twelve tracks and exactly one Jagger–Richards composition, the ballad "Tell Me.") Whatever value their ability to write might have carried, it wasn't an issue that affected sales, as the first LP did twelve weeks atop the U.K. charts; having bumped *With the Beatles*, *The Rolling Stones* stayed at the top until displaced by *A Hard Day's Night*.

Not until two years after their recording career began did the Rolling Stones issue a self-penned single in their homeland. (Like the Beatles, the Who, the Kinks, the Yardbirds, and pretty much any other Brit with a recording career in the 1960s, the Stones recordings sanctioned and issued in the U.K. bore little resemblance to what the counterpart U.S. label issued.) Released in February 1965, "The Last Time" was built around a repeating riff, played by Jones but composed by Richards and based on a Staples Singers song titled "This May Be the Last Time."

The group timed the occasion of their first original single well, for when it arrived, it shot straight to the top of the charts in Britain, peaking at nine in the U.S. (A good showing, to be sure, but not as high as "Time Is on My Side," which had climbed to number six in the fall of 1964.) By this time, they'd expanded their audience to the states, where fans (some of whom were either turned off by the Beatles' mega-stardom, or were genuinely bigger Stones supporters) snapped up their releases and the teen magazines that covered their career alongside that of the Beatles or Herman's Hermits.

It was while in America that they conceived, wrote, and recorded the tune that really set the table for their status as artists on the Beatles' level. While on tour in Florida in May 1965, Keith awoke with a riff in his head, which—as the disciplined writer he was aspiring to become—he duly taped onto a cassette recorder before falling back to sleep. Once he located it again the next day amidst nearly thirty minutes of snoring, he played it for Jagger and announced it was called "Satisfaction." Sitting poolside amidst palm trees, the Rolling Stones' signature song was completed quickly.

What made "(I Can't Get No) Satisfaction" work was the deft blending of a number of elements. First there was the riff itself, which drove the whole thing; played through a fuzzbox, it gave the song an edgy sting that caught listeners' ears and didn't let go. Yet if Richards had had his way, we never would have heard it in this form; he envisioned the riff played by a horn section, completely underscoring its inherent Memphis flavor. Second, there was Jagger's delivery. For most of their recording career thus far, Jagger had channeled American singers: Solomon Burke, Wilson Pickett, Muddy Waters. But on this track, he truly came into his own, projecting tension, attitude, and swagger with a whiff of menace in a performance that made explicit what the song's lyrics only suggested.

Despite Jagger's assertion in *Rolling Stone* in 1968 ("I don't think the lyrics are that important"), "Satisfaction" represented the Stones' discovery of their artistic voice. They'd been inclined toward an anti-Establishment bent anyway, evidenced by their careful nurturing of their image as the anti-Beatles. But they were also studying Dylan closely, and by internalizing his pointed, accusatory rhetoric and ably adding their own implicit sexuality, drawn from the blues, they crafted something that appealed to the head *and* the gut—a diatribe you could dance to. "(I Can't Get No) Satisfaction" was their quintessential single, the very encapsulation of the Rolling Stones experience. At last, they'd produced a track that lived up to the image that they'd worked so hard to project. It went to number one on both sides of the Atlantic and became the biggest-selling single of 1965.

(Less impressed with their accomplishment was Dylan, who felt the need to tell Richards to his face that while *he* could have written "Satisfaction," the Stones could not have written "Mr. Tambourine Man." Recognizing that revenge is best served cold, Jagger responded years later by saying that, while he accepted Dylan's point, Bob couldn't have *sung* "Satisfaction.")

Having now set expectations so high, where to go next was destined to be a challenge. Without repeating themselves musically, the Stones deftly took the socially critical voice of "Satisfaction" and presented it with a Dylanesque meter atop a "Twist and Shout" chord progression in the service of an anti-consumerism rant. The anthemic "Get Off Of My Cloud," empowered by a call-and-response vocal line, became their second straight trans-ocean chart-topper. Rearranging the same elements to produce equally appealing results without overtly repeating themselves was no small feat; but having done so, their position as rock royalty had at last been secured.

By 1966, with "19th Nervous Breakdown" and "Paint It Black" extending their streak, the Stones had definitely proven their mastery of the hit single. But the Beatles had been busy moving the goalposts: *Rubber Soul*—featuring mature compositions like "Norwegian Wood" and "In My Life"—represented an artistic advance that reverberated around the pop / rock world; it was one that every serious creator from Jagger–Richards to Brian Wilson recognized as the challenge it represented. Wilson took up the contest, responding with *Pet Sounds*; while the Stones, who'd began work on their next LP the very week *Rubber Soul* was released, suddenly found that they had to dig deep if they were to keep up.

Aftermath, released just after the Beatles started working on *Revolver* in April 1966, raised their game considerably. The first collection to contain nothing but Jagger–Richards originals, it showcased the band's continued flirtation with exotic instrumentation, notably the dulcimer on "Lady Jane" and the marimbas featured on "Under My Thumb" and "Out of Time," as well as their misogynistic streak (present on virtually every track, but most notably on "Stupid Girl" and "Under My Thumb"—though Jagger took pains to explain with the latter that it was the *girl* that had been the oppressor, and that he was only turning the tables).

Other "innovations" for them came in the form of the sprawling five-minute-plus duration of "Out of Time"; it was shortened to a more conventional length when issued in the U.S. on *Flowers* in 1967; and the bluesy "Goin' Home," which was nearly double that length at 11:13. Though in its time *Aftermath* was considered to be the record that established the band as masters of their game, it is seen today as an important transitional milestone, given that so much of the material is still rather overly derivative.

The purported rivalry between the Beatles and the Rolling Stones persisted as a media-fueled myth, while behind the scenes, friendships flourished. With Paul as the London-based Beatle during the 1965–1966 period, it was he that interacted the most with them, especially Mick, who made it a habit to drop by Paul's Cavendish Avenue home. The two groups, recognizing their positions at the top of the British-rock food chain, took care not to blunt each other's chart performances by staggering their release dates, giving each other wide berth so as not to compete head to

The Beatles were photographed during the Revolver *sessions with a copy of the Stones' latest, though it's doubtful that* Aftermath *influenced their direction in any way.*

head. Privately, there had been some talk around this time of putting together a jointly owned recording studio for their exclusive use, but in the end it amounted to nothing.

John maintained his own ties with Mick, Keith, and Brian, and did not fail to compliment the Stones' work whenever it came up in interviews—at the time. With Paul, he would contribute backing vocals to their summer of '67 single, "We Love You," as well as accept the Stones' invitation to appear in 1968 on their *Rock and Roll Circus* television special. That said, his pride in the Beatles' accomplishments was matched by a decided antipathy toward what he felt was undue praise of the Stones' work, which in his view was far too often an echo of something the Beatles had already done first. He would articulate this quite forcefully in the resentment-fest that was his 1971 *Rolling Stone* interview: ". . . I'd like to just list what we did and what the Stones did two months after; on every fuckin' album and every fuckin' thing we did, Mick does exactly the same. He imitates us."

On the other hand, John had no problem praising artists that he didn't perceive as a threat. One frequently cited when the Beatles were asked was a quintet that became a quartet in 1966. The Byrds, as will be discussed later, figured in some pivotal events in the Beatles' career, notably the occasion in Los Angeles that sparked the writing of "She Said She Said," as well as the schooling of George Harrison in the works of Ravi Shankar. This was only fair, since the core of the band that became the Byrds found their musical direction at the same moment that, without exaggeration, lives were changed for millions before TV sets on a Sunday February night in 1964.

Comprised of Jim (later "Roger") McGuinn, Gene Clark, David Crosby, Chris Hillman, and Michael Clarke, the ensemble had been rooted in folk until the Beatles wave roared across America; suddenly, the possibilities of expressing themselves with electricity and drums didn't seem like slumming amongst bubble-gummers cranking out musical inanities. After checking out *A Hard Day's Night* in theaters that summer (and noting the gear they used, zeroing in on George's twelve-string Rickenbacker), the Jet Set, as they'd been calling themselves, went into the studio and recorded a single, "Please Let Me Love You." It sounded something like what Buffalo Springfield doing a Beatles cover might yield.

Issued in October 1964 by the "Beefeaters," a tag that Elektra Records head Jac Holzman gave them to capitalize on the Anglophilia sweeping the country, it was heard by virtually no one. Their next move, after bringing aboard Hillman on bass and Clarke on drums, was to sign with Columbia—Bob Dylan's label—and connect with producer Terry Melcher. Their manager, Jim Dickson (a former recording engineer who'd worked with oddball comedian Lord Buckley), had brought them an acetate of Dylan's "Mr. Tambourine Man," a song written in early 1964 that was notable for its psychedelic imagery. (It was believed by some to have been written after Dylan's first LSD trip, but research indicates it came before, though not by much.)

Dylan had not yet issued it (but soon would on *Bringing It All Back Home*), and the group didn't exactly rush to embrace it—at first. But they worked up an arrangement built around McGuinn's twelve-string picking, trimmed it down to two verses, and changed the time signature from Dylan's 2/4 to the rock standard 4/4. The results were stunning; as Dylan himself noted, "You can dance to it." (At the session, only McGuinn and his Rickenbacker were allowed to perform, as the others were judged to possess a Pete Best–like level of musicianship: suitable for live dates but not studio work.)

Released in April 1965, the song became the debut single of the Byrds (now featuring a playful misspelling, in the Beatles' tradition). Though technically preceded by San Francisco's Beau Brummels, who issued "Laugh Laugh" in December 1964, the Byrds' recording of "Mr. Tambourine Man" is widely acknowledged as the recording that kicked off the folk-rock movement. Though in a few years they would pioneer country rock as well, this was the Byrds' key contribution to the world. Bridging the gap between the folkies who'd held sway among the masses earlier in the decade and the Beatles, who represented the future, the sound that they created led the way in establishing the hottest subgenre in rock during 1965–1966. To generalize the achievement, "Mr. Tambourine Man" made rock palatable to a lot of folk fans that derided the genre as primitive, while expanding the horizons of rock fans that looked at folk as something passé to which their older siblings listened.

The song topped the charts on both sides of the Atlantic, making the band stars in Britain as well as the United States. The Beatles were among those listening closely, especially George. Later that year he would take their arrangement of "The Bells of Rhymney," a Pete Seeger song about a Welsh mining disaster that had been issued on their debut album, and use it as inspiration for *Rubber Soul*'s "If I Needed Someone." The Byrds drew special notice as an American act that had taken something from the Brits, added to it, then sent it back. At a time when those keeping track of such things assumed that most innovation in rock would

A flock of hits found a home in a Byrds album!

Everything's going for
COLUMBIA RECORDS ®

The Byrds' debut album featured four Bob Dylan songs; three tunes from Gene Clark; a pair of Clark–McGuinn originals; one each from Pete Seeger and Jackie DeShannon; plus the wartime standard "We'll Meet Again," heard at the end of the film **Dr. Strangelove.**

necessarily come from Dylan or the Beatles, the Byrds explored a number of disparate paths that they would ultimately weave into their sound. Taking Dylan material—which they would frequently do—and giving it the sheen of accessibility placed the Byrds, Beatles, and Dylan into a common pool of influence exchange, where each act gave and took from the other in equal measure.

The Byrds went to England in July 1965, where—contrary to assurances from their publicist, Derek Taylor, who was keen on showing his former employer, Brian Epstein, what he'd been up to—they faced a backlash. Though their singles had sold well, their less-than-stellar live performances and inability to engage (they were frankly exhausted and would have benefited from some rest before flying over) gave critics the opportunity to dismiss them as overhyped wannabes. The criticism stung, but the Beatles sang their praises—and brought them into their inner social circle, introducing them to the Rolling Stones.

One key element that strengthened the connection between the two bands came from some direct musical enrichment. David Crosby was a fan of Indian sitar maestro Ravi Shankar, playing his recordings endlessly to his bandmates (along with records by John Coltrane) in the hopes that their exoticism would, through osmosis, manifest themselves in the Byrds' music. As it happened, George had encountered a sitar in early 1965 on the set of *Help!* Whether he'd taken his intrigue any further before reconnecting with McGuinn and Crosby in August 1965 is unknown; but before leaving Los Angeles, he would become thoroughly smitten with Indian music, largely through Crosby's enthusiastic endorsement.

Shankar had recorded at World Pacific Studios, a Hollywood facility where the Byrds' earliest recordings had taken place (as would the Doors', later on). Crosby had actually witnessed a Shankar session, and, using his guitar, illustrated for the enthralled Beatles how Indian scales differed from Western ones by bending notes. To say that something clicked inside George on this occasion would be an understatement: within months, the first fruits of this encounter would manifest themselves on *Rubber Soul* with "Norwegian Wood."

Around the same time that *Rubber Soul* was released, the Byrds' second long-player, *Turn! Turn! Turn!*, arrived. The title track was another Pete Seeger cover (with lyrics drawn from the Book of Ecclesiastes), which readily flew to number one in America. The collection didn't really represent much of a major advance from their debut, excepting perhaps that the band had gained some proficiency on their instruments. It contained two Dylan covers, five originals, and a rendering of Stephen Foster's "Oh! Susanna." While McGuinn had served as the group's frontman to this point, it was Gene Clark that was composing the bulk of the group's original material; furthermore, it tended to be more sophisticated than the more derivative compositions written by McGuinn and Crosby. Clark possessed uncommon lyricism that gave the Byrds some Dylanesque resonance; his departure forced the rest of the band to raise their game.

The Byrds' major artistic leap forward came with their next single. Crosby's efforts at getting his bandmates attuned to post-folkie paradigms bore fruit with "Eight Miles High," an abstract retelling of their unpleasant U.K. tour experience. Lyrically, the song was purposely impressionistic (the "eight" miles high referred to their flight over; and though McGuinn was an aeronautics geek who knew that actual flights were more in the six-mile-high range, the group felt it didn't "pop" as well), but the real innovation came with the song's opening riff and instrumental passages. McGuinn unleashed a series of controlled improvisations on his twelve-string, tapping Coltrane's modal explorations while evoking Shankar's otherworldly timbre, all presented within a rock template.

It was one of the most groundbreaking pieces of pop / rock that had ever been issued. No one had ever offered such an overtly experimental piece of work to a Top Forty audience before; had the song not included the word "high" in the title and drawn criticism for encouraging drug use, resulting in a ban from some radio stations, it might have fared better than its peak of fourteen. With the Beatles paying close mind to the Byrds' work and soon to be preparing their own next release, it had to have been encouraging to see what was possible in striking a balance between

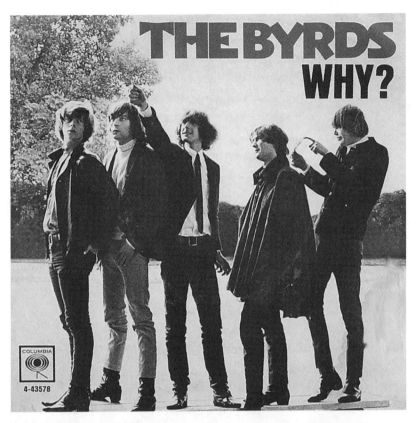

The flipside of "Eight Miles High," "Why"—written mostly by David Crosby—juxtaposed Motown-esque verses against Ravi Shankar–inspired improvisational twelve-string passages.

staying within the accepted boundaries of commerciality and following one's muse. (As work on *Revolver* proceeded in April, their first takes of "And Your Bird Can Sing" came off as blatantly Byrdsian until they rethought issuing so obvious an homage, and scrapped it.)

Also worth a mention is the B-side of "Eight Miles High": called "Why," its genesis began with David Crosby, but it contained key input from McGuinn. If anything, the soloing heard on the track was even more blatantly raga-esque, sounding like a torrent of Indian scales. (It may have been a little *too* exotic, as the track was remade in a more toned-down form for inclusion on 1967's *Younger Than Yesterday* album.)

As for the Byrds, turmoil within their ranks made it difficult for the band to savor their achievement. Gene Clark, feeling resentment as the member who pulled in the biggest checks (for his songwriting efforts) and who furthermore possessed an aversion to flying, left the band in February, before the single was released. Though it was speculated that the Byrds' management encouraged the split in order to have *two* acts, Clark's solo career never rose above cult interest. The Byrds' next album, *Fifth Dimension*, was released in June. Reeling from Clark's absence, it was an uneven work, but still contained a few fine tracks—including the title cut, "Mr. Spaceman," and a cover of "Hey Joe," a song that saw no fewer than four covers issued that year (the others coming from Love, the Leaves, and the Jimi Hendrix Experience).

In 1965, Dylan was an inescapable presence on the AM airwaves, with covers by the Byrds ("Mr. Tambourine Man"); the Turtles ("It Ain't Me Babe"); Cher, and the Byrds ("All I Really Want to Do"); and the Four Seasons ("Don't Think Twice") in play. Additionally, Joan Baez's cover of "It's All Over Now, Baby Blue," and Manfred Mann's of "If You Gotta Go, Go Now," were hits in Britain.

Moreover, he released his most radical, rocking single to date, "Subterranean Homesick Blues" in March; by year's end, "Positively 4th Street" would make the U.S. Top Ten. In between lay his signature song, "Like a Rolling Stone," the recording that—like "(I Can't Get No) Satisfaction" did for the Rolling Stones—defined the Bob Dylan experience. It was sprawling six-minute allegory, one that came to fruition in fits and starts and only with

A 6-MINUTE SINGLE?

WHY NOT! when you have 6 minutes of **BOB DYLAN**

singing his great new song **"LIKE A ROLLING STONE"** ON COLUMBIA RECORDS

Clocking in at 6:09 on the single (and four seconds longer on the album), "Like a Rolling Stone" was initially pressed for deejays by Columbia Records as a "part 1" and "part 2" seven-inch single, until popular demand forced the label to release all ensuing copies featuring the unbroken, full-length recording.

great difficulty. But in the end, it had become ". . . something that I myself could dig"—an important distinction to its author.

"Like a Rolling Stone" was as much a game-changer for Dylan—who was ready to quit music at that point, following the tumultuous tour of England he'd endured that spring, and facing fan expectations at odds with his interests—as it was for rock itself. Beyond dispute is that it married together elements of folk, rock, pop, and blues seamlessly, in support of lyrics that ran far deeper in meaning than its surface level narrative of a socialite fallen on hard times. It's doubtful that every fan that bought the single in numbers that drove it to number two on the U.S. charts that summer (blocked from the top by the Beatles' "Help!") understood even a fraction of what Dylan was trying to say, but in opening minds on a mass scale to accept the notion of rock as a vehicle for expressing universal truths in timeless poetry, it fully earned its immortality.

Dylan had grown in ways that paralleled the Beatles during the 1964–1966 period, prompting much respect from them, not to mention the impetus to raise their game. His word craft shaped the use of language in masterful ways, while "going electric" likewise showed that those resistant to accepting that rock could ever deliver anything of cultural importance needed to reexamine their sense of values. The Beatles, Bob Dylan, and the Rolling Stones have long been regarded as the Holy Trinity of 1960s rock, from whom every important development and innovation flowed. Though certainly at the top of the heap, they would never make that claim themselves, as each has noted individually that they—like any artist—didn't operate in a vacuum, and were susceptible to the influences of everything going on around them.

One would have to look very hard to find another time in the history of popular music where not only were the greatest talents of a generation enjoying the zenith of their popularity, but also creating their most enduring work while directly connected with their contemporaries on a personal basis. There was a community very much in evidence during this time, where, though competition existed, equally abundant was a sense of camaraderie and the feeling that anyone could take something from anyone else and learn from it, expand upon it, and use it as a creative starting point. There is substantial reason that so much of what was created during those years is still embraced, imitated, and admired.

Included on **Blonde on Blonde** *was the song "4th Time Around," a rare example of Dylan parodying a song inspired by his work in the first place, in this case "Norwegian Wood." John later said the Dylan song made him "paranoid."*

3

JUST A STATE OF MIND:
CHEMICAL INFLUENCES

"In the physical world we live in there is always duality . . . good and bad, black and white, yes and no. There's always something equal and opposite to everything. That is why you can't say LSD is good or bad, because it's both good and bad."

—GEORGE HARRISON, 1967

There was nothing exceptional about the Beatles' drug use. Hamburg was their crucible, where a group of direction-less adolescents transitioned into pre-adulthood autonomy. Given the physical demands placed upon them as performers, amphetamines (Preludin, or "purple hearts") weren't just a pleas-ant diversion to make bearable their oppressive working condi-tions, they were a necessity, enabling the boys to sustain endless high-energy sets that pulled out all the stops while engaging their well-lubricated audience.

Further enhancing their hyperkinetic stage personas were the cases of beer regularly sent their way by appreciative onlookers. The Beatles quickly learned that refusing the hospitality only in-sulted the rough, unpredictable denizens of the city's red-light dis-trict. So, with little reservation, they adopted a "when in Rome" attitude. A tidal wave of German beer, coupled with their speed-freak habits, helped to produce a compelling act that knocked audiences out wherever they went. The rough edges may have been smoothed over once Beatlemania hit, but their taste for al-cohol had not. Scotch, usually mixed with Coca-Cola, was their favorite drink during those frantic years of being whisked from one locale to another.

Though sent to the Bahamas for the filming of Help! *as a tax dodge, the Beatles found the island commonwealth a hospitable environment to pursue their love of weed with a vengeance.*

The group moved on to a much more efficient means of getting their buzz on with less effort, and without the inevitable hangovers, courtesy of Bob Dylan. In one of rock's most fabled vignettes, Dylan, on a courtesy call to the group during their August 1964 return visit to the states, turned them on to some marijuana at New York's Hotel Delmonico. (It was believed by many that they had never experienced a joint before that day, but years later, George laid that canard to rest, recalling their baptism in Southport back in 1962 when a drummer from a rival Liverpool band offered them a smoke before they took the stage. "It was like that old joke where a party is going on and two hippies are up floating on the ceiling, and one is saying to the other, 'This stuff doesn't work, man.'" Though initially unimpressed with the drug's supposed magical powers, George did note, "We all learnt to do the twist that night . . .") Dylan had seen through the teen adulation and recognized the artful creativity behind the Beatles' sound—and admired them from afar. But his mishearing of the line "I can't hide . . ." in "I Want to Hold Your Hand" as "I get high . . ." caused him to assume—incorrectly—that they had been regularly indulging in weed. They weren't, but following this encounter, it became hard to get them to stop.

Thoroughly sold on the powers of grass, the Beatles quickly became full-time stoners. Within their circle, "Let's have a laugh" became code for "let's get high." They limited their indulgences to their off-hours for the most part, preferring not to work while baked. "It was good to take it the day before—then you'd have that creative memory—but you couldn't function while under the influence," Ringo noted. "When we did take too many substances, the music was shit, absolute shit." This deliberate effort to keep reefer out of their work life did not extend to film, however, and by the time the Beatles began work on *Help!* in February 1965, it had become rare when they *weren't* stoned.

This time, actor Brandon De Wilde was their enabler. Fresh off the set of Otto Preminger's *In Harm's Way*, De Wilde had starred in *Shane* as a child and was a major Beatles fan as well as an aspiring musician. (It has been said that no one but Emmylou Harris ever sang harmony better with Gram Parsons than Brandon did.) The actor caught up with the Beatles on a charter flight to the Bahamas for the shooting and soon after, ingratiated himself with them by offering "a big bag of reefer," recalled George. "We had Mal smoking cigars to drown out the smell."

The group threw themselves into a regimen of pot consumption that bordered on compulsive. "We were smoking marijuana for breakfast. . . . Nobody could communicate with us. It was all glazed eyes and giggling all the time," John would confess to *Playboy* in 1981. Many scenes in *Help!* were spoiled due to the musicians' inability to remember their lines or, more likely, avoid collapsing into a heap of hysterical laughter over absolutely nothing. Paul and George remembered their putting director Dick Lester's patience to the test while filming the Buckingham Palace scene, so beyond performing even the simplest of tasks were they. In *Anthology*, Ringo described filming the curling scene in the Austrian Alps, wherein he and Paul were instructed to run when one of the stones being swept was actually a bomb about to detonate. "Well, Paul and I ran about seven miles . . . just so we could stop and have a joint before we came back. We could have run all the way to Switzerland."

Statistically, the Beatles were only slightly ahead of the curve in their marijuana use. Public knowledge of their drug habits had been slow to make it to the mainstream, though there were certainly suspicions, especially among those who possessed actual firsthand pot experience (instead of the propaganda). By the time the Beatles and their manager at last came out to publicly declare their support for its decriminalization in July 1967, however, they had largely moved on, with weed slipping from first place in their choice of recreational pursuits.

Lennon would eventually declare that *Rubber Soul* was their marijuana album, while *Revolver* was their LSD album. This may be overstating things, but not by much. Despite its title, the former release had more in common with the Byrds and Dylan than it did Motown or Stax—the opening "Drive My Car" being an obvious exception. Much of *Rubber Soul*'s introspective mood, particularly on the songs he wrote, supports Lennon's observation nicely.

If the two LSD trips that had by this time experienced impacted the Beatles musically on *Rubber Soul*, it left no obvious fingerprints. There are no songs bearing psychedelic imagery; it's generally accepted that the collection's reflective nature (principally on John's songs: "Norwegian Wood"; "Nowhere Man"; "Girl"; "In My Life") was much more a result of pot consumption than hallucinogens. Their marijuana use, according to Paul, had the positive effect of stirring deep discussion. "Instead of getting totally out of it and falling over, as we would have done on Scotch, we'd end up talking very seriously and having a good time till three in the morning."

One possible exception might be "The Word." The tune was striking as it cast its principal author, John, in an evangelical role, spreading "love" as his own personal revelation. Direct evidence is scant; Paul later claimed that he wrote it with John in a fog of weed. (Paul told Barry Miles in *Many Years from Now*, "We smoked a bit of pot, then we wrote out a multicolored lyric sheet, the first time we'd ever done that. We normally didn't smoke when we were working. It got in the way of songwriting because it would just cloud your mind up.") He further stated that the project had been an attempt to compose a one-note song.

But by the time the Beatles entered the studio in October 1965 to begin recording *Rubber Soul*, LSD had become a part of the mix. John and George were the first among them to trip, though involuntarily. On March 27 of that year, the two were invited (along with their wives, Cynthia and Pattie) to a dinner party given by Dr. John Riley, a dentist friend of the Beatles. Riley had cultivated friendships with some creative notables, including filmmaker Roman Polanski (for whom Riley would one day craft fangs for use in *The Fearless Vampire Killers*). The two couples met up with the dentist and his girlfriend, London Playboy Club "house mother" Cindy Bury, at his Hyde Park residence.

The Beatle couples enjoyed their dinner and were ready to leave in time to catch Klaus Voormann's trio, Paddy, Klaus & Gibson, who were scheduled to play their debut gig that night at

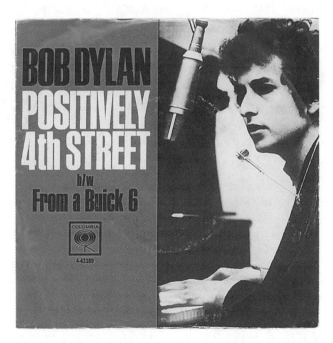

Released as a non-album single in the U.S. around the same time as "Yesterday," "Positively 4th Street," a prototypical Dylan "finger-pointing" song, was a favorite of John Lennon's, turning up on his personal jukebox.

the Pickwick Club, located in London's West End. But the dentist and Ms. Bury weren't about to let them leave just yet, insisting that they have coffee first. Unbeknownst to the Fabs, each sugar cube dissolving in the hot liquid contained LSD.

The host couple's insistence that the guests stay after drinking their coffee raised the suspicious antenna of Lennon, who immediately concluded that they had been set up with an aphrodisiac to participate in an orgy—an activity in which he'd had a bit of experience. No, it was actually something else: Riley informed them that they'd just been given acid, and it would be best if they stuck around. Among the four, John was the one most familiar with the implications—and it unnerved him.

The foursome immediately bolted, squeezed into Pattie's Mini Cooper S, and set out for what ordinarily would have been a less-than-fifteen-minute ride through London traffic over to Leicester Square, followed by Riley and Bury in their own car. Having unleashed four dosed adults (among them two Beatles) on an unsuspecting London on this spring Saturday night, the doctor at this point might have been expected to feel at least *a little* panicked.

In her autobiography *Wonderful Today*, Pattie describes what happened next: "All the way over to the club, the car felt smaller and smaller." They arrived, parked, and quickly went inside. After seating themselves and ordering drinks, George was suddenly hit by "the most incredible feeling . . . I had an overwhelming desire to go 'round the club telling everybody how much I loved them—people I'd never seen before." No sooner had he begun processing his euphoria than he was disrupted by the realization that the club had closed and the staff was cleaning up.

From there, the giddy foursome made their way over to the Ad Lib, a familiar stomping ground located just around the corner which was frequented by their peers. (On the way, Pattie suggested breaking some shop windows.) The club itself was located on the fourth floor of the building, necessitating a quick elevator ride up. John picks up the story in a 1971 *Rolling Stone* interview: "We all thought there was a fire in the lift. It was just a little red light, and we were all *screaming*—it was hysterical. . . . The lift stops and the door opens and we're all going 'Aaahhhh.'"

The opened doors revealed Ringo, Mick Jagger, and Marianne Faithfull (the latter two were not yet dating). John told them that they'd been "spiked," and the party ventured into the discothèque, seating themselves at a table that appeared to elongate before them. With the intensity of the drug rising steadily, John still possessed enough presence of mind to recognize that what was happening was similar to accounts he'd read of opium users hallucinating.

George took the wheel of the Mini for the ride home. Though it was about an hour's drive from the city to Esher, they traveled, by John's reckoning, about ten miles an hour the entire way. (Upon passing some goalposts in a sport field along the road, Pattie suggested they get out and play soccer.) They reached Kinfauns, whereupon George and Pattie passed out and slept "for three years," while John commandeered the "submarine" that the house had become. Cynthia sat terrified for the duration of the trip, surrounded by talking plants and people that looked like ghouls.

The evening left Cynthia traumatized, and without fail she would describe the event in the years ahead as the beginning of the end of her marriage as John drifted into hard-drug use. John and George saw things more positively: though objecting to the circumstance of being sent on a trip against their free will, they nonetheless recognized that their lives had been changed for the better.

To some close to the Beatles in their pre-fame days, George had been a high-spirited fellow: not the "Quiet Beatle" of public myth, but a hard-partying live wire with a dry, irreverent wit. But after two years of sustained Beatlemania, exposure to mind-expanding drugs, and his initial explorations into Eastern philosophy, he had sobered considerably. LSD, he pointed out, had helped him to reach his epiphany. As noted in *The Beatles Anthology*, George described his experience like this: "In ten minutes I lived a thousand years. My brain and my consciousness and my awareness were pushed so far out that the only way I could begin to describe it is like an astronaut on the moon, or in his spaceship, looking back at the Earth. I was looking back to the Earth from my awareness."

This shift from fun-loving pop star to lofty Seeker of Truth marked when George began coming into his own as both an artist and as a human being. As he would tell it innumerable times throughout the rest of his life, acid might have opened the door, but it was not the destination unto itself. "It can help you to go from A to B, but when you get to B, you see C. And you see that to get really high, you have to go it straight. There are special ways of getting high without drugs—with yoga, meditation, and all those things."

John, however, was another case. According to Pete Shotton, once the group reached the conclusion that tripping could be a positive force that brought users closer to understanding life's meaning, George and John pursued it with abandon, especially John. "They quite literally used to eat it like candy," he said. "I must have had a thousand trips," John told *Rolling Stone* in 1970. "I used to eat it all the time." George begged to differ about the number of trips John took while conceding, "I think we didn't realize the extent to which John was screwed up."

Between March and August 1965, John and George steered clear of acid. By the time they were ready to take it again—this time "deliberately"—Ringo was along for the ride. Though Paul was the Beatle most attuned to London's thriving underground art scene, which of course encompassed the latest mind-altering substances, his conservative Liverpool upbringing stopped him from joining the others for well over a year, despite their constant cajoling (and mockery). The prospect of permanently altering his brain, not an unreasonable concern, frightened him. Ringo expressed his approval for the experience thusly: According to *The Beatles Anthology*, Ringo said, "It certainly makes you look at things differently . . . It brought me closer to nature, in a way—the force of nature and its beauty. . . . My outlook certainly changed—and you dress differently, too!"

George noted the connection that he experienced with John after their shared acid explorations: "I felt closer to him than all the others, right through until his death." Despite the passage of years, he recognized when they crossed paths after the Beatles' split something enduring ". . . by the look in his eyes." This bonding sparked by LSD would at last be shared by John and Paul by accident, when the former inadvertently took what he thought was speed during a *Sgt. Pepper* session, nearly two years to the day after he'd first been dosed. (Coincidentally, this was also the night that future famed acid casualty Syd Barrett and his group Pink Floyd popped by for a quick visit.)

On March 21, 1967, the Beatles (minus Ringo) gathered at Number Two studio to track backing vocals on "Getting Better."

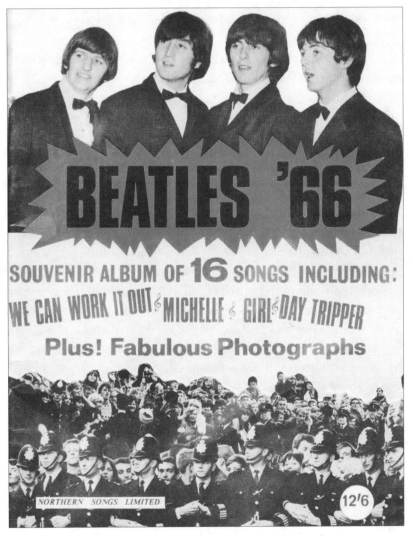

Beatles '66 *collected the music of* Rubber Soul *and their latest single.*

Present that night was their biographer, Hunter Davies, who—unaware of John's chemically altered state—reported that the group sounded flat. John later recalled in *Rolling Stone* ". . . all of a sudden I got so scared on the mic." George Martin, blissfully in the dark about his client's habits, noted something amiss and asked if he needed some air. With legions of fans laying siege to the facility, he quickly decided that the best place for John was up on the roof. So it was that Martin nearly became the agent of John's destruction by placing the tripping Beatle three stories up with nothing but a small parapet standing between him and eternity.

In time John duly returned, but it was clear that he was in no state to work. They decided to end the session, and John was brought over to Paul's nearby Cavendish Avenue home. In a singular act of camaraderie, he decided to join John on his journey. Paul had at last been turned on in November by the ill-fated Guinness heir, Tara Browne, whose death in a car accident a month later sparked the initial inspiration for John's "A Day in the Life." With Paul, acid's effects merely served to further fuel his ambitions to turn the world on with sounds no one had ever heard before. Until this night with John, he hadn't repeated the trip; but in the interim, he had composed some enduring songs.

Like George, Paul was measured in his praise of the drug. On the one hand, he noted to Barry Miles, "Sometimes it was a very, very deeply emotional experience, making you want to cry, sometimes seeing God or sensing all the majesty and emotional depth of everything." But other times it was less profound: he likened it to sitting and waiting for a train that didn't always arrive, leaving you with nothing but "a sore bum." One thing the Beatles were in unanimous agreement on: "I remember John saying, 'You are never the same after it,' and I don't think any of us ever were." On this particular occasion, as evening turned to morning, the two Beatles were drawn closer that they had been in years. "We looked into each other's eyes, the eye-contact thing we used to do, which is fairly mind-boggling," Paul recalled decades later. "You dissolve into each other."

While Paul never composed a song overtly about his acid experiences, George did: in a break from his directly Indian-influenced material, he wrote the gloriously celebratory "It's All Too Much," which describes his acid revelations in a childlike way. Recording began late in the *Pepper* sessions and was completed the day the album was released. (It eventually emerged among the "orphaned" material issued on the *Yellow Submarine* soundtrack in early 1969, but by then it was well past its sell-by date, if the Beatles ever had one.) With its blaring brass flourishes and playfully random vocal backings, it didn't come off as overtly advocating hallucinogens—by design. "We didn't really shove the LP full of pot and drugs, but, I mean, there *was* an effect," John said in 1968. "We were *more* consciously trying to keep it *out*." (Emphasis added.) As for John, his "Day Tripper"—though obliquely evocative by its very title—wasn't a drug song per se, concerning itself instead with what he termed a "weekend hippie."

Among the Beatles' closest artistic peers, references to LSD tended to lie between the lines (such as on the Rolling Stones' February 1966 single, "19th Nervous Breakdown"—a song about a spoiled rich girl finding it hard to cope with life—which contained the lyrics "On our first trip I tried so hard to rearrange your mind / But after awhile I realized you were disarranging mine"). Though the Byrds were acid users, not a hint of their experiences was evident until "Eight Miles High," their March 1966 hit—and even that tune wasn't really about tripping *per se*. While the song's exotic ambience had more to do directly with their application of Indian modes and John Coltrane–style improvisations to their underlying folk sensibility, they revealed decades later that the song could not help but be drug-*influenced*, given their state of mind while composing and producing it.

Despite their protests that it was not intended as a "drug song," the group found themselves subjected to harsh criticism and airplay bans around the country from authorities offended that they'd be so direct. The negative attention was furthered with their next single, "5 D (Fifth Dimension)," written, Roger McGuinn explained, as an attempt to articulate Einstein's Theory of Relativity to the masses. But with lines like "I opened my heart to the whole universe / And I found it was loving," a non-

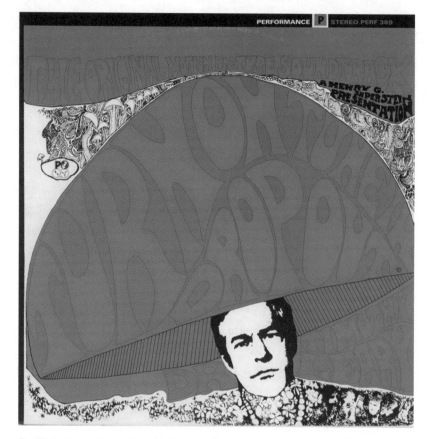

Dr. Timothy Leary's advice to "tune in, turn on, drop out" made him a
counterculture darling and anathema to most everyone else. This 1967 spoken
word / psychedelic soundscape remains a fascinating curio of the era.

acid-based interpretation was a tough sell. Or perhaps, as George
once observed in a similar situation, McGuinn was ". . . writing
his cosmic songs without noticing."

At around the same time John and George's dentist sent them
tripping, Brian Wilson also took acid for the first time and ended up composing the melody of "California Girls"—not that its
influence was readily evident. His continued LSD use, coupled
with a fragile psyche, would eventually render him artistically
paralyzed.

By the summer of 1967, as LSD use was starting to peak
among the world's youth, Paul was questioned by an interviewer
about it. What ensued stirred nearly as big a media commotion as

John's "bigger than Jesus" faux pas a year earlier. No one among his peer group—at least in Britain—had previously publicly admitted to using the drug (which had been perfectly legal in the U.K. until October 1966), making this a big story unto itself. But then he went on to express admiration for its wonders. "We only use one-tenth of our brain," he explained to *Life* magazine in 1967. "Just think what we could accomplish if we could only tap that hidden part. It would mean a whole new world."

The negative reaction was swift. The *London Mirror* accused him of acting like an "irresponsible idiot," suggesting that he both get his head examined and lawyer up, in that order. The timing couldn't have been worse, coming in the afterglow of warmth directed toward the band in the weeks following the release of *Sgt. Pepper* and just days before the Beatles represented Great Britain in the *Our World* live satellite broadcast, showcasing the group before millions around the globe as they sang "All You Need Is Love."

But strangely, though the press was filled with stories of rock stars getting out of hand with their drug habits, most notably the Rolling Stones' bust and subsequent conviction that year for relatively minor offenses (that nonetheless carried draconian penalties), Paul and the Beatles seemed to escape with only negligible damage. First, the group and their manager rallied around him, declaring that they too had tried LSD, and what about it? Second, Paul deftly managed to defuse accusations of encouraging drug use among the fans by pointing out the obvious: it was they— the media—that was spreading the word, not him. "I'm quite prepared to keep it as a very personal thing if you will too. If you'll shut up about it, I will." It was a far cry from the prolonged pillorying that John had suffered one year earlier for his remarks on religion. No one was burning copies of *Sgt. Pepper*.

The impact of the Beatles' drug intake on their art was most readily apparent over the course of the four albums issued between December 1965 and December 1967. (The six new songs released on *Magical Mystery Tour*—the remainder of the album iteration being fleshed out with 1967 singles—represented the group's last excursion into anything overtly psychedelic.)

Use of recording-studio technology to fulfill and make tangible the promise of the Beatles' compositions began in earnest with *Revolver* and peaked with *Sgt. Pepper / Magical Mystery Tour*. Though they would always maintain a close eye on technical developments within their industry (their tasteful application of the Moog synthesizer to cuts on *Abbey Road* being an obvious example), they never again seemed as determined to pursue sonic innovation for its own sake. The real focus, starting with *Rubber Soul* and reaching full flower with *Revolver*, became the songs themselves; and as George's excursion's into Eastern spirituality led the group into the study of Transcendental Meditation, the Beatles issued an about face on their much-discussed drug use. At a news conference with the Maharishi Mahesh Yogi, to whom they'd shifted their allegiance after moving on from Timothy Leary, they "renounced" their use of hallucinogens, declaring that "to get really high, you have to do it straight." Paul laid out the group position: while regretting nothing they'd tried, he likened continued use of chemicals to "taking fifteen aspirins a day without having a headache."

PART II

●

PULLING THE TRIGGER

The Beatles have a new one.
You know what that means.

Paperback Writer
b/w *Rain*
5651 Capitol RECORDS

Though the Beatles were depicted in concert mode in the U.S. advertising and 45 sleeve for "Paperback Writer," it was a song they struggled to reproduce live.

4

MY HEAD IS FILLED WITH THINGS TO SAY: WHERE THE SONGS CAME FROM

"When Paul and I write a song we try and take hold of something we believe in—a truth. We can never communicate one hundred percent of what we feel, but if we can convey just a fraction, we have achieved something."

—JOHN LENNON, 1966

For most of their commercial existence, the Beatles—that is, John and Paul—had had to endure the steady pressure of coming up with both sides of a single three times a year, as well as an album's worth of music semiannually. An ongoing chart presence, as well as personal appearances and (in their case) motion-picture duties, were deemed necessary to maintain a career at that level. By the end of 1965, their energies were already flagging: *Rubber Soul* was completed with a *Help!* leftover, "Wait," as well as what appeared to be a sloppily executed filler track, "I'm Looking Through You." (Upon close listening, one finds extraneous feedback, a missed snare beat, and a dropped tambourine, not to mention the false start heard on U.S. stereo copies. Nothing else on the album comes close to the apparent lack of care heard here; it all seems too random to have been merely an attempt at Dylanesque "looseness.")

Ringo was not expected to contribute material. "What Goes On," his first writing co-credit, was another *Rubber Soul* track contrived out of need. The last attempt to write a fresh "Ringo" track, *Help!*'s "If You've Got Trouble," had been an unmitigated disaster, prompting the hasty selection of a contemporary country-and-western hit, Buck Owens's "Act Naturally," to serve in its place. Rather than risk the embarrassment of another contemporary cover, the boys elected to dust off an unfinished original going back to their Quarry Men days (or so claimed John), completed by the addition of lyrical input from the drummer.

By putting aside all previously held beliefs about their studio limitations in approaching record making, the group was acting upon a tacit decision to create something literally unheard of with *Revolver*. It was therefore manifest that the obligatory Ringo

The U.S. issue of the "Yellow Submarine" sheet music replicated Capitol's advertising artwork for the single.

cut would require considerably more effort than had been typically expounded to this point. While lying in bed one night, in
that ethereal zone of pre-sleep semi-consciousness, Paul was
hit with an inspiration: "We all live in a yellow submarine." It
evoked at once a childlike simplicity and a utopian ideal, with
a hint of psychedelic imagery thrown in, making it a perfect fit
for the album; all the more so when delivered through Ringo's
Everyman voice, thereby deflating any suggestions of pretension.

Once the establishing lick had been settled upon, the details
needed to be sketched in. Paul knew that such a catchy sing-along
chorus made it ideal for children, and he therefore took care not
to populate the lyrics with too many multisyllabic words. (Ringo,
in his delivery, actually altered one line to read, "Every one of us
has all we need" instead of "all he needs"—grammatically incorrect, but aesthetically spot on.) While still a work in progress, Paul
premiered the song to Donovan, who helped complete it by offering up the "sky of blue, sea of green" line.

Rife with undersea imagery as well as an overlay of communal
contentment, the song quickly found an audience upon its release
as a single. Children naturally latched onto it, quickly making the
"Yellow Submarine" refrain a familiar playground motif. Adults
not normally disposed to pay the Beatles much mind likewise
appreciated the group's efforts at engaging a broader audience
with a tune not far removed from the novelty entertainment of
their youth.

What *was* surprising was the counterculture's embrace of the
song. Students protesting at Berkeley in December 1966 began
singing "Yellow Submarine" at a mass meeting that followed a
campus strike. Organizers picked up on the implied theme of a
magical vessel that would sweep everyone up, friends and all, and
take them to that perfect world beneath the turbulence.

But identification with disaffected youth cut both ways. A
certain segment of the population was convinced that nothing
the Beatles said could ever be taken at face value—not after
their "bigger than Jesus" blasphemy that year. The barbiturate
Nembutal (notorious for its role in Marilyn Monroe's death) was

contained in yellow capsules, leading some folks to the ill-founded conclusion that the Beatles were trying to promote downers.

Exactly *why* the group would frame an advertisement for a deadly narcotic in the guise of a children's song was anyone's guess, but similar accusations had been made three years earlier against Peter, Paul and Mary for "Puff the Magic Dragon," a wistful meditation on the loss of childhood innocence now being heard as an advert for marijuana. (The following year, even stronger charges arose when it was discovered that the admittedly trippy "Lucy in the Sky with Diamonds" happened to possess the initials "L-S-D"—something its author swore to his dying day was purely coincidental.)

George, meanwhile, had been stealthily working on his song-craft. Though it would be a long time before his senior Beatle partners would come to regard him as anything approaching an equal, proximity to the two masters had certainly accelerated his learning curve. Thematically, George's material tended toward conveying disapproval ("Don't Bother Me," "You Like Me Too Much," "Think for Yourself")—not usually the stuff of which pop hits were made. *Rubber Soul*'s "If I Needed Someone," on the other hand, caught both the *au courant* folk-rock wave as well as a thematic complexity found elsewhere on the album. It marked the beginning of George's ascent to world-class songwriter.

Work began on a follow-up four months after *Rubber Soul*'s release. Suddenly, George's approach to songwriting had shifted: not one of the unprecedented *three* songs he contributed to *Revolver* could be called a traditional love song. Instead, he offered up a topical rant ("Taxman"), an exotic sermon ("Love You To"), and self-analysis of his own inarticulateness ("I Want to Tell You"). What had changed during those five months? Ongoing experimentation with LSD, for starters; Eastern philosophy, for another. Along with the accelerated maturation that came with being a Beatle, all of these factors sharply directed his worldview inward—a course upon which it would remain for the rest of his life.

First, though, material-world concerns beckoned. "Taxman" marked George's transition from addressing the nonspecific "you" or "my friend" in his songs to an all-too-familiar nemesis: Britain's Inland Revenue. George was historically pegged as the Beatle most preoccupied with monetary matters. (Valid or not, this was precisely how he was typed throughout *Help!*) Typically, in business meetings, it was George who asked questions as the others' eyes glazed over. Given his diminished earning power alongside John and Paul—lacking their songwriting infrastructure—this is completely understandable. Naturally, once he glommed onto the fact that their income was being taxed at the un-Fab rate of 95.6 percent, he was incensed. It wasn't that he felt he wasn't taking home enough; he'd addressed the fact that his material needs had been met in the pages of *Melody Maker* in 1965 ("I know I'm okay"). Rather, it was the principle of the thing, the feeling that he was being punished.

"Taxman" revealed the depth of his fury, though his struggle to articulate his sense of injustice took considerable honing to get it into the shape presented to the public. His original lyric draft (reproduced in the pages of *I Me Mine*) reveals a number of ideas initially considered but eventually rejected. "So give in to conformity" read one line—certainly anathema to the Beatles generally and George specifically.

One couplet read: "You may work hard trying to get some bread / You won't make out before your [sic] dead." George clearly was struggling to express the cradle-to-grave nature of taxation, but it took a contribution from John to arrive at the final, succinct summary: "Now my advice for those who die / Declare the pennies on your eyes." (John later described the burden of helping with a song not started by Paul: "I didn't want to do it. I just sort of bit my tongue and said 'okay.'")

The journey of "Taxman" from composition to recording (wherein Paul contributed the stinging lead guitar) exemplified the symbiosis existing within the group that reached its pinnacle on *Revolver*. Not only did both senior Beatles help shape the finished product, but the track itself was actually selected to open the album: the first—and last—such occurrence for a Harrisong on a Beatles long-player. After *Revolver*, shared input at Beatle recording sessions would take on the air of supporting *individual* rather than *group* efforts.

"I Want to Tell You" might have been an expression of George's attempts to collect his thoughts long enough to express them more clearly in "Taxman," but it was moreover a general commentary on communication breakdown; between individuals, or between the group and their audience—either situation fit. Again, one can read the effect that deliberate consciousness expansion had on George; the faster and more wide-reaching his thoughts came, the greater the struggle to find the words to express them.

The song is notable as an early attempt at matching the music to the message, a formula that he would explore increasingly as his craft developed. Whereas heretofore he was apparently content to let the music and words come together based purely upon pop aesthetics, increased time in the studio spent developing the material had allowed nuance and detail to come to the fore. "I Want to Tell You" featured an off-kilter guitar riff that invited first-time listeners to guess where the beat would fall in. Fading in at the start and out at the end provided a circular effect, perfectly matching the song's lack of resolution.

The track also featured a deliberately dissonant piano that underscored the persistent disorder about which George sang. Though at the time he asserted that "It's only me / It's not my mind" that was confusing things, he later revealed, with the benefit of hindsight, that he should have sung "It isn't me / It's just my mind"—proclaiming that "what we need is to lose [forget] the mind."

George noted to the press that his songwriting learning curve was steeper than John and Paul's had been, since they had had each other to bounce ideas off of and to inspire each other when composing. That his journey was an independent one made the task of keeping up all the more difficult. In *Melody Maker*, he observed that ". . . when you're competing against John and Paul, you have to be very good to even get into the same league." Though he'd solicit their occasional input, he was largely left to himself to find his own unique voice. One tool he did stumble upon to distinguish himself was instrumental innovation: specifically, the sitar.

The first Western pop record to feature a sitar and make it to the marketplace was "Norwegian Wood," issued on *Rubber Soul* in December 1965. But the idea of incorporating the sounds of the distant East into Western youth culture did not originate with the Beatles. In April 1965, the Yardbirds convened at a recording studio with the intent of laying a sitar riff upon a Graham Gouldman composition. Unfortunately, engineering limitations and the inability to get a full, clean sound forced them to abandon the experiment; instead, newly installed guitarist Jeff Beck *simulated* his idea of a sitar sound on "Heart Full of Soul."

By uncanny coincidence, the Kinks were that very same week attempting to inject some Indian culture into one of their recordings. "See My Friends" featured two electric guitars (double-tracked) and employed an open tuning in an attempt to simulate the drone of the Indian *tambura*. Like the Yardbirds' record, this was a purposeful evocation of Indian music without the actual instrumentation. George's work on "Norwegian Wood" was the exact opposite: an Indian instrument in the service of a wholly Western song.

That he encountered the Indian instrument at all was pure happenstance, involving the plotline in *Help!* Having access to the instrument was novel, but only afterward, having become aware of maestro Ravi Shankar, did he actually listen closely to Indian music. What he heard was revelatory—and life changing.

George's Eastern path would lead him to a deeper exploration of all manner of Indian culture, well beyond music. The immediate result of his infatuation with this new world led him to try his hand at a raga, quite early on as he was still getting familiar with the sitar. By any "normal" standard, a novice attempting to impose a pop sensibility upon a classical tradition that went back centuries was a wholly presumptuous move, to say nothing of self-indulgent.

But it was entirely emblematic of the Beatles' innate collective—and individual—confidence to cast aside doubt in their own talents and hold total faith in their creativity. For George, the youngest and arguably most naïve member of the Beatles, to attempt such an ambitious composition at this juncture was a brave move; that he pulled it off was a minor miracle.

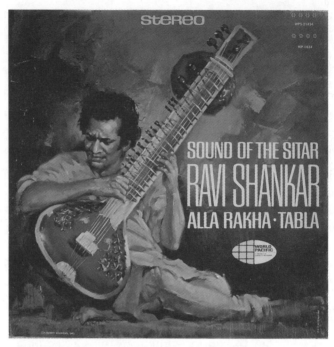

This 1965 release, **Sound of the Sitar,** *featured four lengthy compositions and served as an excellent sampler of Indian classical music, with pieces ranging from an invocation ("Raga Malkauns (Alap)") to an exploration of folk melodies ("Pahari Dhun").*

"Norwegian Wood" represented a tentative first step: earnest but basic. By early 1966, George was ready to tackle an actual raga, albeit within the limitations of rock 'n' roll. It would feature Indian instrumentation almost entirely, including tabla, with Ringo's tambourine and some fuzzed electric guitar added to represent Western musicality. (An acoustic guitar, buried in the final mix, was captured as George's accompaniment when he laid down his vocal.)

Thematically, the newlywed musician wove together a somewhat oblique expression of love directed toward his bride, along with larger concerns regarding mortality and purpose. Thus it was that the Beatle whose reputation would become most inextricably intertwined with philosophical issues beyond the material world took his first tentative step toward the defining characteristic that would follow him for the remainder of his days. (Also written this year, as George's songwriting skills began blossoming, were a pair of compositions recorded after the Beatles' demise: "Art of Dying" was a rumination on reincarnation whose original lyric asserted "There's nothing Mr. Epstein can do / To keep me here with you." The other was "Isn't It a Pity," eventually one of George's best-loved recordings, allegedly ignored by the band because John Lennon dismissed it.)

George's embrace of the East and eventual absorption of its ways of seeing the world represented one Beatle's drive to better his education. But in this he was not alone; at this point in the Beatles' career, Paul differed from the other Beatles in that: 1) he still lived in London; and 2) he was still single. Combined with his own native curiosity, competitive drive, and a desire to catch up on culture that led him to confess to the *Evening Standard* in 1966 that he tended to "vaguely mind someone knowing something I don't know," he was ripe for self-improvement, leading to a major advance in his art.

Credit to the Asher siblings—Jane and Peter—must be given for fast-tracking Paul's cultural enlightenment. In recent years, Paul has frequently (and sometimes clumsily) asserted that, contrary to established belief, it was *he* that was at the forefront of London's artistic and intellectual underground scene of the 1960s, not John. To begin with, there was his involvement with the founding of Indica Gallery. Alongside Peter, Paul's hands-on involvement in setting up the establishment, a partnership between Asher, John Dunbar, and Barry Miles, was total: everything from sawing wood for bookshelves to painting walls; they even collectively designed the shop's wrapping paper. The gallery was a hotbed for exchanges of ideas among the cognoscenti. Beat writers Allen Ginsberg and William Burroughs were regulars; occasional visitors had included notables like Tom Wolfe and Roman Polanski. Paul would hang out at all hours, engaged in deep conversations about philosophy, politics, art, theater—educating himself while expanding his horizons.

Outside Indica, Paul's autodidactic ways manifested themselves in his study of sounds far afield from rock 'n' roll. Jane encouraged his exploration of classical music, but through his friendship with Miles, he soon began picking up other challenging listening:

In moving beyond their origins as hardcore blues interpreters, the Yardbirds alienated lead guitarist Eric Clapton (second from left), who quit before they recorded this Eastern-influenced single with his replacement, Jeff Beck.

avant-garde, typified by composer John Cage; electronic modern, such as that of German composer Karlheinz Stockhausen; and freeform jazz, exemplified by Ornette Coleman.

Any influence Paul took from these artists found form in the sonic textures (rather than actual compositional construction) that he applied to his own work; this was even more true with John's music. After gleaning what he could from the freeform non-pop pieces, Paul set about to create his own *musique concrète* recordings during his non-Beatle time using his portable Brenell tape recorder. The results were collages of sounds unknown in the natural world, having been manipulated by speeding them up or slowing them down and looping them to repeat endlessly. He shared the results with friends, and joked with John that he had half a mind to issue them as an album called *Paul McCartney Goes Too Far.*

As a tunesmith, he was still firmly rooted in pop, staying cognizant (as always) of the latest recordings from his peers. Hearing the sunny sounds of "Daydream" by the Lovin' Spoonful in March 1966 prompted his own "Good Day Sunshine." Though the two records sounded nothing like each other, sonic commonality came from their shared old-timey soft-shoe sensibility. In the Beatles' recording, the lazy, whistling-along ambience of John Sebastian's Spoonful composition was tempered by Ringo's crashing breakthrough on each chorus.

The song was a marvel of simplicity, opening with a pulse of bass and piano suddenly illuminated by a sunburst of cymbal.

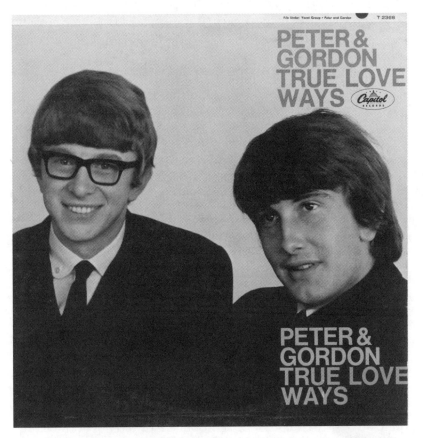

Peter Asher and Gordon Waller maintained a steady presence on the singles charts between 1964 and 1966. "Woman," written for them by Paul under an assumed name (to see if fans would buy their music without an explicit Beatles tie) went to number fourteen in the U.S. in early 1966.

Musically, "Good Day Sunshine" is arguably Paul's least ambitious effort on *Revolver*, but this did not make it valueless; as an adroit evocation of love's luminous serenity, it fulfilled its brief. It also served as foil to "I'm Only Sleeping" on the record's opposite side; whereas John could not bear the thought of daylight rousing him from his slumber, Paul could not wait to embrace the myriad possibilities that a new day—and love—might bring.

No less a sunny evocation was "Here, There and Everywhere." The Beach Boys were peers: musically, as well as corporately (as Capitol label mates). While John had initially made sweeping judgments about American popular culture as he found it upon his 1964 arrival ("What an ugly race"), by 1965 he was prepared to acknowledge that the Beach Boys—or at least their creative leader—had gotten past their surf-and-hot-rod origins to produce decidedly worthwhile, even inspiring, music. (Upon hearing their non-album single "The Little Girl I Once Knew" in late 1965, John gushed in the *Beatles Monthly*: "It's all Brian Wilson. He just uses the voices as instruments. He never tours or anything. He just sits at home thinking up fantastic arrangements out of his head.")

Paul didn't need convincing of Brian's genius. From afar, he'd been an admirer of Wilson's capacity for making full use of his musical palette to capture previously unheard (in rock) sounds. In particular, the block harmonies, borrowed by the Brothers Wilson from the Four Freshmen, caught Paul's ears. This element would figure prominently in the arrangement of "Here, There and Everywhere"—a song directly inspired by Brian Wilson's latest musical effort.

Upon hearing *Rubber Soul* for the first time following its December 1965 release, Wilson was blown away. The Beatles' sophistication had grown discernibly with every release; the summer of '65's *Help!* truly marked the end of their beat-group days. For the first time, they were deliberately filling the grooves with songs that quite obviously could not be reproduced, or did not even belong, on an arena stage. As sequenced by Capitol, the U.S. reconfiguration of *Rubber Soul* dispensed with the overt R&B workout, "Drive My Car," as well as George's jangly "If I Needed Someone,"

KA-208

Between December 1965 and December 1966, the Lovin' Spoonful were a hit-making machine, placing six singles in the U.S. Top Ten, including one number one, "Summer in the City."

Ringo's countrypolitan "What Goes On," and John's "Nowhere Man" in favor of a pair of *Help!* leftovers: "I've Just Seen a Face" and "It's Only Love." The result was a cohesive, acoustic-flavored approximation of the folk-rock experience as offered by an English, American-influenced act.

Wilson took notice: "[*Rubber Soul*] was the first album I listened to where every song was a gas." Accepting the Beatles' implicit creative challenge, he announced to his wife Marilyn, "I'm going to make the greatest rock album ever." With *Pet Sounds*, Wilson certainly came close. Built upon a self-examination into his own troubled psyche (prompted, in part, by his own LSD experiments), Wilson wisely chose Tony Asher—an advertising/

jingle writer by trade—to translate his thoughts into workable, memorable lyrics.

For anyone at all interested in pushing rock's boundaries, the results were astounding. Forsaking all previous formula, Brian Wilson succeeded in raising the bar, delivering a collection of introspective, searching tunes, replete with nuance and depth, but unfailingly catchy and pleasing to behold. Having abandoned touring in 1965, Wilson was free to pursue his muse at his leisure; that time away from the road could result in such astonishing music was a lesson that did not go unnoticed by the Beatles.

Of course, Brian's own band was another matter. Singer Mike Love reacted with open hostility and derision upon hearing the

The sleeve artwork to "God Only Knows" depicted the group minus Brian Wilson, but did show his replacement, Bruce Johnston, who sang on the recording.

work in progress, incensed that Brian would abandon the topics that had been the Beach Boys' bread and butter in favor of pretentious navel-gazing music. He went so far as to force Brian to abandon the original lyrics to an LSD-inspired tune called "Hang on to Your Ego," recasting it as the watered-down "I Know There's an Answer."

If there's an abject lesson here, it's this: Brian Wilson's fragile psychological state and utter lack of support from his bandmates hamstrung him, preventing him from reaching the creative heights he might otherwise have achieved. *Pet Sounds* and "Good Vibrations" depict an artist creating music that no one had ever before imagined. In contrast, the Beatles' *esprit de corps* was never higher than it was in 1966. The creative roll they were on throughout the following year would not have been possible had they been suffering through a similar level of dysfunction.

Paul and John were accorded a special preview of *Pet Sounds* in England, before its actual public release there. It happened at the Waldorf Hotel in London, where Derek Taylor helped organize a listening party for the press and select guests. Bruce Johnston had flown over, representing the group, but it was actually Keith Moon that had contacted the Beatles camp directly with an invite. Rock's noisiest drummer was a huge surf-music fan and had enjoyed the Beach Boys for years—though he privately derided this new masterpiece as "one big drag."

Producer Kim Fowley's account of how the session went was published in Charles L. Granata's *Wouldn't It Be Nice: Brian Wilson and the Making of the Beach Boys'* Pet Sounds. Once Lennon and McCartney arrived, like visiting royalty, the entire atmosphere changed—this in a room whose attendees included Dave Clark, Marianne Faithfull, Moon, Johnston, Taylor, and Fowley, as well as a contingent of British Beach Boys fan-club officers. Quickly sizing up the situation, Paul spotted the fan-club girls at a table, playing canasta. Seating himself, he announced that he would deal before issuing two requests: the first was for absolute quiet while the album spun. The second was for a piano to be brought in.

John and Paul absorbed the sounds emanating from the speakers with complete silence, all the while playing cards. Thirty-six minutes later, upon the album's completion, the two rose and went over to the piano. Quietly, they began tapping out chords, exchanging commentary in hushed tones. Then, as onlookers began to process what they'd just witnessed, Paul called out a cheery "so long," announcing that he and John were headed out to the studio for a scheduled session. (Recording actually resumed the next day, with overdubs for "Got To Get You Into My Life.")

Pet Sounds was released on May 16 in the U.S.; the London premiere occurred the following day. By that time, the *Revolver* sessions had been ongoing for six weeks, and would continue until June 22. John and Paul's exposure to the current Beach Boys album hit them just past the midpoint of their work; late, perhaps, but not too late to have an impact.

Though there is no obvious resemblance, Paul has stated many times through the years that *Pet Sounds*' "God Only Knows"—a track he has deemed the greatest pop song ever—influenced him when composing and arranging "Here, There and Everywhere." The song was written poolside at John's Kenwood home, as Paul strummed a guitar, waiting for his partner to rise. (John was in the habit of sleeping till afternoon when possible; the same *Evening Standard* article that contained the "bigger than Jesus" quote also called him out as "the laziest man in England.") By his account, Paul reported that the song was more or less completed without John's help, but the two "finished it off" once John awoke.

There were some that detected a trace of Beach Boys influence in another song Paul wrote and recorded around this time. Unlike "Here, There and Everywhere"—or most any other Beatle song to this point—it wasn't a love song. "Paperback Writer" was a character sketch, one of Paul's first such attempts to tell a story about fictitious people. As such, it broke new ground, distinguishing itself with a clever arrangement and adroitly arranged vocals.

Taking a page from their own recent past, "Paperback Writer" opened with *a cappella* vocals (recalling "Nowhere Man"), giving way to a heavy guitar riff (echoing "Day Tripper," one side of their most recent single). The song chugged along chiefly on a single chord throughout, but interest was sustained by a number of elements: the layered harmonies; the intricate vocal arrangement, reminiscent of the Beach Boys' work; and the propellant bass, which leapt out of the speakers.

Beyond the apparent sonic nod to Brian Wilson, the song also bore the distinct imprint of Ray Davies's influence. By 1965, the Kinks were sustaining a chart presence with clever, ironic (as well as cynical) material, scoring with such observational hits as "A Well Respected Man" and "Dedicated Follower of Fashion." The latter was issued in February 1966; Paul may have had the notion of trying to something in their style (which in itself bore the unmistakable mark of Bob Dylan, filtered through an English sensibility) in mind, but direct inspiration for "Paperback Writer" is said to have come from an article he'd spotted in the *Daily Mail* tabloid regarding an aspiring writer.

Unlike other songs of his on *Revolver*, Paul's lyrics here were playful rather than profound. "A thousand pages, give or take a few"—that's well above your average paperback. A novel, based on another novel? "By a man named Lear," Paul tells us. Presumably, he was referring to the nineteenth-century English writer Edward Lear, therein suggesting a certain winking satire. Lear, after all, was a purveyor of limericks: clever and full of wordplay, to be sure, but by invoking him, the lasting impression is made of someone unfamiliar with his work nonetheless attempting to display their erudition. (Even John, who might be expected to know about such things, confessed in *Anthology* that he knew the name but little else.)

Some have read the song as a take on John's side work; after all, he was the "literary" Beatle. But more likely, Paul was sending up the culture of the times, which asserted that anyone could become famous—if even only for Warhol's fifteen minutes—and that notoriety for notoriety's sake was a worthy goal. The song's protagonist needs a break, but what he's shooting for—success on the lowest rung of the literary ladder, as paperbacks were felt to be—doesn't suggest he's aiming for high art.

Jane Asher's impact on Paul's music wasn't limited to aesthetic enrichment. During their five years together, the two shared a tempestuous relationship, with arguments occurring on a fairly regular basis. Jane was a woman not given to suffering Paul's inherent chauvinism gladly, and though she inspired her share of love songs from her beau, Jane just as often seemed to prompt songs of resentment. "I'm Looking Through You" was particularly vitriolic, and while it's not recorded how she felt about Paul creating art from their life together, his drawing inspiration from their relationship to write a particularly chilling breakup song couldn't have gone unnoticed.

Work on "For No One"—or as it was originally titled, "Why Did It Die?"—began while Paul and Jane were on a skiing holiday in Switzerland in early 1966. Odd to think that what would become one of Paul's most starkly unsettling compositions would originate on a pleasure trip—in the loo, to be exact. (Paul would one day note that he could recall the details of how his *Revolver* songs came to be written better than he could recall recording them.)

It was while in the lavatory that he began conceiving a tune built upon a descending bass line (an effect which would be borrowed by John the following year for the verses to "A Day in the Life"). Perhaps it was the confining environment in which he found himself that suggested a Baroque-era drawing-room feel, with appropriately mannered first-draft lyrics: "She takes her time and does not feel she has to hurry," he sketched out on the back of a manila envelope.

While the finished product exuded denial on the part of the song's protagonist as originally drafted, the song's original lyrics voiced bewilderment. "Why did it die? / I'd like to know / Cry . . . and blame her." Characteristically, he denied any culpability for the romance's end. The original third verse offered a warning, much in the manner of John's "You're Going to Lose That Girl": "You wait; you're too late as you're deciding why, the wrong one wins / The end begins and you will lose her."

It's hard to know at this distance if Paul ever intended these as serious lyrics or mere placeholders until he got a handle on what he wanted to say. The good thing was that he did extensively rewrite the song (apparently without John's help), sharpening its focus to bloodless clarity with his depiction of the process of love's bitter end. Rarely was Paul so utterly bereft of fancy in his lyrics as he was here; this was an incursion into Lennon territory.

Receiving the MBE honor was something about which the Beatles always had mixed feelings.

Perhaps it wasn't without reason that John declared the song to be "a nice piece of work."

It may be indicative of the esteem John held for another of Paul's songs, perhaps the latter's highest profile contribution to *Revolver*—"Eleanor Rigby"—that John uncharacteristically tried to claim greater input into the song's composition than can be confirmed by others. During his 1980 *Playboy* interview, John conceded that the song was "Paul's baby" while insisting that he ". . . helped with the education of the child." Furthermore, John expressed his genuine offense when Paul, during the song's lyric-writing phase, avoided directly requesting his help and simply tossed it out to anyone that was around, which included George and Ringo as well as the group's road managers, Neil Aspinall and Mal Evans, as though *anyone* could be a Paul McCartney collaborator. "That's the kind of insensitivity he would have, which upset me in later years."

But John's account of the creation of the song's lyrics was disputed: not only by Paul, but also by John's boyhood friend, Pete Shotton, who was also present during the tune's creation. While John's recollection of the song's genesis being a group effort appears to be correct, with George contributing the song's refrain—"Ah, look at all the lonely people"—and Ringo suggesting Father McKenzie's evening preoccupation ("darning his socks"), it was Shotton that came up with the key development of having these two lonely people cross paths only in death, when the priest officiates over Rigby's funeral. (Also according to Shotton: Lennon scoffed at this proposition, insisting that in creative matters, his friend was out of his depth.) John's actual input on the final form was declared all but "nil" by both Paul and Pete.

The names within the song arrived in their finalized form only through the process of some lengthy discourse. Paul originally began the second verse with "Father McCartney," a name that scanned beautifully while containing a ring of realism. But as the song evolved and the blank plotline began to come into focus, it occurred to its writer that perhaps listeners—always on the lookout for some insight into deeper meanings within Beatle lyrics—would read a little *too much* into the name and assume Paul was writing about his own father. Over John's objections, Paul consulted a phone book to find another name that rolled off the tongue equally well, with "McKenzie" winning out.

But it's the inspiration behind the title character's name that has drawn the most scrutiny through the years. Paul has explained it this way: originally, "Miss Daisy Hawkins" was the woman who picked up the rice. But at a time when authenticity ruled, he felt that building a song around such a contrived-sounding persona would undermine the entire premise. "Eleanor," a name taken from the actress Eleanor Bron, who'd starred with the Beatles in *Help!* in 1965, seemed perfect—but only if coupled with a "real"-sounding two-syllable surname.

In January 1966, Paul paid a visit to Jane Asher while she was performing in a play with the Bristol Old Vic Company, *The Happiest Days of Your Life*, at the Theatre Royal, about 120 miles outside of London. While in the neighborhood, he spotted Rigby & Evens Ltd., Wine &Spirits Shippers, located on King Street, just across the street from the venue. According to Paul, the last name "Rigby," when coupled with Eleanor, possessed the virtue of flowing well *and* sounding uncontrived. This aspect of the song's development was explained.

No one questioned Paul's story until the 1980s, when a headstone marking the mortal remains of one Eleanor Rigby, who died at forty-four in 1939, was discovered in Liverpool. In itself this would have been scarcely noteworthy, but for the fact that she lie in the graveyard adjoining St. Peter's Church, Woolton—the location where John and Paul met for the first time in July 1957. That an Eleanor Rigby lay beneath a massive monument in a specific locale known to have been frequented by John (at least) was deemed too remarkable to be a coincidence; Paul surely had to have been aware of this, at least subconsciously.

It probably would have served no useful purpose to point out to anyone questioning Paul's veracity that the song that became "Eleanor Rigby" had yet another name attached to it at the very beginning: one that, it's safe to assume, isn't likely to turn up in any Merseyside bone yards. Donovan recalled Paul showing up at his door, guitar in hand, and playing an embryonic version of the tune to him. It went like this:

> *"Ola Na Tungee, blowing his mind in the dark*
> *With a pipe full of clay, no one can say"*

This version predated the eventual motif of loneliness and alienation, instead being of an entirely different Asian-Indian flavor and containing a rather explicit suggestion of drug use. In 1966, Paul was not quite as willing as John to directly telegraph his thoughts on recreational substances (as the latter was doing with "Doctor Robert" on this same album). But drug use *was* an ongoing part of Paul's life, one he felt compelled to incorporate into his music. Unlike John, he would do it more subtly.

"Got to Get You into My Life" was a bold, brassy slab of American-styled R&B, fulfilling what the title of their last album merely suggested. The finished track would feature an overlay of horns, something previously unheard on a Beatles record—but a sound that would pop up repeatedly throughout the rest of their career. Paul's vocal was as exuberant as anything he would ever record, and listeners could certainly be forgiven if they took his joyful expression of desiring to be with "you" at face value. Thing was, though, he wasn't singing about a romantic interest; he was singing about weed.

If John had ever known this, he may have forgotten by 1980 when he opined that Paul was offering a salute to LSD use. Paul did in fact take his first trip later that year, well after the others had, though he set the record straight in *Many Years from Now*, stating: "It's actually an ode to pot, like someone might write an ode to chocolate, or a good claret."

John was, of course, much less coy about relating his drug experiences in song. Though he never sank to the level of being "gross" (his word) enough to actually advocate drug use per se, he had little problem with all but openly pronouncing his endorsement. "Doctor Robert" was direct and unambiguous: "If you're down, he'll pick you up / Doctor Robert." Over the course of the song's two minutes and fifteen seconds, listeners were treated to a virtual sales pitch for the doctor's mood-elevation services, making you "new and better," man.

While it's probable that most of the millions of fans hearing this song for the first time (on *"Yesterday"* . . . *and Today* in America; on *Revolver* everywhere else) gave little thought to its specific meaning, others did not, making a parlor game out of guessing who the title character was in real life—assuming the party wasn't wholly fictional. Bob Dylan may have been one suspect, given his status as the one who'd turned the group onto their first collective joint in August 1964 at New York's Delmonico Hotel; however, this was not yet common knowledge in 1966.

Another suspect was London art dealer Robert Fraser, who in 1967 would share the distinctions of: 1) helping art direct the *Sgt. Pepper* album cover; 2) getting busted at Redlands for drugs along with members of the Rolling Stones; and 3) introducing Paul McCartney to cocaine (which Paul later confessed in an interview with *Uncut* magazine to using with abandon throughout the *Sgt. Pepper* sessions). Lennon himself was no help in the mat-

In addition to the cover art for Revolver, *Klaus Voormann also produced a series of sketches that were used on various* Revolver *sheet-music issues in the U.K.*

ter, one day offering that he was writing about *himself* in "Doctor Robert" (a claim he often made about certain songs when pinned down about specifics), further stating that among the group, it was *he* who most often served as drug mule, dispensing pills upon request. But in another interview, John actually described a real person they'd met in America while on tour, marveling at their setup. "It was a big racket. He kept New York high."

Two real-life personas suggested themselves as John's model for the song. The first was certainly well-known to the Beatles and celebrities of the day: Dr. Max Jacobson. The notorious "Dr. Feelgood" treated his extensive list of famous clients (who included, most notably, President Kennedy, but also everyone from Tennessee Williams to Mickey Mantle and the Warhol crowd) to injected cocktails of vitamins and amphetamines until his license was pulled following a death in 1969.

However, he did not bear the virtue of being named "Robert"—unlike Dr. Robert Freymann, who made his living performing similar services. Speed-laced B-12 shots were his specialty, and among the musicians that made up a large portion of his clientele, he was something of a legend, having signed the death certificate of jazz great Charlie Parker back in 1955. Either man fits the description; most speculation, Paul McCartney's included, leans toward the latter possibility.

In the early days of the group, John and Paul set out to craft listener-friendly tunes designed to appeal to the biggest audience possible, one single after another. Their first several efforts were deliberately simple, using basic pronouns as keywords (me, you, I) and repeating instrumental motifs until they recognized the danger of those getting stale. During this time, the two chief songwriters took full advantage of their forced proximity (through a series of vans, hotels, and buses) to write constantly, creating a body of work big enough to suit the ever-increasing demand of the fans (while shopping any leftovers to other artists).

As success piled upon success, and it was becoming evident that their staying power was assured, the pressure to write together lessened. Both partners kept up their joint productivity, to be sure, though the resulting compositions had begun to take on more individual flavors. Well before *Rubber Soul* it had become easy to divine (mostly) who had written what song; still, their input on each other's compositions remained critical. John, for example, had contributed the "I love you, I love you, I love you" bridge to Paul's "Michelle," providing just the right amount of soulful grit to keep the song from completely sliding into twee hokum.

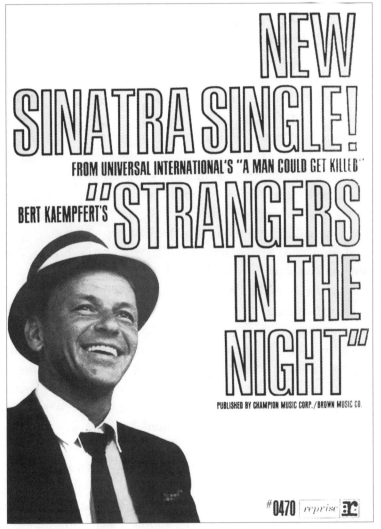

Despite the international success of "Strangers in the Night," Frank Sinatra professed to despise the song and refrained from singing it in his numerous TV specials.

Both men recognized the value of each other's ear and therefore maintained the partnership, despite the slackened pace. By 1966, the group's artistic goals had shifted: they were increasingly drawn to producing work whose merits would not be determined by the dictates of the Top Forty marketplace (or its translation into live-performance constraints, for that matter).

To that end, John and Paul continued to meet regularly to craft material. This oftentimes took place at John's Weybridge home, Kenwood. Despite the fact that Paul was the bachelor Beatle given to clubbing into the night, it was John that had the most trouble getting himself out of bed in the morning. Without delving too deeply into armchair psychoanalysis, it isn't hard to conclude that John was suffering from an ennui that possibly crossed the line into depression.

In later interviews, he spoke of this time as his "fat Elvis" period—certainly photos show his face fuller than it would ever be again. Only after the Beatles ceased touring later that year, and his recreational drug use began an uptick as he cast about for some sort of purpose, did he shake off his slothfulness and become something resembling the John of old, displaying flashes of ambition and regularly frequenting the artistic hotspots into which Paul was already hardwired. Nonetheless, he was sufficiently moved to defend his somnambulatory habits in song with "I'm Only Sleeping."

Initially, John's lyrics were a quite literal account of his need for slumber: "Try to sleep again / Got to get to sleep." But they soon found their groove as an evocation of purposeful daydreaming: escaping from the world's transient but persistent demands in favor of turning off his mind, relaxing, and floating upstream. This was an early expression of what would evolve into "bed peace" in three years time.

If the finished recording didn't drive the point home clearly enough, the song's rough draft underscored it. John began composing the words on the back of a "past due" notice from the General Post Office, the vendor who'd supplied his "radiophone"—an early car telephone. The letter threatened to cut off his service in seven days unless payment of twelve pounds, three shillings was made forthwith. One can assume that someone roused the sleeper just long enough to sustain his utility.

One pursuit that did stir John from hibernation was reading. While visits to the heady Indica Gallery bookstore were frequent, he could also be drawn into any less weighty content that crossed his path. There's circumstantial evidence that a profile of Frank Sinatra by Gay Talese that ran in the April 1966 issue of *Esquire* magazine connected with John enough to inspire a song, "And Your Bird Can Sing."

Through the years, there were some that speculated that the composition, originally titled "You Don't Get Me," was somehow a veiled take on the Beatles' creative rivalry with the Rolling Stones, going so far as to assert that the "bird" in question was none other than Mick Jagger's girlfriend at the time, chanteuse Marianne Faithfull. But there's no evidence whatsoever to support this.

Talese's article, a brilliant example of what was becoming known at the time as "New Journalism," refers repeatedly to Frank's use of the word "bird" as a synonym for the male member. With Frank, it was practically a verbal tic—a device for the Chairman of the Board to exhibit machismo while connecting with and putting his toadies at ease. In other words, fairly standard alpha-male behavior.

Author Jonathan Gould, in his magnificent cultural history of the Beatles, *Can't Buy Me Love: The Beatles, Britain, and America*, has put together a pretty convincing hypothesis that "And Your Bird Can Sing" was a slam at Sinatra, aimed squarely at Little Frank, specifically. To begin with, there was the matter of timing, with Sinatra having just beat out the Beatles twice at the Grammys (held on March 15) in two categories: Album of the Year (*September of My Years* over *Help!*—*Rubber Soul* was not even nominated) and Male Vocal of the Year ("It Was a Very Good Year" over "Yesterday").

Perhaps equally galling to John may have been Talese's depiction of Sinatra as "the fully emancipated male . . . the man who can have *anything* he wants" as the writer went on to describe the man's wealth and status. Though he'd one day ask the world to

Written by Jack Nicholson, The Trip's *principals—Fonda, Dennis Hopper, and director Roger Corman—all prepped appropriately for the film, but Corman later needed to have a "bad trip" described to him, since he hadn't had one.*

"imagine no possessions," John was running neck-and-neck with Sinatra in the acquisition category, as Maureen Cleave told the world in the infamous "How Does a Beatle Live?" article which, coincidentally, hit newsstands around the same time as Talese's.

Finally, the article followed Sinatra as he was preparing for a major television broadcast. Talese quoted the press release promoting *The Man and His Music* (which had aired in November 1965): "If you happen to be tired of kid singers wearing mops of hair thick enough to hide a crate of melons . . ." To John, this may have been the final insult (though he may have delighted in the article's mention of the fulltime staffer charged with maintaining Frank's *sixty* "remarkably convincing" hairpieces).

Gould suggests as further evidence: 1) the fact that the typically forthcoming Lennon was unusually dismissive of "And Your Bird Can Sing" in later years, as though he was less than proud of a song born of spite; and 2) the early take, issued on *Anthology 2*, where John and Paul collapse in fits of giggles as they try to get through the song. Their mirth is easily understood if they were being mindful of John's meaning. And your bird can *swing*, baby!

As discussed elsewhere, for those looking for it, *Revolver* is permeated with suggestions of LSD use. Not until Paul's revelatory 1967 interview did knowledge of the group's use of the hallucinogenic become public, but there were clues in ample evidence beforehand. "Tomorrow Never Knows" was a fairly explicit guide to tripping properly, while "She Said She Said" used as its starting point John's second LSD experience, which had occurred in Los Angeles on August 24, 1965.

During a stretch of five days off in the midst of their second American tour (between Portland and San Diego), the group rented Zsa Zsa Gabor's Beverly Hills home. There, they entertained numerous guests, including the Byrds' Crosby and McGuinn, actor Peter Fonda, and actress Eleanor Bron from *Help!* (with whom, rumor had it, Lennon was having a romantic interlude).

The two Byrds bonded quite easily with their musical counterparts over acid; those taking the trip included John, George, and—for his first time—Ringo. (Paul demurred.) Lacking a musical angle with which to engage the others, Fonda at first sought to impress them with a parlor trick: jumping into the deep end of the swimming pool and then proceeding to walk across the bottom to the opposite end. Neil Aspinall recalled their reaction: "Wow! Could you do that again?"

When this did not bring about the desired camaraderie, Fonda upped the ante, attempting to interest them with the revelation that, following a gun accident at the age of ten, he had actually knew what it was like to be dead. (The incident in question was no joke; the bullet had managed to pierce practically every vital internal organ before exiting. The boy was pronounced dead on arrival, until an attending gunshot-wound specialist was able to restart his heart and revive him.) Fonda would later report that it was in the interest of comforting George, who appeared to be experiencing some anxiety, that he brought up the episode at all.

But for two of the tripping Beatles, the actor was harshing their mellow. Given their proneness to paranoia and general lack of comfort around actors (George later reported his "hate" toward Lee Marvin, whose latest film, *Cat Ballou*, starring Peter's sister Jane, was being screened in the house while the Beatles tripped), John and George made their displeasure known. "Stop! We don't want to know," John recalled telling Fonda. "Who put all that crap in your head?" Though unsettled at the time with the encounter, John recognized Fonda's "I know what it's like to be dead" line as a keeper.

Coupled with his own "You're making me feel like I've never been born," John had the makings of a memorable vignette around which to build a song. It did take him awhile before he altered the gender from the original "He Said He Said" to its final form (a device he'd employ on "Sexy Sadie" two years later: originally written as "Maharishi," he feminized that song's title as well once his anger had cooled). But another noticeable motif that popped up was John's evocation of his childhood; one that, as every fan knows, was less than idyllic. In contrast to his negative reaction to the Fonda encounter, childhood was a time when "everything was right."

John seemed to be attacking the sanctimony of those "in the know" that feel they have the right to impose their knowledge upon others. (In "Tomorrow Never Knows," he turned the motif around by offering to impart what *he* knew.) As for Fonda, he's stayed a good sport, appreciating his immortalization in a John Lennon song while acknowledging years later that that the musician "was not very fond of me." A year after the encounter, he starred in the Roger Corman exploitation picture, *The Trip*, a film that effectively sensationalized the LSD experience.

Another John song that emerged during the sessions offered some perspective gleaned from acid: that the material world we live in is merely an illusion—"just a state of mind." John's "Rain"—containing more input from Paul than is commonly supposed—used the mundane topic of the weather as a vehicle to express the view (embraced by regular users of acid) that external appearances, and the sway that they have over people's moods, are irrelevant. What *really* matters is the meaning of within—as John would expound upon in another song. Given its allegorical lyrics, manipulated sounds, and droning, trancelike vibe, "Rain" can rightly be regarded as the group's first explicitly psychedelic song.

While that subtext would define the greater part of George Harrison's work well into his solo years, it was already a familiar one with John. As far back as "There's a Place," he sang about the escape to be found internally: "In my mind there's no sorrow." But with "Rain," he not only underscored the point by using metrological conditions as his metaphor; he also made the very conscious decision to express his willingness to share what he knew with those who hadn't yet traveled down the same mind-expanding path.

His lesson from the acid experience was that the way to escape the weight of materialistic thinking was to recognize it as the illusion that it was. For those willing to follow, he would lead the way: "I can show you"—"Can you hear me?" (This implicitly Messianic message echoed the one present in "The Word," released a few months before: "I'm here to show everybody the light.")

As recorded, "Rain" displays more than a trace of Indian influence. Though containing no Indian instrumentation, the overall droning effect throughout, achieved in part by slowing down the instrumental track (explored further on in this book), was purposely evocative, suggesting the exotic in a manner befitting the song's theme.

Secondly, John's singing on the words "rain" and "shine" during the choruses was an example of what's called "gamaka" in Indian music: the technique of applying "ornamentation" to a note.

On April 1, 1966, John, Paul, and Barry Miles paid a visit to Indica Bookshop and Gallery, on a mission to secure a copy of a book by an author named "Nitz Ga." After several frustrating moments, Paul and Barry divined that what John was really looking for was a copy of *The Portable Nietzsche*. Whether or not he purchased it became irrelevant, for what he *did* buy took on almost immediate and certainly long-lasting significance. It was a copy of *The Psychedelic Experience: A Manual Based on the Tibetan Book of the Dead*, published in 1964 and written by Timothy Leary, Ralph Metzner, and Richard Alpert.

Leary had spent over half a year in the Tibetan Himalayas, learning what he could directly from a Buddhist Lama Govinda. The so-called *Tibetan Book of the Dead* (the actual title translation is *Liberation Through Hearing During the Intermediate State* or *Bardo Thodol*) is a sacred text used to prepare and calm the dying during their transition from this world to the next. In Leary's case, it was the death of *ego* associated with LSD use that he was trying to help ease.

In 1966, this was pretty heavy stuff, essentially being a user's guide that drew upon venerable Eastern philosophy in order to steer experimenters away from bad trips. At this distance in time, it's probable that many contemporary readers will have difficulty grasping that, caricatures of tie-dyed hippie stoners aside, many young adults of otherwise earnest, inquiring dispositions possessed genuine curiosity in discovering for themselves a more satisfying handle on life's meaning than that which had been handed down to them by their elders.

Among Western youth, interest in the occult, in non-Western thought, and in "mind-expansion"—chemically induced, if need be—was on the upswing. Most of those digging deepest weren't

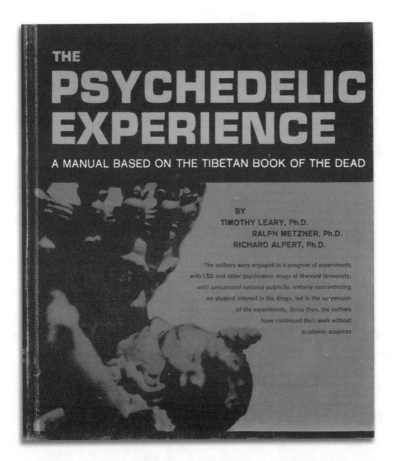

THE

PSYCHEDELIC EXPERIENCE

A MANUAL BASED ON THE TIBETAN BOOK OF THE DEAD

BY
TIMOTHY LEARY, Ph.D.
RALPH METZNER, Ph.D.
RICHARD ALPERT, Ph.D.

The authors were engaged in a program of experiments
with LSD and other psychedelic drugs at Harvard University,
until sensational national publicity, unfairly concentrating
on student interest in the drugs, led to the surpension
of the experiments. Since then, the authors
have continued their work without
academic auspices

*First published around the time of the Beatles' first marijuana experience
with Bob Dylan,* The Psychedelic Experience *remains the classic work
on the topic, and is in print to this day.*

doing so on a mission to find the latest kick so much as they were
attempting to make sense of a world where the means of bringing about instantaneous global destruction far outstripped the
human mind's ability to wrap itself around the implications of
such. It's worth noting that, rather than being on the vanguard of
such thought, the Beatles were reflecting what was already going
on within a segment of their generation. (Or, as John would one
day express it in *Playboy,* "Whatever wind was blowing at the time
moved the Beatles, too.")

Whether or not John digested all 159 pages or not, he at least
made it to page 14, where readers were advised: "Whenever in

doubt, turn off your mind, relax, float downstream"—a much more poetic impression than the line it followed: "Trust your divinity, trust your brain, trust your companions." Elsewhere, he took the concept introduced in the book as "the void"—the ultimate reality "beyond the restless flowing electricity of life"— and similarly evoked it. Indeed, "The Void" is widely but incorrectly believed to have been the working title of "Tomorrow Never Knows"—in fact, it was called "Mark I" at the time it was recorded. But with the finished product being so atypical for the Beatles and (John felt) susceptible to being blasted for perceived pretentiousness, its author settled on a Ringoism to take some of the weighty edge off of it.

At a February 1964 news conference upon their return to London following the group's *Ed Sullivan Show* debut, Ringo was asked about an unpleasant experience at the British Embassy in Washington, wherein a guest actually attempted to cut off a lock of his hair. He summed up the incident by stating with a shrug, "What can you say? . . . Tomorrow never knows!" Prompting laughter at the time, John must have filed away the quote for future use.

5

EVERY SOUND THERE IS: CREATING *REVOLVER*

*"The best thing about this group is that we all work everything out between us.
It doesn't matter who is playing what. If someone thinks
of something, then we'll try it."*

—RINGO STARR, 1966

A t around 10 AM on Monday, February 11, 1963, the Beatles commenced work on their debut LP, *Please Please Me*. With four sides representing two singles already in the can, ten numbers were needed to complete the task, though eleven were attempted; the thirteen takes of "Hold Me Tight" were ultimately deemed unusable, and their tape destroyed. This made their intended roster one song short, till—after conferencing—they decided to tackle "Twist and Shout," long a highlight of their club act.

The problem they faced, however, was the deteriorating condition of John's vocal cords. Suffering from a head cold (as was Paul) and the worse for wear after a full day of recording, odds did not favor what promised to be a single shot at nailing a useable take. But fortified by a couple of Zubes cough drops and a swig of milk, John gamely went for it, shredding what was left of his pipes in the process and ensuring that the second take they attempted would be worthless.

History records that EMI got their 600 pounds' worth out of the boys that day.

Three years later, the entire situation had changed. Whereas in 1963, the Beatles were given a single day to produce an album, EMI now allotted as much time as they needed. Three years before, the band was expected to lay down a studio version of their club act; now, they were given latitude to produce songs that they had no intention of ever reproducing live. In 1963, George Martin told them what was what; but in 1966, producer and artists functioned on the level of collaborators and co-explorers, pushing their imaginations as far as the limits of technology would allow them to go.

In this last effort, they were fortunate enough to have secured the services of an engineer as innovative and bold as the five of them: Geoff Emerick. Though Emerick has been the first to say that it was a matter of luck and good timing that placed him at their service just as they set down to work on such a significant project, it is beyond question that his willingness to push the envelope to find the sounds with which the Beatles tasked him paid dividends.

Perhaps one factor that inclined Emerick toward breaking rules was his youth. He was nineteen when George Martin asked him to work with him and the Beatles on *Revolver*, replacing Norman Smith, who'd been promoted by EMI to producer. Emerick was something of a company prodigy, having started his employment (albeit unpaid) the very same week of the Beatles' very first session back in June 1962 (Pete Best's last with the group).

He soon found a position as tape operator, and assisted on several overdub sessions for the group's first three LPs. From there, Emerick rose to the position of "lacquer cutter," mastering acetates—records of the day's work so that artists could take them home and listen to in the days before convenient, portable taping devices existed. This took him off the recording floor, though on at least one occasion during the *Beatles for Sale* sessions, he was pressed into service to act as assistant engineer on their *second* single-most productive day: one that saw them knock out eight tracks—half the album, plus one side of their next single.

Much of what we know about the details of the *Revolver* sessions comes from Emerick's 2006 memoir, *Here, There and Everywhere: My Life Recording the Music of the Beatles*. While a highly entertaining book, the perils of writing an account of events forty years after they happened are manifest. Emerick's tome includes dialogue, vivid anecdotes, and plenty of opinion; it also offers up

Melody Maker *editor Ray Coleman, a journalist friend of the Beatles who would one day pen bios on John, Paul, Brian Epstein—and Gary Numan— wrote this cover story in late 1966, anticipating the group's musical ambitions.*

some vignettes that are demonstrably incorrect, as evidenced by what has emerged from the oft-bootlegged multi-track masters. (Fellow engineer Ken Scott called him out on the inaccuracies in an Internet flame war, asserting that Emerick reached out to his fellow EMI engineers after securing a publishing contract, confiding that he really couldn't remember enough to fill a book.)

Emerick had been plucked from disc-cutting duties when a balance-engineer position opened up. Among his first successes was work with Manfred Mann on "Pretty Flamingo," a single destined to hit number one in the U.K. one month after the

Revolver sessions had begun. It's likely that Emerick was chosen by George Martin to work with the Beatles because the two got along so well; furthermore, as someone not yet twenty, he probably posed far less of a threat to Martin's position than any of the other staff, the majority of whom were past forty.

The first song slated to be recorded for what became *Revolver* was John's "Mark I" (since Lennon's preferred title, "The Void," was judged to be a little too obviously drug-connoting). It was composed in evident haste, given that the book that had inspired it had been purchased less than a week before. (Just after bringing *The Psychedelic Experience* home, John taped himself reading passages from it, and then took his third trip, intending to follow the instructions therein to the letter.)

From the onset, it was evident that some pretty heavy demands were going to be placed upon the engineering team. John had often complained about the quality of his voice, insisting that Martin douse it with tape echo whenever it might possibly suit the material. This wasn't often the case, and so John was compelled to make do with double-tracking: in this case, singing each song twice so that the vocals could be doubled up upon each other, resulting in a fuller sound. (The effect could also be applied to an instrument: George's leads, for example, were sometimes double-tracked, though accomplishing this with absolute precision was sometimes tricky.) But the sheer tedium of this chore annoyed him, and he constantly exhorted the staff to find some other way to obtain a usable vocal track without him being forced to replicate what he'd already done once.

It is astonishing that the Beatles were able to summon up revolutionary innovations on demand, but this was exactly what happened with the creation of ADT (Automatic Double Tracking), invented by technical engineer Ken Townsend. It operated on the principle of a tape delay, wherein a signal could be diverted during the mixing process into a second tape mechanism and then rerouted back to the track where the original signal was bound, superimposing this second signal upon it with just the slightest variance in timing, controlled by an oscillator, resulting in the effect of a single performance sounding double-tracked. With stereo mixes, the "two" performances could be (and often were) panned to opposite channels.

Another innovation employed with abandon at this juncture was vari-speed. This was nothing more complicated than altering the speed with which recorders burned up tape while laying down a track. The results of performing a song at a faster tempo than desired with the intention of slowing it down at playback tended to add a layer of texture that it was not possible to acquire through the normal process. Conversely, recording a song with the tape running slowly before playing it back at normal speed added a quality of lightness to the finished version. This latter approach would in a couple of instances ("Here, There and Everywhere," "I'm Only Sleeping") be applied to vocals on *Revolver*.

Sometimes controlling the speed of the tape simply enabled the performer to deliver a quality take that might have been too difficult to play in real time. George Martin's Baroque-sounding keyboard solo on "In My Life" from the *Rubber Soul* sessions was the serendipitous result of him recording his piece with tape rolling slowly in order to nail it. Upon the faster playback, the sped-up piano evoked the sound of a harpsichord.

Another tool for coloring their recordings came with the application of "tape loops." Through their publisher, Dick James, each Beatle had received a Brenell portable reel-to-reel tape recorder. (The idea was that any stray musical ideas they might unexpectedly come up with could be captured on tape; this was something of vital importance to the publisher, a man whose fortune was built upon the group's compositional abilities.) Paul, well into his Stockhausen phase, was given to experimenting with the device, and quickly learned that the erase head could be removed. Once the tape had been spliced to create an endless loop, sound could be added to it indefinitely without erasing what had been recorded before, thereby allowing the user to saturate the tape with sound—though Paul quickly learned that important sounds should be added last, lest they become masked by audio recorded thereafter.

Though the technology itself was not new, applying it to pop recordings (Beatle recordings in particular) was. Paul used the

As evidence of his interest in the avant-garde and electronic composing, Paul was fond of namedropping Karlheinz Stockhausen. This 1963 album, **Gesang der Jünglinge** *("Song of the Youths"), was said to be his favorite recording.*

recorder to capture any random sounds that caught his fancy: talking, laughter, instruments played in unconventional ways, ambient noises, and so forth. These found sounds, which he'd been in the habit of playing for his artsy friends as a sort of primitive *musique concrète*, would find the perfect setting on the very first song they attempted, but only after being reversed and played back at every speed but the original.

The use of reversed tape became ubiquitous during the making of *Revolver*. There is disagreement as to from whom the innovation originated: John related the story of coming home stoned while the band was working on "Rain" and declared that his less-than-clear-eyed state led him to put the tape on back to front. Hearing the performance from end to start entranced him, leading him to later declare his wish to issue the entire song *just like that*. Wiser heads prevailed.

On the other hand, George Martin was no stranger to experimenting with tape, going back to his comedy-record days, as well as an electronic recording he'd issued under the name Ray Cathode back in 1962 called "Time Beat." English record producer Joe Meek, of whose work the band was certainly cognizant, was also pioneering use of the very effects being explored at this juncture at Abbey Road.

Whether due to their expanded consciousness or simply recognition that so many records being made by their American counterparts sounded superior to what the Abbey Road facility was producing, the Beatles were adamant that something be done about what they believed to be evident shortcomings in EMI's recording capabilities. In fact, with classical recordings as their bread and butter for many years, EMI invested very carefully in top gear, including microphones with image fields that enabled three Beatles to record vocals at once, thus saving the necessity of reduction mixes to free up track space. Still, with rock's rapidly shifting paradigms, the inability of their equipment to keep pace with their expanding imaginations was becoming painfully evident.

Plans were actually in the works to fly the Beatles and their production team over to the states to record this album at the Stax studio in Memphis. There, the group believed, they would benefit from the loose but solid vibe they had heard on records by artists such as Otis Redding and Wilson Pickett. To that end, Brian Epstein flew over in March to personally make the arrangements. The famous Stax facility at 926 East McLemore Avenue was booked for two weeks beginning April 9, while an estate on Walnut Avenue belonging to a banking investor was selected as their residence for the duration. Unfortunately, word leaked out. Stax Studios became deluged with gawkers before the group ever actually arrived, while the town's tunesmiths besieged Stax personally with custom-crafted material in the off chance that the Beatles were interested in recording some authentic American R&B.

Epstein had seen enough and canceled the engagement, citing security concerns. (It has also been suggested that inflated rates for studio time were a factor.) Initially, a fallback plan to then relocate to Atlantic Records' New York City studios was considered, as was Motown, before the whole notion was quietly shelved. Among those disappointed by the turn of events was Stax guitarist / engineer Steve Cropper. "Who knows what might've happened? 'Taxman' could've been 'Staxman,'" he wryly noted.

In any event, Martin and Emerick proved themselves to be up to the task of fulfilling the group's desire for greatly improved sonic quality, as well as pushing the boundaries of everything they'd achieved to this point. In addition to the ADT's capacity for beefing up vocals and instruments with less effort, a vast improvement in capturing the bass was developed by the resourceful Emerick.

The bottom end found on Motown recordings was the envy of the music business. Much of it came from the talents of the then largely unknown James Jamerson, an uncredited but essential member of the "Funk Brothers," the Motown house band heard on virtually all of the label's hits. Jamerson played a 1962 Fender Precision bass; what few realized is that he barely maintained the instrument, feeling that the heavy-gauge flatwound strings that he took care to *never* change were essential to his tone.

The equally innovative Paul McCartney matched Jamerson's inventive, melodic style; the trouble was that few could truly hear it since his playing was often difficult to discern in the mix with any precision. Paul's choice of an instrument hadn't helped: the 1963 Höfner 500/1, an iconic violin-shaped hollow-body semi-acoustic (warm toned though it was), simply didn't have the testicular fortitude to propel the group into fulfillment of their sonic aspirations—at least on record. Also, it tended to go out of tune with itself the further up the neck he ventured. Within the noisy environs of their live work, the Höfner worked just fine—as Paul's signature bass guitar.

One potential remedy came with the arrival of the Rickenbacker 4001S solid-body bass, presented to Paul in Los Angeles during their 1965 tour. Paul was eager to try out the beast, a *heavy* long-necked behemoth, quickly mastering it and using it to great effect throughout the *Rubber Soul* sessions. Still, though tracks like "Drive My Car" and "Think for Yourself" (the latter featuring *two* bass lines, one played through a fuzz effect) hinted at the possibilities, Paul was relentless in pressuring the EMI team to come up with a way to make his parts pop.

Geoff Emerick provided the solution. Putting his career at EMI in jeopardy (by "abusing the equipment," as management would have it), he reasoned that the cone of a bass speaker could be used as a microphone, since the difference—in theory anyway—between a microphone and a speaker was the wiring path. A mic translated the incoming air of sound into electronic impulses that could be amplified or recorded, while a speaker took those electronic impulses and pushed them back into the air, making them audible. By reversing the wiring, Emerick reasoned, a bass speaker could become a large microphone, surely capturing much more of the loud bass signal than the typical small mic placed in front of a cabinet. It was worth trying, anyway.

A similar epiphany struck Emerick when it came to capturing the impact of Ringo's beater upon his kick drum. Though Norman Smith's technical expertise had proven invaluable for documenting the pedal's squeak on innumerable recordings, its actual percussive force had often been elusive thus far. Emerick had noticed Ringo's habit of dampening his snare drum's head with a cigarette pack. The engineer wondered if applying some sort of muffling to the kick would result in a more powerful sound on tape.

Removing Ringo's bass drumhead (bearing the famous dropped-T logo), he inserted a thick sweater inside. (This wasn't just any jumper: it was a four-necked pullover, apparently connected in some way with the *Help!* film—which had been, after all, originally titled *Eight Arms to Hold You*. Emerick surmised that Mal Evans must have kept it around to use as packing material.)

Next, he replaced the drumhead and brought the microphone as close to it as he dared—about three inches—despite EMI policy demanding a two-foot distance be maintained. (The potential for destroying the delicate inner workings of the expensive ribbon microphone was great—as were the grounds for termination.)

Last, he pushed up the faders on the drum track while applying a Fairchild Limiter; this last electronic filter had the effect of compressing the signal so that the peaks were lopped off, resulting in a more evenly focused, punchy sound.

As it happened, with the Beatles' rhythm section now taking this quantum leap forward sonically, the first track to be laid down seemed to forecast the techno ethos of a future era (complete with tape loops, sampling, and upfront bass and drums): the fittingly titled "Tomorrow Never Knows."

"MARK I" a.k.a. "TOMORROW NEVER KNOWS"
(Recording begins: Wednesday, April 6, 1966)

For some time, the Beatles had aspired to create a song around a single note, "Like 'Long Tall Sally,'" Paul explained. "We get near it in 'The Word.'" With "Tomorrow Never Knows," John essentially rode a C major throughout the duration, although the illusion of relief was applied during the second half of the verses by the introduction of flattened sevenths—a subtle change that broke up the underlying monochromatic drone.

John's freshly composed paean to the wonders of lysergic acid diethylamide became the first song attempted at the sessions. From the onset, John was very clear about the sound he wanted, if not on how to go about getting it. "I want my voice to sound like the Dalai Lama chanting from a hilltop," he informed Martin. He also required, in the background, the sound of "a thousand monks chanting." Given that John's last recorded originals had been rather straightforward material like "Run for Your Life" and "The Word," George Martin's astonishment at the rather leftfield request is fully understandable.

Without so much as a titter, Martin soberly assessed his options. He recognized that what John wanted was the effect of distance, rather than mere slap-back echo. "He said he wanted to hear *the words*, but he didn't want to hear *him*." To his credit, the producer "got" what John was asking for and set to work fulfilling this brief.

Given that the invention of ADT coincided with the recording of *Revolver*, and that its use is well-documented on Beatles recordings from this point forward, it might be an easy conclusion to draw that it was applied to Lennon's vocal on the first half of "Tomorrow Never Knows," while the well-chronicled application of the Leslie speaker came in the song's second half. Virtually every Beatle book asserts this as gospel; and while some authoritative writers have gone along with such, it simply isn't true.

For the first half of the song, concluding with the line "it is being," the effect applied to John's voice was simply good old-fashioned double-tracking, not ADT. (Hearing the stereo mix through headphones reveals this.) There were elements that *did* get that treatment, namely Paul's guitar solo (at least in the mono mix). After the instrumental break, a distinctly different effect is heard on the vocal: the Leslie speaker. The Leslie was a rotating device enclosed in a cabinet, designed and built for organs. They delivered an oscillating effect, something that Emerick judged would be worth trying out on the vocal to see if it evoked the Tibetan hillside well enough for John's liking.

The Beatles and their producer saw John's composition as something special that required a different approach than anything previously attempted. In the time between their last album and this one, each Beatle had absorbed influences that seemingly prepared them for this moment. With George, his Indian studies allowed him to recognize the latent exoticism of this single-chord song. He was quick to suggest a tambura drone to enhance the ambience; John quickly agreed.

Take one of "Mark I" was officially issued in 1996 on *Anthology 2*, giving fans at long last a glimpse into the development of this highly experimental track. It featured Ringo in a straightforward performance, absent the tom-tom syncopation heard on the finished recording, along with Paul on bass. It is *not* a tape loop; slight but discernible variances confirm this. Accompanying the rhythm section are three tape-looped instruments slowed down from their original recorded speed: an organ fed through the Leslie speaker, a guitar through a fuzz effect, and a thumping tom-tom.

John's voice was added next. It's heard processed entirely through the Leslie speaker and lacks the extra "oomph" to which we're accustomed, being very likely a guide vocal. It falls out of synch in places, which is completely understandable, given the difficult-to-follow backing. (The Leslie mode was set to "choral" for the vocal and "vibrato" for the guitar, resulting in what George quite accurately described later as an "underwater" effect.) The results of this first pass, though undeniably hypnotic, represented a good start, but something short of a keeper.

The remake (slated as "take three") ended up as the foundation of the finished track. Ringo and Paul were now locked together, with the former's thunderous, repetitive tom-tom beats giving the song a foreboding, apocalyptic tone. (The heads had been loosened for the occasion, adding an almost timpani-like resonance.) His steady wash of cymbal, used here for ambience rather than accent, provided a metallic and slightly alien feel, one that was amplified by George's atmospheric tambura.

The process of layering sound upon this solid backing began in earnest with the introduction of Paul's tape loops. He arrived at the studio the following day bearing a plastic bag that contained a number of his sonic experiments. (It is believed that the others likewise contributed: George with sitar samplings, John with Mellotron.) Of the loops, there has not yet been a universal consensus as to exactly which tapes made the final cut, but it does seem that a combination of the following five were settled on by group and producer:

1. A sped-up recording of Paul's own laughter, resembling the sound of seagulls.
2. A "sampling" of an orchestral B-flat major chord; later identified as coming from Jan Sibelius. (His Seventh Symphony pops up in "Revolution #9.")
3. and 4. Two separate sitar parts, heard backwards and at twice their performed speed.
5. Some Mellotron voicings, believed to be strings and brass. (Others have said flute.)

It has also been suggested that a tape of Paul running his finger along the brim of a wineglass reached the final mix (said to be heard—once—at 0:53). Given that virtually every sound heard on this track was distorted in some way, we will likely never know. (Paul's wineglasses *did* make a better-documented appearance on an album years later, as a segment within the "Hot As Sun / Glasses" track on his solo debut.)

The Mellotron can be thought of as a primitive synthesizer in that it enabled its user to simulate an array of instruments. It came loaded with tape samplings ranging from flute to Spanish guitar (both of which eventually ended up on Beatle records), accessed through a keyboard. John had accepted delivery of one back in August at his home in Weybridge. As moving the behemoth was precluded by its great size, John created some loops and brought them in. (The Mellotron heard on "Strawberry Fields Forever" was not John's home machine; that particular instrument would not be heard from again on vinyl until 1968's *Two Virgins*.)

Recording the tape-loop track required the use of many tape decks and many hands. As someone (a Beatle or George Martin) directed the faders up or down at the desired points in the song, engineers were busied holding pencils or glasses to maintain the tension on the tape loops as they moved across the play heads. It was, as Emerick related later, a surreal scene.

Other, more traditional elements were eventually incorporated: a tambourine here, an organ chord (playing the B-flat that came during the repeated lines at the end of the verses) there. A Challen upright piano occupied Studio Three, so it too was pressed into service. What made it unique was the built-in "jangle box" mechanism: a brass-tipped strip of felt that, with the touch of the third pedal, moved between the hammers and the strings to add a staccato, percussive sound, otherwise known as "tack piano" (from when the same effect had been achieved by actually inserting tacks into the hammers). During an early take, George Martin had pounded out some incongruously merry-sounding notes; the performance would find use in the song's outro.

Not until the afternoon of Friday, April 22 were the final elements put into place. This included John's vocal: it was double-tracked through the instrumental break before being sent through the Leslie speaker for the song's concluding verses. Though the recording at this point was richly laden with all manner of audio coloring, at this juncture a guitar solo was deemed necessary, and not just any one: it would be presented backwards and performed by Paul.

Ian MacDonald asserted in the book *Revolution in the Head* that the wildly psychedelic obbligato heard here was merely Paul's "Taxman" lead sped up and turned back to front. To be sure, to anyone so interested in deciphering it, it does indeed seem to match the tone and voice of Paul's work on George's song recorded one day earlier. But home-recording technology has come so far in our day that it doesn't take much ingenuity beyond digital programs like Audacity or Audition to deconstruct what's here, place it at its recorded tempo with the backward tape forward, and assess.

The conclusion? It's similar—but different. Seeing as how Paul recorded the "Taxman" solo one day earlier, one could conclude that: 1) it's an outtake that was preserved and flown in for use on "Tomorrow Never Knows"; or 2) Paul kept his settings until the next day, when he laid down this solo in a style similar to his earlier one.

The differences between the mono and stereo mixes are worth noting. The tape-loop effects are livelier in stereo; indeed, to anyone raised on this mix, the mono sounds somewhat spartan in comparison. The mono version, which of course would have been the common currency at the time, appears to have run the guitar solo through ADT, suggesting that this was how the group preferred to have it heard. But stereo listeners were treated to a bonus element not heard in the mono mixes: a bell-like ringing tone of feedback at 1:28—the exact midpoint of the song.

Though the array of sounds seemingly coming and going at random may have struck some fans as chaotic, there was very much a method to what had been put together. It was therefore a big deal when, upon the album's release, John discovered that the mix of "Tomorrow Never Knows" pressed in British mono copies sold on the first day of issue was not the one they'd intended to release. A mastering error left the wrong mix ("Remix 11") in place, forcing a recall and a substitution ("Remix 8") at George

Martin's behest. Nowadays, of course, this rare pressing commands premium prices. (For those wondering: Remix 11 features a hotter vocal mix and longer fadeout, among other variances.)

All in all, "Tomorrow Never Knows" was an audacious start to the as-yet-untitled album's sessions. Nowhere was the band unity at a higher point than here, where each member contributed something vital to the greater whole. As a measure of how far they'd come and the direction they would give to others that followed, it was an achievement of inestimable value.

"GOT TO GET YOU INTO MY LIFE"
(Recording begins: Thursday, April 7, 1966)

Next up was an R&B–styled shouter, complete with the brass and production that Paul may have had in mind back when the group was still contemplating recording at Stax. Though this was indeed how the finished recording ended up, this was not at all how it had started. On the same evening that the tape loops were applied to "Tomorrow Never Knows," a basic track was attempted for this number of Paul's. This work in progress was also eventually issued on *Anthology 2*, offering a peek at what might have been.

As this attempt (take five) was abandoned before it was completed, we'll never know how it would've sounded in finished form. But at this early stage, it came across as more Haight-Ashbury than Memphis, sounding much more airy pop than gritty soul. This take of "Got to Get You into My Life" possessed elements rethought (and removed) from the final version: hearty harmonies from John and George, as well as a "need your love" interlude and Paul's exclamation of "somehow, someway" following the refrain. The overall impression heard here tended to camouflage the song's true inspiration as an ode to marijuana with the trappings of your garden-variety love song. Paul may have recognized this, and therefore opted for ambiguity rather than deception in the final product.

One day after laying down this version, it was decided to revisit what had been considered the best take, and start again from scratch. The prominent organ part played by George Martin the previous day was toned down in favor of guitar, specifically

John's. George occupied himself with a tambourine, dropping in his guitar parts later. The band quickly settled into a groove that jettisoned the extraneous elements in favor of a slimmed-down performance that dropped all the vocals except for those coming from Paul. Three takes completed over the course of a seven-and-a-half-hour session produced the keeper: take eight.

Beyond assists from George Martin and—occasionally—Mal Evans, the Beatles had spent the bulk of their recording career handling all the instrumentation themselves, multitasking when necessary. Some fans believe that 1965's "Yesterday" marked the first occasion where outside musicians were conspicuously employed on a Beatles record; others note flautist Johnny Scott's contribution to "You've Got to Hide Your Love Away," which was recorded earlier for the same album. (Technically, of course, both are wrong: session star Andy White had famously supplanted Ringo on one version of "Love Me Do" back in September 1962.)

But with *Revolver*, session musicians were contracted with abandon. Nothing underscored the rather obvious decision the Beatles had made with their music than this: no longer would they be bound to record only what stood a decent chance of being reproduced on stage. From now on, whatever was needed to fulfill what they were hearing in their heads would be found, live presentation be damned. George later said that it hadn't occurred to them to even consider augmenting themselves with other musicians onstage, so accustomed were they to doing at least this aspect of their job the way they always had.

For "Got to Get You into My Life," five horn players (three trumpets and two saxophones) were recruited to provide some jazzy brass. Two were pulled from the ranks of Georgie Fame's Blue Flames—Eddie "Tan Tan" Thornton (trumpet) and Peter Coe (sax) —augmented by Liverpudlian Ian Hamer, trumpet; Les Condon, trumpet; and Alan Branscombe, sax. All were older men whose careers predated the Beatles by a number of years; and though live dates were their bread and butter, the Blue Flames personnel had scored a few hits of their own, notably 1965's "Yeh Yeh."

The most time-consuming element audible on the finished recording is the brass arrangement. Normally, scoring multiple instrumental parts was all in a day's work for George Martin, who took care of such tasks from the beginning with great alacrity and finesse. But neither he nor Paul were entirely sure exactly what they wanted. As Coe recalled later, it was the *feel* that they were going for rather than the exact pitches, and a great deal of time was spent trying different approaches as Paul pounded out notes on the piano. Eventually something magical was hit upon, stirring John to dash out of the control room, giving all the thumbs-up.

With an air of experimentation permeating the proceedings thus far, it was natural that getting the sound on tape for this song would also require a fair amount of trial and error. Following the path he'd taken by close-miking the drums, Geoff Emerick tried a similar tack with the brass, going so far as to place the mics into the bell of each horn. Again, this was something that was simply not done—normal procedure dictated a four-foot placement from the source. But group and producer were pleased with the added bite gained in this fashion.

Once the horns were heard on tape alongside the group's backing track at the mixing session, however, Paul was concerned that the sound was not fat enough, and asked George Martin if perhaps another layer might be necessary. Worried that they'd already spent a considerable sum on musicians' scale, Martin and was loath to run up the tab further. Once again, Geoff Emerick came up with a solution: doubling the horns by tape (in effect, applying ADT), achieving the desired sound without expending further effort. However, this effect was applied only to the mono mix.

The mono / stereo differences heard on the remastered CDs are otherwise minor, principally audible at the song's fadeout. There, Paul's ad libs vary between the two mixes, with different ones employed on each. (Also, the mono fadeout is slightly longer.) Much more tantalizing is the 1970s-era vinyl stereo mix heard on U.S. Apple pressings. There, Ringo's drum fills leap from the speakers. It is mystifying that this superlative mix has never made it to digitization (legally, anyway).

"GRANNY SMITH" a.k.a. "LOVE YOU TO"
(Recording begins: Monday, April 11, 1966)

The first George composition laid down for *Revolver* was also the most ambitious. Less than half a year after placing a primitive sitar line onto John's "Norwegian Wood," the guitarist was now ready to offer up a composition *written* on sitar and performed just about entirely on Indian instruments. He had been taking lessons in London from a tutor contracted through the Asian Music Circle, a North London organization founded by Ayana Angadi in the 1950s. George Martin was familiar with the organization, having hired some of its members in the past for a Peter Sellers recording requiring an authentic Indian backing. Though George had not yet met Ravi Shankar at the time the *Revolver* sessions had begun, he was well steeped in the maestro's recordings.

By the time he was ready to take on the challenge of recording his *khyal* (a short-form modern Indian musical composition built upon an unharmonized melodic line, with distinct slow and fast movements), he had the arrangement sketched out in his head, but no title. To keep a handle on the track, Emerick dubbed it "Granny Smith" after his favorite variety of Apple—the same one that would emerge as the Beatles' corporate logo in two years time. The session began with George performing the song on acoustic, Ringo on tambourine, and Paul providing high harmony. This last element eventually fell by the wayside.

To this day, there are some that question whether George handled the primary instrumental duties himself. The sitar line on "Norwegian Wood" was quite simple, but it had been recorded before he'd had any proper schooling on the instrument. Some believe that the apparent complexity heard on "Love You To" was beyond his capabilities, at least in spring 1966. But others point to his single-minded diligence in mastering the instrument, as well as his study through private lessons, proximity to accomplished musicians, and close listening to pertinent records.

Others were brought in to handle specialized parts, however. To capture a live go of the tune rather than resort to multi-tracking and tape reduction, George recruited another sitar player as well as someone to handle tambura, *swarmandal*—a zither-like Indian harp—and the tabla, the Indian hand drum. Thankfully, the percussionist—Anil Bhagwat—was credited on the album; why the others were not is one more Beatle mystery. Mr. Bhagwat later told Mark Lewisohn that he had no idea who was summoning him to the session, but the Rolls-Royce that arrived to take him to the studio clued him in that it was *important.* Swarms of girls camped out at the facility confirmed the presence of pop stars.

He further related that, once settled in, George was direct in explaining what he wanted: a sixteen-beat rhythm (Ravi Shankar-style), encouraging him to improvise. "It was one of the most exciting times of my life," Bhagwat reported. The finished track was indeed a groundbreaking undertaking, making explicit the Indian influence implicit throughout the entire album: from the single-chord drone of "Tomorrow Never Knows" to the Indian-styled attack of Paul's solo in "Taxman" to the melisma of "Rain."

ADT was applied to the vocal in places. Mono / stereo variances are confined largely to the length of the fadeout. Just as the song shifts into high gear for the improvisational movement, the number ends, though mono listeners are given an extra thirteen seconds.

"PAPERBACK WRITER"
(Recording begins: Wednesday, April 13, 1966)

Recording what was slated to be the Beatles' follow-up to the "Day Tripper" / "We Can Work It Out" single began with the unusual lineup of Paul on "lead" guitar (there is no real soloing); George playing second guitar; Ringo, drums; and John, tambourine. The song was built around a singular riff, composed by Paul; it can be read with hindsight as the furthering of an unhealthy tendency that started with "Another Girl" on *Help!* (wherein Paul similarly usurped George's role) that would eventually lead to antipathy between the second and third Beatles. But for now, it is probable that expediency dictated that the person most capable of performing the riff do so, especially since his own primary part (bass) was slated to be added later anyway.

"Paperback Writer" marked an occasion for Geoff Emerick to maximize the bass to an unheard-of level on a Beatles record. He picked the perfect song to which to apply this treatment, for Paul's nimble lines, played high up on the neck, seldom demanded to be heard as they did on both sides of this single. Though capturing the muscular sounds proved to be the easy part, once Emerick's experiment of recording through a speaker was shown to have paid off, there was still the issue of getting the single mastered that concerned EMI's engineering staff.

They feared (with good reason) that too powerful a signal cut so deep in the grooves would cause the needles to bounce right out of the records. It would not do to have the purchasers of the latest Beatles single return them en masse as defective. Therefore, as had occurred virtually every other time some technological limitation stymied progress on the *Revolver* project, a new innovation custom-created to serve the Beatles' artistic vision came into existence. In this case, it was something called Automated Transient Overload Control (ATOC) that did the trick, enabling the stylus cutter to present the full depth of bass without causing any issues.

The song itself was recorded quite quickly (two takes), without any rethinking necessary. The arrangement was deceptively simple, employing two chords judiciously implemented over the course of two minutes and eighteen seconds. The layered *a cappella* vocals that comprised the song's chorus were expertly arranged; they were not innovative, perhaps, but effective, especially when doused with taped delay at every other occurrence. Cleverer were the "Frère Jacques" backing vocals from John and George, a musical *non sequitur* that served as countermelody. (These were recorded at half speed at Paul's request in order to be played back at higher than their normal range.)

The only elements documented to have been tried and not kept were two keyboard parts: a Challen "tack piano" track, routed through the Leslie speaker; and a Vox Continental organ part. These both had been played by George Martin. George Harrison applied some lead-guitar fills to augment Paul's riffing, which itself was supplemented with ADT.

He would later note that, even though this song was as straightforward a recording as they would manage in 1966, they still fell short when attempting to reproduce it live. When horrendous harmonies and all-around lack of coordination plagued performances of "Paperback Writer" in Tokyo later that summer, George would simply wave wildly to the crowd, eliciting a big enough outbreak of screams to mask the group's all-too-obvious musical shortcomings.

Differences between the mono and stereo mixes of "Paperback Writer" are manifest. The tape delay on the choruses is much more pronounced in mono; the overall running time is longer, too, with more repeats of the refrain at the finish. Really, there is simply no comparison between the two formats; since the song was built for AM airplay, to be enjoyed through tiny transistor speakers, the mono mix is premium. Between this song and "Revolution," if anyone ever needs convincing of the merits of monaural mixes, these tracks make the case quite forcefully.

"RAIN"
(Recording begins: Thursday, April 14, 1966)

Assuming that U.S. single releases didn't count—since there were so many of them—precedent established on their two previous singles mandated that the Beatles would couple a "John" song with a "Paul" one on the opposite side. (George's moment for single space would not arrive for another two years, with "The Inner Light" as the flip side of "Lady Madonna.") "Rain," written mostly but not entirely by John, was tabbed to back Paul's hyperkinetic A-side. Also echoing prior example, the two sides could not have offered a bigger study in contrasts.

Whereas "Paperback Writer" was a booming piece of extroverted pop, "Rain" was designed to draw listeners into their own heads, to reexamine their perceptions by way of its inherently seductive drone. Though instrumentally conventional, the manipulation of the captured sounds was anything but. This recording was as compelling through repeated listenings as its A-side had been immediately appealing. "Rain" represented a fine example of a song destined for a B-side that nonetheless was produced with the same care it would have been given on the plug side. In this, the Beatles and their producer stood head and shoulders above most of their peers.

This photo was taken on November 25, 1965, at Twickenham Film Studios, during the shooting of the Intertel promo film for "Help!"

It is evident right from the start that the second John Lennon composition taped during these sessions was going to be subject to a certain amount of innovation. The fact that the group purposely recorded the initial takes at a slightly faster tempo (key of B-flat) than they intended the finished product to play back at (G major) strongly suggests the input of their producer, who knew a thing or two about ways to achieve musical texture. By slowing down the backing track after laying it down, the instrumentation would come across as less beat group-y and more dense without sacrificing clarity.

Another aspect that left the overall effect slightly disorienting was the song's innate rhythmic boldness. As Ringo would be the first to attest, John's sense of timing was, to put it one way, adventurous. As far back as their first single, the Beatles had been fond of irregular measures, but on "Rain," this device of nine-measure verses (except for the second verse, which was nine-and-a-half) instead of the usual even-numbered ones resulted in an asymmetrical feel to a 4/4 song. Added to this was John's Dylanesque phrasing of the vocal line *against* the beat. It was a device that helped emphasize the lyrics, one that he would increasingly rely upon in the future.

It is impossible to discuss "Rain" without giving props to the superlative performances delivered by the Beatles' rhythm section. First, there is Paul's virtual "lead bass" playing on the track. Knowing that at last his bass would be heard in all its dynamic glory seemingly inspired him, spurring him toward the previously unreachable heights of glory evident on both sides of this record. While "Rain" was less obvious of a vehicle for displaying virtuosity than its uptempo counterpart, Paul nonetheless was in no way hamstrung by any perceived limitations. Instead, he displayed increasing invention with this song, varying his fills with each repeated chorus and taking advantage of the capability of laying down his part separately once all the other instruments were in place.

Nowhere was the benefit of this heard to greater effect than at the break beginning just before the coda at 2:22. Knowing in advance what Ringo was going to play allowed for Paul to lock onto the percussive fills with precision, heightening the moment's taut drama. It is therefore somewhat curious that the Beatles, Martin, and Emerick chose to never repeat the trick of using a speaker as a microphone after "Rain" was finished, as though it was simply an innovation intended for use on a single and not an album track. For the remainder of the project, bass was recorded in the traditional way; not until the following February (when laying down *Sgt. Pepper*'s title track) did they discover the possibilities of recording the bass through "direct injection": running the patch cord out of the instrument and straight into the recording console.

The Beatles' self-effacing percussionist spent the whole of their career years being quite modest about his abilities behind the kit. But once the rest of the world—well, at least the discerning portion of it—caught up with his singular talents, and Ringo started to be asked about them, he was quick and quite definite about what his personal favorite performance was during those years. Not "Long Tall Sally," "Ticket to Ride," "Strawberry Fields Forever," "A Day in the Life," or "The End." It was "Rain" that he gravitated toward, completely without reservation, as noted in *The Big Beat: Conversations with Rock's Great Drummers*: "I know me and I know my playing, and then there's 'Rain.'"

From the song's opening volley of snare taps, Ringo is in command, punctuating every other measure with a burst of percussive fire beneath the singing. An interesting thing occurs at 0:40, wherein instead of pulling out of the fill before the next bar, he continues on, as if stumbling down a flight of stairs, unable to stop himself. Somehow he manages to reel himself back in before the whole thing collapses into chaos, but it's a telling indicator of the group's collective thinking that they allowed such an unorthodox passage to remain in the finished product.

Ringo would later marvel at his own approach to the fills, saying that on this song he began them by coming off the high-hat cymbal before hitting the drum first (something he'd pioneered as far back as "Wait" during the *Help!* sessions). But now the fills that followed were much more adventurous. Perhaps it would be stretching a point to conclude that his rethinking his approach to his job was directly influenced by his LSD use, but it is at least worth noting that everything we hear him do on this particular record was performed at a faster tempo than the the familiar one heard on the recording.

On the subject of vari-speed, the lead vocal had also been subject to a little tweaking. In addition to the ADT applied to John's voice, it was recorded with the backing slowed down (beyond its eventual playback tempo), which had the effect of making him sound a little airy when contrasted with the more leaden instrumental track. But the biggest innovation came at the song's coda, when the wonders of backward vocals were first introduced on a Beatles record.

As discussed earlier, it's anyone's guess whose idea it was to first turn around the vocal line on "Rain." John claimed (and George seconded) that he hit upon the concept while herbed up and listening to a playback at home on his portable Brenell tape recorder. But George Martin, never exactly known for stealing a Beatle's thunder, has claimed the idea was his. Certainly the execution was his doing, something no one disputes.

However the seed had been planted, Martin did select a portion of the vocal track to reverse and fly into the track's coda beginning at 2:36, pointedly ignoring John's suggestion that they issue the entire performance backwards. Set against the backing vocals (taped on another track) singing "Rain!," John's lead evoked the sound of a blissed-out zealot speaking in tongues in a trancelike state. It was a pitch-perfect capper to an astonishingly pioneering piece of pop.

The song was issued in mono. Not until the need for an LP iteration surfaced (for the 1970 *Hey Jude* collection) was a stereo mix prepared, by which time, presumably, hard-panning the vocals to one channel (*à* la the stereo *Rubber Soul*) was recognized as a bad idea.

"DOCTOR ROBERT"
(Recording begins: Sunday, April 17, 1966)

Having laid down *two* earnest evocations of his drug experiences so far, as the *Revolver* sessions entered their third week John was now ready to offer up a tongue-in-cheek salute to a drug-dispensing physician. In contrast to "Tomorrow Never Knows" and "Rain," however, there wasn't anything particularly tricky or experimental about the studio treatment of "Doctor Robert." Rather, it was a standard guitar workout, colored by a harmonium—the same keyboard instrument John had used not long before on "We Can Work It Out."

The most interesting feature of the song's construction is the subtle key shift. "Doctor Robert" begins in A major and stays there for the first twelve bars, which normally would establish it as an A major song. But the tune then slides into B major at 0:17, just before the repeat of the title and the "you're a new and better man" passage, remaining there for the bridge. This floating key pattern repeats throughout the remainder of the song, displaying the group's gift for keeping things interesting for themselves and listeners well versed in music theory.

Also of interest is the song's Christmas carol–like bridge. The "well, well, well" passages feature group harmonies and prominent harmonium while the drums come to a rest (reminiscent of the choruses in "Rain"). This choirboy interlude, implemented in the service of a song glorifying a pill pusher, underscores a dark sense of irony lurking just beneath the surface.

It took just seven takes, recorded over the course of an eight-hour session, to nail a satisfactory instrumental track. Added overdubs included maracas and some lead guitar; an attempted piano addition was dropped. The issued recording of "Doctor Robert" contains an aspect of mystery about it, concerning the excise of forty-three seconds of recorded music. Some believe it came just before the first bridge; others (among them, writer John C. Winn) at 1:34. Since the familiar recording contains no soloing, it is believed that the original performance included an instrumental interval that was judged superfluous, and cut.

Paul provided some robust harmonies to the verses (beginning with the second) that offered a nice contrast to John's deadpan delivery (which would be subjected to ADT during the mixing process). The U.S. mono mix contained an "Easter egg" of sorts: John saying something that sounds like "okay, Herb" just after the song's cold ending.

Mono mixes were prepared just after an April 19 session that saw the group's final touches put in place; these never saw release. But then on May 12, while *Revolver* was still a work in progress, a call from Capitol sent George Martin, Geoff Emerick, and second engineer Jerry Boys back to the mixing console to rush mono and stereo masters over to America. With the label cobbling together a collection for the U.S. market culled from U.K. singles and spare parts drawn from *Help!* and *Rubber Soul*, *Yesterday . . . and Today* was still short by three tracks. In order to make their June release date, the Beatles' American label was demanding something novel: new, heretofore-unreleased material.

They might have simultaneously kept the new album intact

and spared themselves the creation of more non-album material simply by scooping up the summer of '65's "I'm Down"— recorded the very same day as "Yesterday," by the way—and adding both sides of their spring 1966 single, "Paperback Writer" / "Rain." This latter addition would have provided the added benefit of making the collection much more up-to-date than building it around "Yesterday" had. This did not happen, the result of which led to a compositional imbalance that made the American *Revolver* album the only Beatle release to feature more George Harrison songs than John Lennon ones.

A mono mix that differed from the eventual U.K. one was produced for this American release. But rather than wait for the proper stereo mix to arrive, Capitol instead made the decision to create a fake stereo "Duophonic" mix, channeling low frequencies one way and high ones the other. Given the fact that the stereo market was so much smaller in 1966 than the mono one, this may have been considered a justifiable bit of corner-cutting subterfuge; but by the 1970s, a more discerning breed of listeners demanded—and got—a proper stereo mix, as did buyers of the tape format.

The U.K. mono version has the guitars mixed slightly lower during the verses than its U.S. counterpart. All mixes except the U.S. mono one fade the song just before the actual ending is audible.

"AND YOUR BIRD CAN SING"
(Recording begins: Wednesday, April 20, 1966)

Just a day after the recording of "Doctor Robert" was completed (and two days after John and George took in a set by the Lovin' Spoonful at London's Marquee Club), another John composition was ready to be tracked. Unlike "Doctor Robert," "And Your Bird Can Sing" would undergo a major change in arrangement, perfecting an already good song and making it great by erasing the derivative-sounding approach.

As originally laid down (take two can be found on *Anthology 2*), "And Your Bird Can Sing" came off as practically a Byrds homage, in the key of D major and featuring predominating harmonies supported by some twelve-string Rickenbacker jangle. Juxtaposing the California bands' sound with a composition containing "bird" in the title may have seemed to them, upon reflection, to be carrying a joke too far.

A considerable amount of mirth was caught on tape, much of it evident on the *Anthology 2* release of the song. It came while John and Paul were double-tracking the vocal harmonies; something set off a giggling fit between them that spoils the take, leading the two to abandon all seriousness. Though there are many that supposed it was prompted by a good dose of "tea," as noted earlier in this book, the Beatles were averse to indulging themselves while working, if only because it tended to undermine the quality of their efforts, inevitably leading to do-overs afterward.

Take three (which has gone unheard publicly—so far) has been described by Mark Lewisohn as "a very heavy recording." It is likely that here is where the key was shifted to E major, while the decision was made to ditch the jangle in favor of a twin-guitar harmonized riff. It is this intricate dual picking that took the song to a whole other level, representing a tack that was never attempted again, but one that made "And Your Bird Can Sing" a unique, ferociously guitar-heavy track. Also dropped were the stacked vocals in favor of a leaner approach that emphasized John's lead, with harmonies from Paul limited to the end of each line, making for a much more effective accent.

One very hot topic of debate among the hardcore fans has been: Who exactly is wielding the two guitars? Under ordinary circumstances, one would suppose that George supplied one of them; but at some point during the 1980s, he told an inquisitor that the parts had been played by John and Paul. Now one can take his statement as the final word, except that we find often that George's memory was hardly an infallible instrument of recall, despite his reputation for remembering the past well. For instance, at various times, he forgot which album came first: *Rubber Soul* or *Revolver* (as did John); totally blanked on the fact that the Beatles played Shea Stadium *twice*; and had to be reminded that it was *he* who had played bass on "Golden Slumbers."

In other interviews, he *did* lay claim to it, saying that it took "ages" for he and Paul to get their parts perfected on tape. Still another expresses his uncertainty whether it was he and Paul or he and John. All of which underscores a point made by Paul years after the Beatles ended: the Beatles were too busy creating to mentally keep track of the details over which fans would obsess for decades thereafter.

The fact that much of what would become the final riff is present in the abortive take two, albeit in a slightly less-realized form, leads one to the natural conclusion that George is in fact playing one of the guitars (assuming that it's his twelve-string Rickenbacker, as seems evident; this was an instrument that Paul, for all his superpowers, was not known to have played on a Beatles record).

Compositionally, it certainly has more in common with George's style of guitar playing than John's: crisp, fully articulated notes, and precision bends that are more voice-like than bluesy. About the only signature George element missing is any hint of Indian influence.

While John was certainly a capable lead player when he needed to be (listen to the solos in "You Can't Do That" or "Get Back" for examples), nothing he ever played came close to this level of discipline, much less the focus needed to play it in synch with another guitarist, live, as the tape reels turned. (George and John did double each other on the lead for "Nowhere Man," but that part is a much simpler one to play.)

In *Many Years from Now*, Paul took ownership and declared that it was *he* and George that had been responsible for the harmonized lead. Given his knack for arranging, as well as the guitar-hero aspirations that he increasingly took every opportunity to display, it isn't hard to conclude that it was indeed Paul who harmonized the twin lead with George.

Just as the arrangement required a certain amount of time and effort to be finalized, right up until the tape began to roll, so too did John tinker with the lyrics until right before he laid down the definitive take. Overdubs were few, consisting of handclaps; touches of cymbal; a wildly variant tambourine part; and, of course, Paul's Rickenbacker bass. Beyond the song's central riffing, "And Your Bird Can Sing" is a picture-perfect example of how the group *orchestrated* their parts, arranging so as to provide optimum color and detail without stepping on each other.

The vocals were subjected to ADT in the mixing process, as seems more evident in the mono version. The stereo mix doesn't hard-pan the vocals, which is nice, but the guitars seem slightly rawer in the mono mix, especially the U.S. version. Take ten was the keeper, with Paul's song-ending bass flourish spliced in from take six.

"TAXMAN"
(Recording begins: Wednesday, April 20, 1966)

The second Harrisong tackled benefited mightily from the input provided to George by his bandmates. First, it was John who gave the already-biting lyrics some extra sting, while Paul contributed equally sharp lead guitar. The group began work on "Taxman" on the same evening that the aborted take of "And Your Bird Can Sing" had been recorded. Four takes (of which only two were completed) were attempted before they set it aside in favor of mixing take two of "And Your Bird Can Sing," which at this point was still being considered a keeper.

When work resumed the following day on "Taxman," it began from scratch, as the arrangement was still taking shape. *Anthology 2* offered up a performance that was completed on April 21, the last of eleven takes that took roughly as much time to perfect as it had to lay down *the entirety* of their debut album. Unlike 1963, when the group was expected to come in with their song arrangements fully locked down, 1966 saw a virtual blank check accorded to the unfathomably successful act, wherein they could tinker with their creations at their leisure.

The *Anthology 2* take offers a couple of striking differences from the finished release. To begin with, the chiding "Ah-ah, Mr. Wilson / Ah-ah, Mr. Heath" was not a part of the song yet; instead, a rapid-fire repeat of "Anybody got a bit of money?" sung in falsetto by John and Paul took its place. Though it's likely that had the decision to keep this element intact (as heard on the 1995 issue on *Anthology 2)* been made, millions of Beatle fans would've gotten accustomed to it by now, it comes as a superfluous distraction that doesn't mesh with the rest of the track nearly as well as its eventual replacement.

Another prominent difference came with the cold ending: an exclamation of the song's title sung with gusto by Paul and John. A repeat of the same backing-vocal part that had come earlier in the song (just before the solo and during the last verse at 2:02) was quite effective and dramatic; it also bore an unmistakable evocation of television's then-current *Batman* series (which had first hit the U.S. airwaves on January 12). Some have questioned through the years how it was possible for George to have been familiar enough with Neal Hefti's theme song to have purposely referenced it in this song without having seen the show. (The show was first broadcast in Britain on May 21, 1966—well after "Taxman" had been committed to tape.)

The answer is: he was familiar with the show's *theme song*. "Batman," the song, had charted as a single on both sides of the Atlantic, coinciding with the show's premiere. Versions by both the song's composer as well as by an instrumental band, the Marketts, were in release; the Who, in fact, recorded a cover later that year for release on their *Ready Steady Who* EP. Therefore, it's pretty likely that George was making a deliberate decision to call it out in "Taxman," giving listeners a wink by letting them in on the joke that, real tax issues aside, his rant shouldn't be taken at face value.

There are many readers who have taken issue with a prevailing theme in Geoff Emerick's memoir: namely, that until 1967, George Harrison's skills as a guitarist were somewhat lacking in the studio, requiring either countless takes or much criticism— even to the point where someone (usually Paul) would seize his instrument and play the parts themselves. Emerick's lack of esteem toward George's abilities, framed in a "I'm just sayin'" sort of way, say more about himself than they do about George's well-documented instrumental prowess and refreshing lack of ego.

In Emerick's colorful telling, George simply could not get a handle on the solo for "Taxman," despite hours spent—even with efforts made to record it at half speed. He states further that, with so much time being squandered on a "George" song—something less than a top priority—George Martin finally stepped in and, for the sake of expediency, handed it over to Paul who (naturally) nailed it straight away.

Then there are the recollections of Paul and George. Paul's was more detailed, basically saying that he had an idea of something that he would like to try that was musically fiery in the spirit of early Hendrix: "feedback-y and crazy." George, open-minded as always, told him to give it a go. He proceeded to unleash a torrent of ferocious, feedback-laden notes, deliberately drawing from exotic Eastern scales rather than bluesy Western ones. His angry bloodletting sounded nothing like anything previously heard on a Beatles record, capturing the rage implicit in the lyric while simultaneously getting inside George's own head and speaking a language of which the composer fully approved. It was a moment of unsurpassed artistry, and George knew it. Twenty years after the session, he told *Guitar Player* magazine: "I was pleased to have Paul play that bit on 'Taxman.' If you notice, he did like a little Indian bit on it for me."

So spectacular were the results that George Martin made two decisions with the full consent of the Fabs: firstly, he would fly in a repeat of the solo at the end of the song, perhaps diminishing the impact of that final "Taxman!" but also giving some momentum to the tracks that followed. Secondly, made at the sequencing stage of assembling the master, was that this George Harrison composition would hold the oh-so-important position of opening the album. Not only would the guitarist get an unheard-of *three* songs on the album, but also the very first cut besides. It was an honor that left him "dead chuffed," but one that he would never enjoy again.

Overdubs included tambourine and cowbell, as well as assorted vocals. A gravelly count-in intoned at the onset was imposed over the song's actual one. As yet another point of dispute among fans, there seems to be a divide between listeners who believe it's George delivering the guttural false count and Paul the "real" one, with others reversing this, equally certain of the opposite.

More important than this minor attribution was the implicit statement being made. By deliberately echoing the first sound heard on their debut album, they were quite consciously under-scoring their progress as artists. Three years earlier, they'd invited listeners to their live set. Now, they wanted to have the audience witness a journey made possible through the wonders of studio craft. It was as though they were counting off the next phase of their career, where live performances would be a quaint relic of the past.

Mono and stereo mixes were prepared on June 21, at which time the prominent count-in and ending guitar solo were dubbed in. Variations include an earlier start to the cowbell in mono (0:34 vs. 0:46) and more powerful-sounding instrumentation all around, particularly the bass, than in stereo.

"I'M ONLY SLEEPING"
(Recording begins: Wednesday, April 27, 1966)

The backwards guitar solo heard on "Tomorrow Never Knows" was cut on April 22, one day after Paul performed lead-guitar duties on "Taxman." Upon entering the studio at 6 PM on this Wednesday evening, the first order of business for the group was to prepare mono mixes for the two aforementioned tunes, which were judged to be complete at this stage, as well as "And Your Bird Can Sing."

Though none of the mixes worked on ever ended up actually being used, the exercise did consume many hours of studio time, only after which the band was ready to begin work, fittingly, on John's somnambulant rumination.

One might be tempted to think that the Beatles deliberately put off taping "I'm Only Sleeping" until late at night in order to fall into the proper mood. There's no evidence that this is true, but in any event, some taped rehearsal was the first order of business.

Anthology 2 offers a fascinating taste of something that only sur-vived by the purest happenstance: forty-one seconds of rehearsal that somehow avoided being taped over. (One more run-through and it would have vanished forever.) What's notable about the attempt is the track's use of a vibraphone. This appellation was obviously dropped for the finished take, but the use of vibes here offers a window into the thinking of the group and their

producer: the evocation in sound of the milieu occurring some-
where between full—and the complete lack of—consciousness.

Much less clear is exactly who was manning the mallets for
their performance. The group's resident musical savant, Paul,
is believed to have done the honors, especially as the existing
snippet features drums and acoustic guitar, but no bass. Then
again, it might have been George Martin. In any event, this touch
of atmosphere was ditched, in favor of the increasingly popular
use of vari-speed in the project thus far. Just as when you're a
hammer, everything looks like a nail, so it was in 1966: if you were
a Beatle, every sound was fair game to be sped up, slowed down,
turned backwards, doubled, and otherwise sliced and diced.

Though a much less complicated recording than "Tomorrow
Never Knows," a considerable amount of time and labor was
expended on getting exactly the right touch for "I'm Only Sleeping." Once the actual attempts to create a usable master began
(with John and George on acoustics and Ringo and Paul on their
usual instruments; the latter on his Höfner rather than his Rickenbacker, in order to get those soft tiptoeing sounds between the
chorus and the bridge), the group purposely played it a little faster
(in the key of E minor) than they desired the finished recording
to be. As with "Rain," the master rhythm track was manipulated
to suit the material, in this case providing a more "dreamy" feel.

The band laid down eleven takes before calling it a night
(at around 3 AM). Following a re-listening two days later, all
concerned must have felt that the song could be improved upon,
so a remake was attempted—five takes' worth. (This was on the
reel containing the rehearsals with vibraphone; the fifth pass
ended forty-one seconds short of wiping away all the evidence.)
In the end, these April 29 takes were judged less to be than
optimal, so take eleven of the April 27 batch was returned to and
designated the master.

John's lead vocal was also the recipient of some vari-speed
magic. Once again following the "Rain" template, the vocals
were recorded with the tape rolling more slowly than normal,
raising its range somewhat upon playback and, in its way, suggesting the sleepy, "don't bother me" detachment implied in the

lyrics. The vocal was later double-tracked, and with the addition of the backing vocals, including a yawn from Paul at about the 2:00 mark (a close listen reveals John's command to him about four seconds before), the track was nearly finished.

George's contribution came first, though, and took a considerable amount of effort to perfect. The labor-intensive guitar line provided a sublimely eloquent embellishment, much the same way his sitar had with "Norwegian Wood."

Already having experienced the wonders of backward tape's exoticism with "Rain" and "Tomorrow Never Knows," George was ready to expand on the formula with "I'm Only Sleeping," but with a twist: rather than simply play a solo and reverse it, he wanted to *compose* his backward part first, and then learn to play it forward to get the exact notes in the exact order he wanted on playback. While Geoff Emerick's account of how he did it is rather derisive ("At the best of times, [Harrison] had trouble playing solos all the way through forward . . ."), George could not be deterred, and set about achieving his goal through hours and hours of work.

It has been suggested in some accounts, including Paul McCartney's, that the notion of placing a backwards solo in this song was a happy accident, inspired by a tape operator's wrong-way placement of a spool on the recording deck, resulting in a barrage of unheard-of sound that caused everyone in the room to react with a collective "Ah *ha!*" Given the previous backwards-tape experiments already successfully completed by this time on the work in progress, this hardly seems likely: the Beatles and their producer were already well aware of what sounds could be produced in this fashion. What *was* novel was George's approach to using the newfound tool.

Once he'd composed the guitar lines that he wanted to hear backwards, he had George Martin transcribe the notes, so that he could play them—twice. The first was with a clean guitar; the second featured his Gibson SG run through a fuzzbox. The two guitar lines varied slightly, but when reversed, they added exactly the hypnotic touch needed to give voice to the song's inherent message.

"I'm Only Sleeping" became the third song upon which a quick mix was produced in order to satisfy Capitol's demand for material to pad out the *"Yesterday"* . . . *and Today* release. As with the other two tracks, a mono mix was prepared for American issue, one that would be superseded with a more refined one in Britain; the illusion of stereo was faked for American ears with "Duophonic." The pattern of multiple U.S.–U.K. mixes repeated itself with this track, but the song's novel reversed guitar fills comprised an element that made the differing mixes eminently distinctive.

The mix containing the most backward guitar fills is the British mono mix, currently issued as part of the mono-remaster set. The mix featuring the least is the U.S. mono mix, the first one prepared. There are five mixes in total that were officially issued for this song: two stereo (U.S. and U.K.); two mono (U.S. and U.K.); and the "Duophonic" one. The main differences between them are limited to exactly where and when the guitar part is brought up in the mix. (The U.K. stereo mix was once believed to be so novel in this country that it was included on the 1980 U.S. *Rarities* set. Come the CD era, it became the standard, making the U.S. stereo version upon which it was intended to be a variation the scarce one.)

"ELEANOR RIGBY"
(Recording begins: Thursday, April 28, 1966)

When "Yesterday" had been recorded back in June 1965, Paul initially resisted his producer's desire to arrange it for a string quartet, fearing he was being led into "Mantovani" country: schmaltzy orchestration aimed squarely at pretentious middlebrows. George Martin's desire to record the tune with no other Beatle involvement or rock instrumentation (save the composer's lone Epiphone Texan) prevailed, with results against which no one could argue.

By the spring of 1966, however, Paul had no qualms about using such literate instrumentation, and was in fact excited by the idea. He regarded "Eleanor Rigby" as an artistic breakthrough: something beyond the mere pop stylings in which he'd trafficked

Another piece of Klaus Voormann artwork, seen on the U.K. sheet-music issue.

to this point, a direction that could sustain him well into the future, after "the bubble burst" on his Beatles career.

George Martin's ambitions for this song were grander than what he'd come up with for "Yesterday"—by exactly twice, in fact. With "Eleanor Rigby," a string *octet*—comprised of four violins, two violas, and two celli—would be used. Two violinists who'd played on the earlier session were summoned: violinists Tony Gilbert and Sid Sax. They were augmented by John Sharpe and Jurgen Hess. On violas were Stephen Shingles and John Underwood; the two celli were played by Derek Simpson and Norman Jones.

Before rolling tape, Martin requested that the ensemble run through the piece twice: first using vibrato; the second time not.

Paul had a distaste for vibrato, feeling it was schmaltzy and senti-mental—feelings he wasn't ordinarily known to be averse to. He and Martin opted to go without, each one believing that record-ing the instruments "dry" (minus the vibrato) made for a starker, more dramatic accompaniment.

Emerick's mania for close-miking extended to the strings, which he felt (correctly, as it happened) would better capture the timbre of the instruments. This deviation from standard procedure did make the musicians slightly uncomfortable, as placing microphones so close to where they could acciden-tally strike them with their bows or instruments wasn't exactly conducive to relaxation. For their efforts, each man was paid the standard musician's nine-pound fee.

It took fourteen takes to secure a "best" performance. John and Paul watched from the control-room window upstairs in the Number Two studio as George Martin conducted down on the floor. There was no mistaking the results of the octet's work with mere light pop orchestration: this was full-bore chamber music in support of a rather serious-minded lyric that went far beyond the standards of romantic sentiment, or even topical protest mu-sic. "Eleanor Rigby" did not end on an optimistic note; it was straightforward rhetoric that asked questions without offering answers—in the best Dylan tradition. As such, it was a piece that provoked thought rather than soothing, a sign of the Beatles' growing maturation as artists.

George Martin has asserted through the years that he was in-spired by the work of film composer Bernard Hermann when he scored the strings for "Eleanor Rigby"—specifically, Hermann's work on Francois Truffaut's *Fahrenheit 451*, released in 1966. He may have been influenced by Hermann's work, but given that *Fahrenheit 451* wasn't released until well after *Revolver* hit stores (on November 14, 1966), it would appear that Martin's recall was faulty. The staccato strings are, however, distinctly reminiscent of Hermann's score for Alfred Hitchcock's *Psycho*, a film released in 1960, making it the more likely model. (For his part, Paul believed the scoring was lifted from Vivaldi's *Four Seasons*.)

The following day, on Friday, April 29, the lead and backing vocals were cut. Paul, with John and George supplying support harmonies, finished the task very quickly—or so they thought. Mixes were prepared from the work completed and the group moved on, playing their final live date in Britain on Sunday, May 1: the *NME* Poll-Winners show.

Not until a month later did George Martin call Paul back to add a final touch to the recording: on June 6, he had Paul lay down another refrain ("Ah, look at all the lonely people"), sent through a Leslie speaker and serving as a countermelody to the last "all the lonely people" section of the song. Such attention to detail was an element upon which the group and their producer prided themselves; this level of precision might not have been possible had they still been on the same treadmill requiring them to crank out product on demand to feed the insatiable dictates of the marketplace, as they had been a year or two earlier.

Few things in the story of the Beatles' approach to stereo (and how undervalued that element of their audio presentation was for so long) are as graphically illustrated as they are with this song. The mono mix of "Eleanor Rigby" is perfectly acceptable, with the strings and layers of vocals given sufficient room so as to not come off as crowded; the mix breathes, and the level of care given to it is commensurate with a track selected as a single.

The stereo mix, in contrast, is riddled with sloppy mistakes, most conspicuously when the ADT effect being applied during mixing was not turned off quickly enough after the opening chorus. The opening "Eleanor Rigby" of the first verse was inadvertently subjected to the effect before it was abruptly switched off; similar errors occur thereafter and are best noticed in headphones. In 1966, this might not have mattered a great deal, with stereo still the minority option while mono ruled. Come the shift during the 1970s and this flawed mix became the currency, issued on millions of stereo copies of *Revolver* as well as the *1962–1966* compilation once the mono mix became extinct.

Perhaps equally distracting was the decision to pan Paul's vocal to hard right on the verses, creating yet another annoying stereo listening experience for latter-day fans. This lopsided mix was fixed with 1999's *Yellow Submarine Songtrack*, which at last centered the lead vocal and eliminated the ADT errors; but the remasters, which were executed with a notion to keep such bad decisions preserved intact, perpetuate the errors. (*Anthology 2*, meanwhile, offered up a stereo remix of the backing track, enabling listeners to hear George Martin's Hermann homage with clarity.)

"FOR NO ONE"
(Recording begins: Monday, May 9, 1966)

Following the *NME* show and a few days spent catching up on assorted overdubs and mixing, the Beatles resumed work on tracking new songs with this Paul composition, another non-rocker following closely his previous path of chamber-music excursions. "For No One" would not require any guitars, instead being centered on keyboards and drums. Over the course of ten takes, Paul (playing a slightly echoed Steinway grand) and Ringo quickly nailed their parts.

The next task to be completed was the overdubbing of some percussion (maracas, tambourine, and high-hat cymbal), plus an additional layer of keyboard.

Some discussion as to exactly what was needed for this song had been underway between Paul and George Martin, both men feeling that a harpsichord, used the year prior on the Yardbirds' chart-topping "For Your Love," wasn't exactly it. Martin suggested a clavichord, a Baroque-era keyboard associated with the work of Georg Friedrich Händel; furthermore, it just so happened that he owned one and was happy to lug it down to the studio—for a fee, of course. (AIR, George's production company, billed EMI five guineas.)

A clavichord differs from a harpsichord in how it produces sound. In the latter, the strings are plucked by the mechanisms inside; with the former, they're struck. It takes a different touch to play a clavichord well than it does your standard piano; it is to Paul's credit that he adapted quite quickly to an unfamiliar instrument. (During the '70s, the clavichord's electronic cousin, the clavinet, was often used as musical shorthand for "funk." Stevie Wonder played one often, as did Billy Preston on the title track of Ringo's *Goodnight Vienna*.)

A week after work began, Paul added bass and his lead vocal; unlike with "Eleanor Rigby," John and George were not needed. The track was slowed for the taping, giving his voice a slightly elevated pitch upon playback, with compression added. The last element—arguably the recording's signature sound—was laid down three days later. A French horn motif had been mentally sketched out for inclusion in the song virtually from the moment the tune had been written. Given what Paul had in his head, a truly exceptional musician was needed to pull it off.

In his semi-autobiography, *Many Years from Now*, Paul relates that his and George Martin's first choice, maestro Dennis Brain, had been booked for the session, but was killed in an auto accident before it could take place. He was half right: Brain, considered Britain's foremost horn player, did indeed die behind the wheel of his Triumph TR2—in 1957. Luckily, an equal-caliber musician fully among the living was available: Alan Civil.

The descriptive word most often applied to this larger-than-life character was "Falstaffian." The bearded, somewhat hefty Civil's reputation as *the* preeminent horn player was matched by his renown as an acerbic wit who did not suffer fools and could often be found in his off hours tipping back a few in his beloved pubs, regaling those around him with colorful stories—when not leading sing-alongs around the piano. Given his own celebrity, a call to play on a Beatles session wasn't likely to have intimidated him.

Civil's scheduled appearance came on the same day the group spent the bulk of the daylight hours shooting promos for the "Paperback Writer" / "Rain" single. He arrived at the studio to find George Martin had transcribed his part from Paul's hummed / sang notes. Civil initially thought that he was playing on a piece called "For No. [number] One," misreading the actual title. An oft-repeated anecdote states that after he read through the music, a particular note caught his eye. "George, that's a G!" (The normal top range note of the French horn is F.) In the story's telling, it's said that Martin and Paul merely exchanged giddy smirks and told Civil, "Yes, it is." Ever the professional, Civil merely shrugged and went on to play without issue this particularly challenging piece of music.

Whether this actually happened or, as is believed, he simply performed his part with the tape slowed down in order to accommodate the difficulty and *appear* higher on playback, doesn't really matter. (Some accounts allude to the song having been recorded "in the cracks" between B major and B-flat.) What does is that he delivered a wonderfully sublime performance that accentuated the inherent pathos in the song without descending into cheap mawkishness.

Another canard from the session holds that Paul kept hounding the master musician to extreme agitation by urging him to do it "better" with each pass; this tale has also been connected to Dave Mason on "Penny Lane" as well as Ronnie Scott on "Lady Madonna." It's therefore unlikely, since Civil seems to have reviewed the experience quite positively and in fact played on "A Day in the Life" the following year. With that, "For No One" was complete. Like Anil Bhagwat, Civil soon discovered that prominent credit on a Beatles album jacket brought him into a whole other world of fame.

"For No One" is a song that benefits from being heard in mono, as the vocal seems inordinately prominent in the stereo mix.

"YELLOW SUBMARINE"
(Recording begins: Thursday, May 26, 1966)

To this point in the *Revolver* sessions, now in their eighth week, the Beatles had laid down the bulk of their "serious" material: the art-rock "Eleanor Rigby"; the psychedelic "Tomorrow Never Knows" and "Rain"; the exotic "Love You To." Only "Doctor Robert" exhibited any trace of ironic humor (though it may be argued that "Taxman" represented the strikingly satiric viewpoint of a young millionaire railing against his punitive debt to the state). At last, the group was ready to tackle an undeniably youth-oriented novelty number, something heretofore unthinkable for an artistic collective that saw itself as a breed apart from such frivolous novelties cluttering the charts as "Wooly Bully" (from Sam the Sham) or "You Really Turn Me On" (by fellow Brit Ian Whitcomb).

But given their drummer's public image as something less than serious, assigning him the vocal chores on "Yellow Submarine" adroitly deflected any charges that might have been made about them lowering themselves to the level of common inanity. That the song had an undeniable layer of trippy surrealism (if not to say implicit drug connotations—whether by design or not) certainly assured that the more cerebral members of their fan base weren't likely to be put off by the offering at first glance.

The Beatles' approach to capturing a studio take would hereon be marked by a decidedly freewheeling, pull-out-all-the-stops methodology. It couldn't have hurt that George Martin, a victim of food poisoning, was absent during the initial proceed-

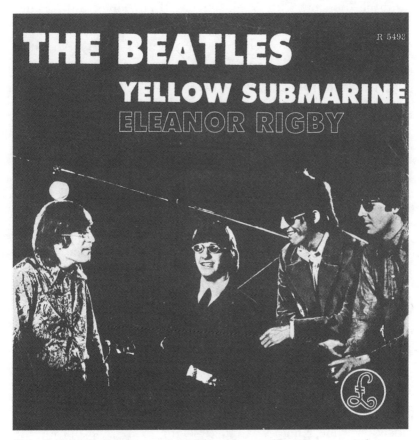

This photo of the Beatles, used on the rear cover of Revolver, *was taken by Robert Whitaker on May 19 as they filmed the studio promos for "Paperback Writer" and "Rain."*

ings. Thus without adult supervision, the foursome was free to explore the possibilities without fear of being told "no." The days' work entailed filling two entire tape reels with rehearsals before attempting four takes, with John on Gibson acoustic, George on tambourine, and Paul and Ringo filling their normal roles. This rhythm track was recorded with the deck running slightly fast, lowering the pitch upon playback, while Ringo's lead and Macca's accompanying vocals were taped with the backing running slow, raising his pitch.

The group waited several days until their producer recovered before proceeding. On June 1, the group reconvened, this time with several guests in tow, including Pattie Harrison, Marianne Faithfull (possibly with Mick Jagger), Brian Jones, and Beatles chauffer Alf Bicknell. Along with the trusty Mal Evans, all were pressed into service to help enhance the track's party-like ambience during the second verse ("And our friends are all aboard"). Those not vocalizing (the normally shy Pattie, according to Emerick, was responsible for the high-pitched feminine cries heard here) were busy with an array of found objects being brought into the mix: Bicknell, for instance, busied himself rattling chains, while others clinked glasses, shook (and dropped) coins, rang bells, and otherwise added to the merriment where needed. (The revelry climaxed with a conga line around the studio led by Mal, marching bass drum strapped to his chest.)

Given the song's aquatic theme, water sounds were required. Rather than conduct field recordings or rely purely on EMI's sound library, creativity ruled. John manned the straws, blowing air through them into a bucket of water, while George sloshed water around in a metal bathtub. Keeping in mind that it was a piece of military transportation that the song was describing, it became necessary to add the appropriate commands from the "crew" to provide that extra layer of "authenticity" to the proceedings. Lacking a bullhorn, John, the son of a seaman, shouted out orders into the echo chamber behind Studio Two ("Full stern ahead!") while Ringo was taped yelling in the hall outside the facility ("Cut the cable!").

According to Emerick, John had very much wanted to capture his voice singing underwater, and went to a lot of trouble to achieve his goal. After attempts to sing while gargling (which nearly choked him) and requests for a tank big enough to sing in went nowhere, Emerick hit upon the idea of recording him with a submerged microphone. George Martin seemed to recognize the folly, but patiently acquiesced to the experiment after Mal Evans waterproofed the expensive mic with a condom, which was then placed into a milk bottle full of water. Unfortunately, the results weren't remotely "hydrosonic"; only muffled sounding, which ended the pursuit.

Another notion enacted that likewise went south was the spoken-word introduction recorded for the song. To the accompaniment of marching feet (actually, coal shifted around in a box),

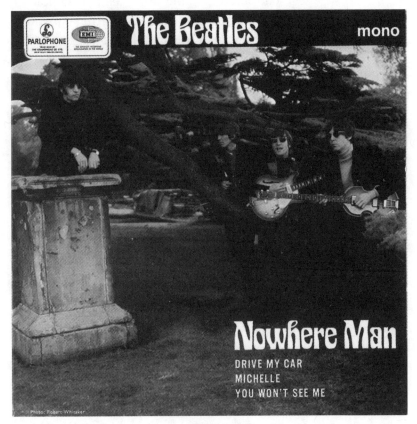

This photo was taken at Chiswick House on May 20, during the shooting of the "Paperback Writer" / "Rain" promos.

Ringo intoned a brief poem composed by John, describing a trek "from Land O'Groats to John O'Green." Though less than twenty seconds long, ultimately it was judged to be superfluous and ditched. (It eventually turned up as a bonus track on the "Real Love" single.) Though this idea was abandoned, one last piece of business provided the final piece to the puzzle: music from the band described in the second verse.

George Martin was concerned about the expense of the project, and couldn't see hiring outside musicians to provide just a few seconds of sonic color. Therefore, he and Emerick opted to pull some audio from the studio's library to use, something that evoked a Sousa march but that wouldn't be identifiable enough to both distract from "Yellow Submarine" and subject them to paying a usage fee. The solution came from taking a sample of the recording selected, slicing the tape, then re-splicing it in a way that disguised its actual identity. It was then faded quickly during the mixing process.

"Yellow Submarine" proved that the Beatles could compete with the best of the novelty acts on the charts without compromising their integrity. Its skillful production in support of a charming vocal with a captivating chorus demonstrated the group's ability to produce quality recordings in virtually any genre—even for kids.

The mono mix used for the single (naturally) contained a couple of variances from the stereo one. The two most noticeable were the opening guitar strum accompanying the singing at the very start, instead of the delay heard in the stereo mix, and John's repeat of Ringo's singing in the last verse, which starts immediately and not on the second line.

"LAXTON'S SUPERB" a.k.a. "I DON'T KNOW" a.k.a. "I WANT TO TELL YOU"
(Recording begins: Thursday, June 2, 1966)

It has been suggested that George was accorded a *third* composition on this album due to John's not having another song ready at this point. (It had been over a month since his last contribution, "I'm Only Sleeping," had been introduced—and that was a song explaining his lack of industry.) If true, it was a portent of a similar situation that arose in January 1969, wherein George's heightened productivity in bringing in fully realized tunes almost daily was contrasted with John's struggle to keep up, forcing him to revive "One After 909," a song the group had abandoned years before.

If the received anecdote is accurate, John's evident disdain for George's aversion to naming his songs is what prompted Emerick to dub this one "Laxton's Superb." Showing up again with a composition as yet unnamed, John sardonically suggested "Granny Smith Part Friggin' Two." Emerick seized upon this and changed it to a different apple. Later, when pressed for something more definitive, George offhandedly replied, "I don't know," which it indeed was recorded as until he came up with the rather obvious title it should have possessed in the first place.

This third and final Harrisong was probably the easiest to nail. The initial run-through consisted of Ringo on drums; George playing guitar through a Leslie; Paul on piano; and John on tambourine. Five attempts were made, with the third judged the keeper. George's lead vocal was added on a separate track, followed by John and Paul's backing vocals. Another track was filled with extra percussion—more tambourine, plus maracas—as well as some additional piano, playing that repetitive off-balance lick. Once tape reductions had been made of the work thus far, some handclaps were added, along with Paul's bass, and the song was complete.

About the only noticeable differences between the mono and stereo mixes of "I Want to Tell You" are the bass and piano parts, which seem more defined in mono.

"GOOD DAY SUNSHINE"
(Recording begins: Wednesday, June 8, 1966)

For his second song in a row, Paul dispensed with the instrumental services of John and George, cutting another keyboard-driven tune by multitasking most of the parts, excepting the solo and the drums. Paul might've played the skins himself, too, had he had access to more than four tracks with which to work. But thankfully, the do-it-yourself tendencies that served to alienate his fellow Beatles in the future had not yet become fully awakened at this point. (He would indeed re-cut this song practically by himself nearly twenty years later for the soundtrack of his film, *Give My Regards to Broad Street*. While George Martin was allowed to reprise his performance, Ringo, also in the film, was not.)

As a group, the song was rehearsed several times before a proper take was attempted. It must have been time well spent; for after three passes, their *first* try was judged the best. Paul's lead vocal was then laid down, after which he and John recorded backing vocals on a separate track. The addition of bass filled the four tracks, which were then reduced in order to accommodate various additional overdubs: another piano, playing in a lower register; Ringo's cymbal splashes; and added percussion touchups such as hand claps.

Additional bursts of harmony for the song's outro, featuring the group's three principal singers, were laid down before the final touch on "Good Day Sunshine": an old-timey piano break. Paul recognized his limitations here and deferred to George Martin, who nailed the honky-tonk solo with little effort; though, it should be pointed out, he "cheated" by taping it in a lower register at half speed.

Variations between the mono and stereo mixes are few, chiefly centering on the apparent dropout of the bass drum at the end before the song fades away completely. One item of curiosity centering on this song appears in either format: a quickly whispered comment at 1:25, following Paul's "she feels good." There are some that believe it's merely a repeat of those three words; in fact, Paul seems to say just that in the 1984 remake. But a close listening to the Beatles recording reveals that the final syllable contains an *sss* sound, changing perceptions of the actual words from something rather innocuous into a lyric more naughty than previously suspected.

"HERE, THERE AND EVERYWHERE"
(Recording begins: Tuesday, June 14, 1966)

By any measure, "Here, There and Everywhere" was an intricate recording. Though not experimental in the usual sense, it did feature delicate harmonies, a double-tracked lead vocal, and layered, melodic guitar lines. Also, vari-speed was used to great effect on Paul's voice, thereby making the track a culmination of sorts for all that the team had learned over the course of creating together on this album.

Over the course of seven hours on the first days' recording, the group ran through the song four times, with Paul handling rhythm guitar and providing a guide vocal. (The song's soft opening chord progression was echoed seven years later when he composed "Live and Let Die.") Ringo accompanied him, not on brushes as some have suggested, but with a careful recalibration of his approach to sticks; he was a model of control. The fourth attempt was the keeper, initially anyway, and received an overdub of three-part block harmonies.

Two days later, the Beatles endured a particularly hectic work schedule. Their day began with each receiving a cholera vaccination, likely in advance of their touring schedule, due to commence in Munich on June 24. Afterward, the foursome and Brian Epstein piled into John's Rolls-Royce for a trip to the BBC Television Centre for an appearance on *Top of the Pops* to plug both sides of their new single. Following the live broadcast, they headed back to the studio for a late-night session, resuming work on "Here, There and Everywhere."

Unsatisfied with their previous four takes, the group attempted another nine, with George playing his twelve-string Rickenbacker—very likely for the last time on a Beatles record—and Paul, his Epiphone Casino. (John, while present, apparently did not play.) The unused take seven was released in 1995 as a bonus track on the "Real Love" single, featuring a guide vocal and some backings flown in from the finished take. Take thirteen, the final pass, was judged best and became the recipient of overdubs: bass, plus two separate tracks of three-part block harmony (one of which featured finger snaps), stacking the vocals, Beach Boys–style.

For the lead vocal, Paul was double-tracked the old-fashioned way, without ADT. While the backing was slowed down to give his voice a higher pitch on playback, Paul also modified his strategy by getting into character, as it were. "When I sang it in the studio, I remember thinking, I'll sing it like Marianne

Faithfull," he told Barry Miles in *Many Years from Now*. This approach gave his singing a fragile quality, which, along with the inherent wistful romanticism of the lyric, projected a vulnerability not usually heard in his work, at least to this point.

The lead guitar was treated with ADT at the mixing stage. There was also a horn-like flourish of guitar at the song's end, courtesy of George's "Rick-o-sound" effect, which sent the instrument's signal to two different amps. "Here, There and Everywhere" represents an effort wherein the very methods applied to the song while recording it seemed calculated to bring great results with a stereo mix. The spread of the vocals and multiple guitar lines make it one of the few songs of the "mono era" that actually is enhanced in stereo by design, rather than tossed off indifferently as so many early stereo mixes had been.

"SHE SAID SHE SAID"
(Recording begins: Tuesday, June 21, 1966)

Despite decades of research and thousands of books published, there remain a handful of unsolved Beatle mysteries: Why does "Help!" exist with two different lead vocals? What became of Mal Evans's book manuscript? Will "Carnival of Light" ever be released? To that list we can add the recording of "She Said She Said": Why did Paul McCartney, in a fit of pique, walk off *Revolver* just before the finish line?

To be sure, the pressure was on at this point. A deadline for completion of the as-yet unnamed album loomed, as the group were about to resume the Axis leg of their 1966 world tour (to Germany and Japan—they had played Italy the year before), to be followed by their final dates in North America. The album was still not finished, judged to be a track short of the usual four-teen (though *A Hard Day's Night* had somehow skated by with only thirteen songs).

Had inter-band squabbles occurred throughout the band's career thus far? Certainly, though dealing with matters of noth-ing of more than transient importance. The influence of Brian Epstein, though definitely waning by 1966, was not insignifi-cant, nor was that of George Martin. As the designated "adults"

Another shot taken at Chiswick House, this time in the conservatory.

around the Beatles, their respective capacities for keeping egos in check and projects on track kept the operation a disciplined, well-oiled machine; it was not an accident that the band's success stayed steady and on an upward trajectory during Brian's lifetime.

It is therefore baffling that Paul, of all people—the consummate professional and, by reputation, the Beatle most dedicated to maintaining the group's success—would leave the others in a lurch just as a project was closing. The incident has never been discussed in any detail anywhere: no quotes from John, George, or Ringo have surfaced, but there *is* exactly one existing account— from Paul—as an aside within a discussion of *Revolver*.

Recalling the song from a distance (as told to Barry Miles), Paul said, "I'm not sure but I think it was one of the only Beatle records I never played on. I think we'd had a barney or something and I said, 'Oh, fuck you!' and they said, 'Well, we'll do it.' I think George played bass." Now, it must be said, as has been pointed out elsewhere, that Paul's recollections are not to be taken at face value; he, like the other ex-Beatles, sometimes had trouble recalling his own history with one hundred percent accuracy, and appears careful here to qualify what he says with "I'm not sure." But this was neither a particularly flattering anecdote nor something that most people ever suspected had even happened: though George's backing vocals are quite evident, no one was ever given reason to think that something out of the ordinary to explain Paul's absence had gone down. In other words, this wasn't a story that he *had* to tell.

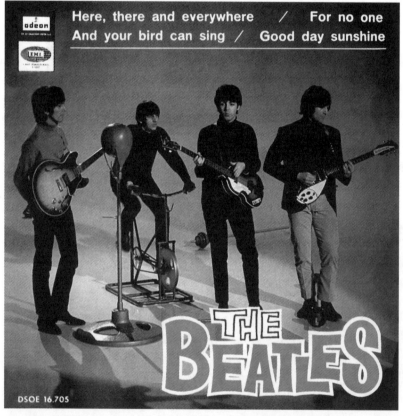

From "I Feel Fine"—another image taken during the filming of the Intertel promos.

For those at all skeptical if Paul knew what he was talking about, or doubting that George could have handled the bass on "She Said She Said," a conversation preserved less than three years later supports these facts. In January 1969, with the group's dysfunction on full display before the cameras and a battery of recording devices, John and Paul were taped discussing how to deal with George's January 10 walkout. A meeting held two days later to resolve things went badly (where he again left abruptly), and two dispirited Beatles, joined by a late-arriving John, were documented discussing events both recent and past while at lunch on January 13.

As part of a dialogue on the negative effect that telling George how to play has had over time, John mentioned "past numbers" (i.e., recordings) where he had allowed Paul to take control in a direction that he, John, didn't want them to go. "My only chance," he explained, "was to allow George to take over because I knew he'd take it as-is"; in other words, George would defer to John on arrangement matters on *his* songs. Paul then chimed in with "She Said She Said" as an example of this.

Was this—an arrangement dispute on a "John" song—the object of contention? There might have been more to it: years later, George himself was quoted in *Acoustic Guitar* magazine as saying that he indeed helped John put the song together. "He was struggling with some tunes, loads of bits, maybe three songs that were unfinished. I made some suggestions and helped him to work together so they became one finished song: 'She Said She Said'. . . . That was a real weld!" Did John's coming into the studio with a song that he'd finished off with George rather than Paul stir resentment from the latter that the partnership was being usurped?

Yet another layer may have been the song's very subject matter. As John would say later, he and George had a tendency to needle Paul about his resistance to tripping with them. "Paul felt very out of it because we are all a bit slightly cruel, sort of, 'We're taking it and *you're* not,'" John told *Rolling Stone* after the Fabs' split. Did John and George push a little too far for Paul's liking on this occasion, leading him to storm out in a huff? Short of some sort of contemporary documentation turning up, such as the session tape, we may never know.

Here's what we know for sure. "She Said She Said" was taped in its entirety in a single marathon session, held less than forty-eight hours before the group departed for West Germany. The session began with rehearsals at 7 PM and did not finish until nearly 4 AM the next morning; it was the only *Revolver* track completed in one session. Paul was apparently present for these run-throughs, and may have been around when the initial attempted takes had been lain down, as the session log records bass and drums recorded one on track; two guitars on another; John's lead vocal on the third; and the backing vocals from John and George on the last.

If accurate, this suggests that Paul was around at least initially for laying down the rhythm tracks but gone by the time the backing vocals were added, since his voice isn't present. The band completed a total of three takes of backing instruments before adding the vocals; at least a couple of well-researched Beatles reference books cite the above track-by-track breakdown, suggesting that Paul *had* to be playing bass since George couldn't very well be playing guitar at the same time—unless they had already switched roles.

But there's a problem with this, discernible by closely listening to the stereo mix. Either the log—and therefore the books—are mistaken, and the drums occupied their own track all along, with the bass added later, or a "Paul-and-Ringo" rhythm track was wiped following Paul's walkout, with the drums recut alone. Most likely, Paul's bass was never cut because he absented himself before this stage; therefore, the only bass on the track was played by George after the initial reduction mix.

As evidence, the stereo imaging shows the drums and bass as separate, distinct entities: the drums are panned to the far right, while the bass is centered in the mix. They therefore were not recorded together; and any source saying otherwise is incorrect. Some doubting this wonder how George could've pulled this off, assuming his taking the part had been unplanned and the only basses at hand were Paul's left-handed models. The answer is: George was documented in the studio with a bass during the sessions, specifically a 1964 Burns Nu-Sonic model.

His handling the bass is shown in photographs taken during the extraordinarily well-documented "Paperback Writer" session, covered by a photographer and writer from *Beatles Monthly*. It is therefore probable that on this occasion, George played bass during rehearsals, while Paul merely demonstrated the riff. In short: George had a bass on the premises. Furthermore, what's heard on "She Said She Said" sounds neither like Paul's Rickenbacker nor his Höfner.

The bass line itself doesn't particularly resemble Paul's style either, inasmuch as it doesn't really draw attention to itself. It is solid and workmanlike during the verses, mostly building off the root notes of the chords; but during the "when I was a boy" section, it gets a little bolder and busier, displaying the kind of imagination into which a guitarist accustomed to composing riffs would have tapped. None of these clues taken singly amount to a smoking gun; but as a whole, they support the case built here that makes George's role pretty well certain.

Final overdubs included an organ part (played by John) and lead guitar. Three mono mixes were prepared just after the final overdub, but they ended up unused. Instead, a mixing session held the next day wrapped up work on "She Said She Said," "Eleanor Rigby," and "Good Day Sunshine," all in mono. Stereo mixes of the aforementioned, plus "Yellow Submarine," "Tomorrow Never Knows," and "Got to Get You into My Life" were completed thereafter.

With that, work on *Revolver* was complete. Said George Martin: "All right, boys, I'm just going for a lie-down."

PART III

●

BANG!

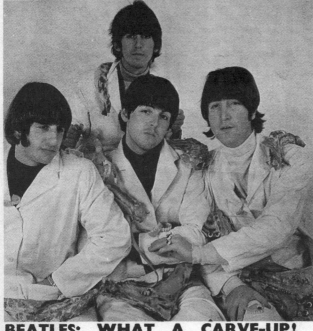

DISC
and MUSIC ECHO 9d
JUNE 11, 1966   USA 25c

MERSEY UPROAR
after 'Whole Scene' attack

SEE PAGE 6

SANDIE
TV miming no CRIME!
Page 7

MERSEYS
jealous of the Hollies!
Page 8

CILLA
I just can't stop myself GIGGLING!
Page 8

BEATLES: WHAT A CARVE-UP!

BEATLES WEEK! They're back with a single, "Paperback Writer" and "Rain"—out tomorrow (Friday).

BUT WHAT'S THIS? The Beatles as butchers, draped with raw meat! Disc and Music Echo's world exclusive colour picture by Bob Whitaker is the most controversial shot ever of John, Paul, George and Ringo.

THE PLACE: A private studio in Chelsea, London. Whitaker is taking some new pictures of the Beatles, and decides that a new approach is needed.

"I wanted to do a real experiment — people will jump to wrong conclusions about it being sick," says Whitaker. "But the whole thing is based on simplicity — linking four very real people with something real.

"I got George to knock some nails into John's head, and took some sausages along to get some other pictures. Dressed them up in white smocks as butchers, and this is the result—the use of the camera as a means of creating situations."

PAUL'S comment after the session: "Very tasty meat."

GEORGE: "We won't come to any more of your sick picture sessions."

JOHN: "Oh, we don't mind doing anything."

RINGO: "We haven't done pictures like THIS before . . ."

Well, what's YOUR verdict? Sick—or super? Six LPs for the best six captions—of no more than 12 words—to the picture above. Send your entry to "Beatles Picture," Disc and Music Echo, 161 Fleet Street, London, E.C.4, before next Friday, June 17.

● PAUL in his own write—exclusive interview: Page 9.

This even more graphic image from the "butcher" session was published vin color on the front page of Disc and Music Echo, *a publication co-owned by Brian Epstein that had grown out of Bill Harry's* Mersey Beat.

6

EVERYTHING WAS RIGHT: *REVOLVER*'S RECEPTION

"Revolver is a revolutionary record, as important to the expansion of pop territory as was Rubber Soul."

—RICHARD GOLDSTEIN, *THE VILLAGE VOICE*

O f the four Beatles, Paul seemed to give the most thought as to how the still unnamed album would be received. "We'll lose some fans with it," he told *Disc and Music Echo* in the June 11 issue, "but we'll also gain some. The fans we'll probably lose will be the ones who like the things about us that we never liked anyway . . ." One issue that alarmed Paul came with his listening to a tape of the freshly completed album while the group was in West Germany. Upon hearing the finished product in its entirety, he was devastated to discover that the whole release was out of tune. It took some persuading from the other Beatles that it wasn't, but given the extensive use of vari-speed throughout, his concerns were fully understandable.

A much more positive—and lasting—moment came around the same time. John and Paul roomed together on the German dates, and as they listened to their work together, John declared, "I think your songs are better than mine." Coming from someone who dispensed compliments the same way a particularly miserly football-team owner was said to "toss nickels like manhole covers," Paul savored the praise ever after.

It was while in Munich that a title for the release was finally agreed upon. *Beatles on Safari*, *Bubble and Squeak*, and *Pendulum* were all considered before being shot down. Initially, the one name that all four Beatles agreed upon was *Abracadabra*. It has been reported in every Beatles book since that this selection was dropped after they discovered that another artist had already used it. (Whoever this unnamed act was has now become lost to history.) With the suggestion of enchantment in the air, Paul came up with *Magic Circle*, prompting John to counter with *Four Sides of the Circle*, and thereafter, *Four Sides of the Eternal Triangle*. (Ringo chimed in with *After-Geography*—a play on the Rolling Stones' recent *Aftermath*.)

Revolver, suggested by Paul, became the keeper. Though guns were the last things on their minds when they selected it—the idea of a twelve-inch piece of circular vinyl being literally a *revolver* when producing sound being foremost—this firearms aspect would be seized upon by Capitol in the states when their ads rolled out. (The cover art was displayed beneath a large pop art–styled "Bang!") The art crowd that Paul hung out with was less impressed, declaring it a "terrible" title, recalled Barry Miles. But as John Dunbar pointed out, he hadn't liked "Rubber Soul," either.

Robert Freeman, the photographer who'd shot all of the group's album covers from *With the Beatles* through *Rubber Soul*, was given leave to produce the jacket art for *Revolver*. Working the rotating-disc theme, he came up with a circular collage that featured the faces of all four. (It is reproduced in the *Anthology* book.) When spun, so the idea went, the four faces would meld into one. (How one would achieve this, short of cutting up the album cover and placing it on a turntable, was not explained.) In the end, the concept was scrapped, and their association—never formalized in the first place—ended amicably by mutual agreement.

John then approached their friend Klaus Voormann with the offer. The group's friendship with the German graphic artist and musician went back to 1960, to within weeks of the Beatles first setting foot on Hamburg soil. Though yet not a rock fan on the evening that he first discovered them at the Kaiserkeller, he soon became one, enthralled at first by their sound, then later, their personalities. In the years since being first drawn into their orbit, Klaus had taken up the bass, schooled at first by the supposedly completely untalented Stuart Sutcliffe (a perception that Klaus has tried to dispel through the years).

After a brief stint at a London ad agency (during which time he shared an apartment with George and Ringo), Klaus returned to Hamburg. It was 1963; the following year, he joined his first band, a five-man outfit called the Eyes. Attrition pared the ensemble down to a trio, which quickly rebranded itself Paddy, Klaus & Gibson. (Gibson Kemp, the drummer, had replaced Ringo in Rory Storm's Hurricanes. He later married Astrid Kirchherr.) The threesome was signed to a management deal with Brian Epstein, who quickly secured them a record contract, which fell apart after three singles. It was precisely at this juncture, when Klaus was trying to figure out his next move, that John came calling.

Despite the fact that he hadn't created artwork in several years, he decided to give it a go. The opportunity hadn't been presented to him as a given, and it wasn't. After brainstorming, coming down to the studio to hear the work in progress, and producing some preliminary ideas, Klaus submitted a number of concepts (he believes ten or fifteen). The Beatles liked the idea he'd floated of focusing on their hair —for a large segment of the population, their most distinguishing feature. Having heard some of the music they were working on, he was adamant that the art match the sound as a sort of bridge from their past into the future. To him, "Tomorrow Never Knows" represented a step toward the avant-garde. To that end, he was determined to render his creation in stark black-and-white, thereby going against the convention of the time, which dictated extravagant use of color—the more, the better.

Working from memory, it took him a couple of weeks to complete the drawing of the four faces. The most difficult one to capture was George's; in the end, he cut a mouth and eyes out of a newspaper and glued them in to get it just right. The collage was completed with help from John, Paul, Pete Shotton, and a pile of newspapers and magazines. (Ironically, some of Robert Freeman's work made it onto the cover after all: photos he took that were published in the Beatles' 1964 and 1965 U.S. tour books made it into the mix.) One shot of Ringo, taken by Dezo Hoffmann in 1963 and depicting him in a old-fashioned, striped bathing suit, is seen as oddly distorted. This one was clipped from a magazine showing a Beatle fan's bedroom wall; it's a poster, taken from an odd angle—thus the distortion.

Klaus brought the finished art over to George Martin's office at EMI in Manchester Square. Without ceremony, he set it up atop a file cabinet for the unveiling before Martin, Epstein, the four Beatles, and a secretary. There was momentary silence as they took it all in, a heavy void that only served to stir Klaus's nervousness with every passing second. It was finally broken by Paul. "Hey! That's me sitting on a toilet!" Everyone gathered closer to peer at what he'd spotted. He was right; there he was, in a photo taken in Hamburg. George Martin *tsk-tsk*ed and said, "Well, we can't have that." "No, it's great," Paul protested. (Suffice to say, the offending image was removed.)

That, as Klaus later related, broke the ice. Singly and as a group, the four Beatles heaped praise on Klaus and his work. He'd captured them all perfectly, with self-awareness of their

Nationally, the "Yellow Submarine" / "Eleanor Rigby" single did not top the charts in America, though it was a different story in individual markets.

image apparent, while simultaneously suggesting the explosion of ideas that were pouring out of their heads—something even more evident within the grooves of the release. He immortalized, as Paul Morley wrote in the U.K. *Guardian*, the "post-beat sophisticates that would curate *Sergeant Pepper,* and accelerate toward mutually agreed self-destruction."

Only Brian remained silent; and when Klaus caught his gaze from across the room, he noticed he was crying. His first thought was of alarm, but when Brian began to speak, he told him, "Klaus, this is exactly what we needed. I was worried that this whole thing might not work, but I know now that this [is] the cover, this LP will work. Thank you." For his efforts, Klaus was paid a princely forty pounds. This seemingly modest sum may have been made up for by the Grammy Award Klaus received on March 2, 1967 in the category of Best Album Cover / Graphic Arts.

On May 19 and 20, the Beatles took a timeout from recording to fulfill some promotional duties in advance of the release of their newest single. Two days were set aside for shooting video accompaniment to the "Paperback Writer" / "Rain" single, with the intent of covering all anticipated needs for TV "appearances" on both sides of the Atlantic, as well as the world over. At this stage of their career, the group was well past the point of showing up on every television show that demanded their presence. Instead, they created clips that may or may not have provided the illusion of an in-person appearance, serving the need to plug their latest product without succumbing to the grind of nonessential travel and / or demands on their time.

This approach to getting airtime for their product without having to actually show up and play was born of necessity. Pop artists were expected to turn up on the tube each time a new single dropped, but with success coming at such a high level and the pull of so many networks coming the world over, Brian Epstein recognized that a suitable solution to satisfying everyone's needs could be achieved with a little creativity. Dick Lester's film work pointed the way to creating exciting, visually engaging musical interludes that dispensed with any pretense that the group was actually performing. With that thought in mind, in November 1965 Epstein arranged for the group to shoot clips depicting themselves lip-synching to their last several singles. Produced in one day and with no evident planning other than to get through the requisite two to three minutes, these primitive videos marked the real beginning of what we view now as standard visual musical presentation.

The results of that shoot have become known among Beatle scholars as the "Intertel Promos." They were filmed at Twickenham Studios (where the *Let It Be* project would begin in 1969) and directed by Joe McGrath. McGrath was a Dick Lester associate who'd worked on *A Hard Day's Night* and *Help!*; he was also associated with Peter Sellers and would direct him in *Casino Royale* (1967) and (with Ringo) *The Magic Christian* (1970). Over the course of several hours, the Beatles ran through "I Feel Fine" (shot twice); "Ticket to Ride"; "Help!"; "We Can Work It Out"; and "Day Tripper" (the last two, three times each), with changes of clothing and / or set.

There was little in the way of deep conceptual thought put into the clips, other than to try and capture the Beatles' innate charm and mirth. (They are seen goofing off throughout: John is shown deliberately going out of synch or, as seen on "We Can Work It Out," trying his level best to crack Paul up—and succeeding. Things at last got out of hand with the second take of "I Feel Fine," wherein the group was depicted consuming fish and chips, with only the most token of efforts being made to mouth the song's lyrics.)

By the time the Beatles were ready to try again, they were prepared to take the process a little more seriously. The first day's shooting saw them videotaped at EMI's Number One studio. Director Michael Lindsay-Hogg, an American who'd made his reputation for capturing music on *Ready Steady Go!*, dressed the set to resemble a darkened soundstage rather than a recording facility, illuminated by colored set lighting and with randomly placed boom mics providing "atmosphere" scattered about. Ringo was perched atop a riser, while the others were situated on stools for the color shoot and standing for black-and-white. In the color versions, they sported dark glasses; also, a timpani was placed among the group as an aesthetic touch.

Perhaps to foster the illusion that they really made multiple appearances (should a viewer happen to see more than one broadcast), the Beatles changed clothes between setups. The most curious detail about the entire undertaking was also the least consequential. Sharp-eyed viewers can easily observe damage to Paul's front left tooth when he's shown singing. (Once your eyes lock onto it, it's hard to see anything else.) It begs the question: Why did the Beatles (indeed, why did Brian Epstein allow them to) expend the effort on so high profile a task with so obvious

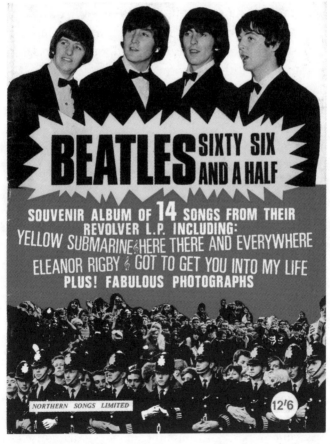

The Beatles' music publisher, Dick James, sang Revolver*'s praises in this songbook, calling it "their most spectacular and imaginative" release yet. He probably meant it, too.*

and easily remedied a distraction in plain sight? To contemporary viewers, it seems like a blatant slipup, unless of course they *intended* it to be seen. (Further confusing things is the fact that in the black-and-white "Paperback Writer," Paul appears to have a broken tooth in some shots and not others, as though he was toying with a loose crown between takes.)

The story is: back in Liverpool during the 1965 holiday season, Paul was joyriding on a moped along with friend Tara Browne, who'd come up to visit. They'd already shared a joint, and possibly spent time in the pub that evening as well. In any event, they were tooling around in the dark. Paul later claimed he was distracted by the full moon and wasn't watching where he was headed when a rock in his path threw him over the handlebars, his face hitting the pavement. His carelessness cost him a broken tooth and a split lip, requiring stitches. (Google around and you'll find a photo taken of him before being attended to.)

A check of the records for the date in question (Boxing Day) does not support the "full moon" story, but we'll let that pass. What is interesting is that Paul's telling of the incident was offered as the explanation for why he grew a mustache (to hide the scar). The trouble is, this particular bit of facial hair didn't arrive until late 1966, just as the *Sgt. Pepper* sessions got underway *about a year after the accident.* Maybe it took that long for the scarring to appear; but in any event, the reasoning doesn't make much sense, timing-wise. Why his teeth would appear so imperfect before the video cameras, yet cosmetically flawless only two months earlier at the so-called "butcher cover" session, remains another Beatle mystery. (Paul's accident and efforts to somehow disguise elements of it would, in 1969, be cited as "evidence" that he had, in fact, been killed three years before.)

The day after the studio shoot, the Beatles, accompanied by their usual entourage (Brian Epstein, Mal Evans, Neil Aspinall, Alf Bicknell), arrived at Chiswick House in West London. This eighteenth-century London landmark, spread over sixty-five acres, encompasses a magnificent neo-Palladian exhibition venue, as well as sprawling gardens and a glass conservatory. It was an inspired location in which to film them in 35-millimeter color, given the rich greens of the English spring and stately classical statuary. The group once again mimed their two songs, this time within the exedra. Recognizing that no one would be fooled into thinking they were actually performing, Lindsay-Hogg didn't bother having Ringo's kit set up. Instead, the drummer simply nodded in time along with the music his mates pretended to make.

Though both recordings feature Paul's Rickenbacker bass, he used the Höfner for all the videos shot, perhaps recognizing its iconic visual value. John was depicted with his newly acquired Epiphone Casino, the same one he'd later use extensively throughout the "White Album" sessions and *Let It Be* (though by the time it was seen in the "Hey Jude" / "Revolution" promos, it had been stripped down to its natural wood finish). George played his 1964 Gibson SG, another recent acquisition he was using extensively on the *Revolver* sessions. It would last be seen in his hands during the filming of the "Hey Bulldog" session in 1968; at some point afterward, he passed it on to Badfinger's Pete Ham. (Its exact whereabouts became something of a mystery following Ham's suicide in 1975. Rumored to have been sold at a "garage sale" for pocket change, it in fact turned up at Ham's brother's home. In 2004, it sold at auction for over half a million dollars.)

Compared to the Intertel promo clips prepared six months before, wherein the group had mimed their way through ten performances with an array of props ranging from a sawhorse to an exercise bike, the Chiswick House clips were high art. Lindsay-Hogg established a visual rhythm that fit the music, especially on the "Rain" clip, which also depicted shots taken in the conservatory and outdoors with some schoolchildren in the background. When reintroduced to the public in 1995 within the *Anthology* documentary (albeit in reedited form), the Chiswick House clips seemed startlingly fresh and *au courant*. Given that so many Britpop bands popular at the time took their visual cues straight from *Revolver*-era Beatles, this isn't at all surprising.

"Paperback Writer" was released in America on May 30; in Britain, on June 10. Five days before the latter date, the color studio footage was screened on *The Ed Sullivan Show*, complete with a personal introduction from the group that they'd filmed back on

May 19. On the show, Ringo explained their in-person absence by noting that *everybody* was busy these days "with the washing and the cooking." Interestingly, they are first seen covering their faces with large pieces of plastic film; when seen in close-up as the singing starts, the celluloid is revealed to be transparencies of the infamous "butcher" version of the *"Yesterday"* . . . *and Today* album cover.

Though the black-and-white versions of the two songs were intended for British television, *Top of the Pops* opted to broadcast the Chiswick promos—in black-and-white. The A-side aired on June 2, the B-side on June 9. One week later, the Beatles broke with long-standing precedent and actually appeared on *TOTP* in person, miming both songs before heading back to the studios to work on "Here, There and Everywhere." The appearance, which depicted John, Paul, and George grouped around Ringo before blazing rings of marquee-style lights, was extensively document-ed in still photos, which only seems to underscore the damnable decision by the BBC to wipe the broadcast videotape.

The single topped the charts in both Britain and America, dislodging Frank Sinatra's "Strangers in the Night" in the for-mer country and the Rolling Stones' "Paint It Black" in the latter. Much was made of the fact that it didn't go *straight* to number one in England, as had every one of their singles since "She Loves You" in 1963, as though this was evidence of their waning popu-larity. The Beatles shrugged off the suggestion, long accustomed to the press prematurely penning their obituary. The Sinatra single ended their two-week run atop the U.S. charts, while the Kinks' "Sunny Afternoon" dislodged the Fabs after just one week of reigning supreme in their homeland. To the extent that they cared about such matters, their streak of number-one singles in the U.K. (since "Love Me Do") remained unbroken.

The Beatles knew that they were taking a calculated risk as they moved further away from the sound that had gotten them where they were. Though their fan base had stayed with them to this point, they were now navigating deeper waters; there was no guarantee that their audience would keep up. It is therefore a tangible measure of both their self-confidence and their belief in their art that they did not flinch from moving in a direction that might not satisfy everyone. That said, the alternative—standing still or repeating themselves—was simply not in them.

In response to the standard "What do you think of the Beatles' new record?" query addressed to subscribers in the June 4 issue of *Disc and Music Echo*, most respondents expressed a positive impression of the A-side, less so the B-side. One reader, a Miss Penny Valentine, insightfully noted that the group had, in a way, put themselves in a paradoxical position: had another, lesser group recorded the songs, they may have been regarded as something special. But since the Beatles had set such a high standard for themselves, any release that wasn't simply amazing was seen as a letdown.

Meanwhile, the group toiled away to complete the album before setting out on the road. If they had any misgivings about the pioneering direction in which they were headed, and any potential alienation of their fans this record might cause, they may have drawn inspiration for sticking to their artistic guns from Bob Dylan, who was about to release the sprawling two-record set *Blonde on Blonde*. He had been in town the week before; and on May 27, John and George attended his concert at the Royal Albert Hall. Bob's tour of the U.K. had been marked by some epic hostility from folk fans that felt that by "going electric," he'd sold out his musical values for the allure of rock's bigger audience—and sales.

Though he had charted five singles showcasing his new sound, and a pair of albums (*Bringing It All Back Home* and *Highway 61 Revisited*) that featured one side and nearly all (respectively) electric material, fans in Britain seemed particularly resentful that the Woody Guthrie-esque singer of 1963 appeared only briefly as part of a brief acoustic opening set. Events came to a head with the legendary heckling incident that occurred on May 17 at Manchester's Free Trade Hall. Dylan had just finished performing "Ballad of a Thin Man"—the song that would be cited by John in "Yer Blues" two years later—and was about to perform the final number when a male audience member yelled out, "Judas!" The audience, as one, roared in response, prompting Bob to sneer into the mic, "I don't believe you!" Jangling the opening chords to "Like a Rolling Stone," he added, "You're a liar!" The tape and film rolling that night then caught the entire exchange, as well as Bob's hissed instructions to the band: "Play fucking loud!"

It was a singularly chilling moment in rock, as artist and audience battled over expectations. The event crystallized Dylan's metamorphosis from an earnest folkie to an evolving troubadour whose poetry was enhanced by the rock-solid foundation with which he'd chosen to present it. The point of following your muse wherever it led in the face of fans resistant to evolution was not missed by the two Beatles observing the proceedings from the VIP box at the Royal Albert Hall show. At this point in their respective careers, they were still very much in awe of Dylan's

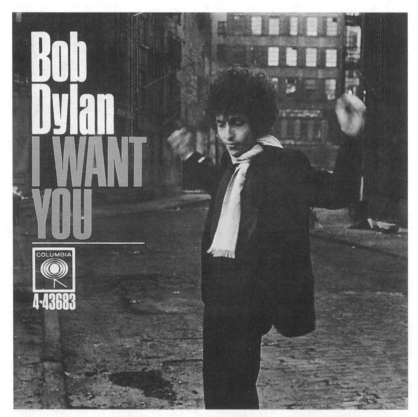

Blonde on Blonde's *release was preceded by the issue of "I Want You,"* *a song believed by some to be about Anita Pallenberg, the actress girlfriend* *of Brian Jones, and later the commonlaw wife of Keith Richards.*

talents. (George would remain so for the rest of his life, taken to quoting his lyrics, as someone once observed, the way some people quote scripture.) The Beatles' own day of reckoning with their fans was coming soon, but when it did, it wasn't about their music as much it was about how the public perceived the group's estimate of their own popularity when measured against that of the Almighty's.

Paul's relationship with Dylan in 1966, such as it was, seemed to be that of the eager pupil seeking the cool teacher's approval. Marianne Faithfull was on hand when the Beatle showed up at Dylan's Mayfair suite, clutching an acetate of the work in progress. Once ushered into Dylan's presence, he placed the disc on the turntable. Marianne described the scene as "Tomorrow Never Knows" began blaring through the speaker: "Paul was obviously very proud of it and stood back in anticipation, but Dylan just walked out of the room." (This might have been better than Cilla Black's reaction. When she was given a preview of the track, she laughed.) Despite the chilly reception, Paul recognized the crosscurrents between his band and Dylan: ". . . we're getting more interested now in the content of the songs, whereas Bob Dylan is getting more interested in rock 'n' roll . . . we're both going towards the same thing, I think."

Revolver was released on Friday, August 5 in the U.K., and the following Monday in the U.S. Breaking with tradition and standard U.K. practice, the single issued alongside it, "Yellow Submarine" / "Eleanor Rigby," was pulled from the parent album, instead of being fresh material separate from the long-player. The Beatles, Brian Epstein, and George Martin had until now been quite deliberate in giving fans value for their dollar (or pound) by offering material on singles that didn't duplicate album tracks, thereby sidestepping accusations of cheating the public by selling them the same songs twice. (Though it could be argued that this forced completists to shell out even more money.) The economics of record purchasing was well delineated in Britain: those who couldn't spring for an entire long-player were served by EPs containing the four most popular tracks.

No such distinctions were felt in America, where Capitol

apparently had no qualms about marketing singles *and* albums to the same purchaser. The logic from the Beatles camp for departing from precedent at this juncture is interesting. "We just thought we may as well put it out instead of sitting back and seeing dozens of cover versions all getting hits," said George in response to the question. If the Beatles were determined to reap the economic benefits of scoring hit singles with their own recordings by heading off the competition, their choice of these two particular tracks calls into question their reasoning.

Early reviews compared "Eleanor Rigby" to "Yesterday," the single most-covered song of all time. True, both recordings departed from rock convention by the use of string sections in place of more standard instrumentation. Also, both were Paul songs, but that's where the similarities ended. "Yesterday" bore obvious commercial universality with its time-honored theme of a love gone wrong. But "Eleanor Rigby" was a somewhat unsettling composition devoid of traditional romanticism, calculated to stir thought rather than soothe. That the Beatles had the notion that other artists would rush to cover it and steal their thunder is a curious line of thought. Perhaps they saw the song as an artistic breakthrough (which it was) and sought to capitalize on the attention it was destined to draw before anyone else had the chance to.

Likewise, "Yellow Submarine" was a highly idiosyncratic composition, as well as Ringo's first vocal showcase issued in this form. (Earlier that year, he'd gotten B-side exposure with "What Goes On," the flip side of the U.S.-only "Nowhere Man" single.) But novelty songs don't tend to stir covers by other artists. (At best, they may inspire "answer" records.) It is therefore somewhat baffling that, if the intention was indeed to score the hit before another artist did, the band didn't select some of the more obviously commercially appealing songs. "Here, There and Everywhere," "Good Day Sunshine," and "Got to Get You into My Life" were all the stuff from which hit singles are made, being catchy, engaging, and melodically well crafted.

Of the covers that came in the wake of *Revolver*'s release, only one really constituted a hit. Perhaps not coincidentally, it was an effort sanctioned by its writer. Cliff Bennett and the Rebel Rousers, a Parlophone act managed by Brian Epstein, were first out of the gate with a cover of "Got to Get You into My Life," which was produced by Paul himself. It peaked at number six in Britain while giving the group their second and final Top Ten hit. On the other hand, the Tremeloes, the band that beat out the Beatles for a Decca recording contract in 1962, made "Good Day Sunshine" their first release following the departure of lead singer Brian Poole. It did not chart. They fared better the following year when covering Cat Stevens's "Here Comes My Baby."

Though the Beatles' issue of these two *Revolver* tracks effectively preempted any competing versions, it's interesting to note that two months after they pulled out all of the promotional stops to plug their previous single, they did not go to the same efforts on behalf of "Yellow Submarine" / "Eleanor Rigby." No promo films were produced and no television appearances were scheduled. Granted, they were on the road while the single was in release, which should have stirred enough media attention in itself to keep public awareness heightened, though of course no *Revolver* material was performed. Even without any special efforts expended, the single went to number one in Britain, occupying the top slot for four weeks.

America was a different story. In the United States, the single peaked at number two, blocked from the top of the *Billboard* Hot 100 by the Supremes' "You Can't Hurry Love." The Beatles might have prevailed, if just for a week, had they not found themselves embroiled in controversy just as the single dropped. In late July, Art Unger, publisher of *Datebook*, an up-and-coming player in the teen-magazine market, sent reprints of the Maureen Cleave Beatle profiles to conservative radio stations throughout the South. Though Unger was on good terms with the Beatles and their entourage personally, he recognized media dynamite when he saw it. (Unger in fact had been alerted to the Cleave articles in the first place by Beatles publicist Tony Barrow, who suggested that Unger see about licensing them for American publication. Barrow evidently overlooked all the red flags within the articles, or else purposely operated on the "any publicity is good publicity" theory.)

"Paperback Writer" did indeed top the national charts on both sides of the Atlantic, but not in every local market. Fondness for Tommy James's "Hanky Panky" kept it from similarly going to number one in Chicago, for instance.

It didn't take long for the most reactionary broadcasters in America to take the bait. Whatever antipathy they had heretofore largely kept in check against the Beatles, their hair, and their latent Negro tendencies (evidenced by their fondness for black artists) had at last been unleashed. Not only did a number of stations announce a boycott of Beatles music on the airwaves ("We're not going to forget what they said . . ."), but plans were soon announced in Birmingham, Alabama, for a public burning of their product. Chapters of the Ku Klux Klan leapt into the fray, undoubtedly pleased at the novelty of having somebody other than blacks and Jews to threaten. All of this might have stayed a local concern, but for the UPI wire service picking up the story and taking it national.

Suddenly, breathless reporting of the group's "blasphemy" had gone viral; and by the time *Datebook* hit the newsstands on July 29, a large and vocal segment of the Beatle's Bible Belt fan base had turned against them. On August 5, Brian Epstein was forced to make a statement, insisting that John's remarks had been taken out of context. Technically, that was not true: the articles ran more or less intact as received, but the magazine had isolated John's most damning comment ("I don't know which will go first—rock 'n' roll or Christianity!") and placed it on the cover, alongside an equally provocative quote from Paul ("It's a lousy country where anyone black is a dirty nigger!"). Unger had in fact expected Paul's comment to incite a reaction, influencing his decision to run the most popular Beatle's photo on the cover. He was as astonished as anyone in an era of heightened civil-rights sensitivities that Paul's remark was ignored while John's touched a raw nerve.

If *Datebook*'s editors wished to sell a few extra copies with this calculated effort to stir the hornet's nest, they succeeded beyond their wildest dreams. Unfortunately for the Beatles, the timing of the story could not possibly have been worse, just as a new single and new album were entering the marketplace on the eve of their North American tour. With Brian's statement failing to quell the storm, the Beatles and their manager became all too aware of the many millions in lost revenue they were potentially staring down. Thus was the scene set for John's humiliating act of contrition upon arriving on U.S. soil at a Chicago press conference on August 11.

As he tried to explain it, first: he was referring specifically to a decline in church attendance in England, not anywhere else.

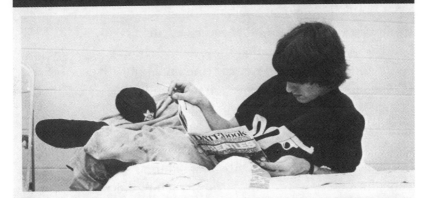

Despite what one might think, the Beatles maintained a good relationship with the publishers of Datebook *magazine. John even autographed a copy of the issue for Art Unger, signing it "John C. Lennon."*

Second, his observation asserting that the "Beatles were bigger than Jesus" was not a boast; it was a quantifying statement citing an example of something that held more sway with youth than Christianity did. Those capable of recognizing nuance took him at his word, while the rest of the media hoped to string the story along a little longer, basking in the light projected from the Beatles' star.

Though the boycotts ended once the attention of the press was diverted elsewhere (stories recently in the news included Charles Whitman's sniper rampage at the University of Texas, as well as the death of comedian Lenny Bruce), the controversy could not help but depress the group's record sales. It's hard to escape the conclusion that a pair of songs as popular as "Yellow Submarine" / "Eleanor Rigby" would have topped the American charts had enthusiasm not become clouded by nonmusical matters. (By way of comparison, "Paperback Writer" sold 750,000 copies within a week of its release. Four weeks after its issue, "Yellow Submarine" had sold 1,200,000 copies: overall, good numbers, but a substantial slowdown.)

Certainly, the attendant bad publicity seems to have affected ticket sales, which were well down from the year before. A year after first playing Shea Stadium, their 1966 date there saw them at 11,000 seats short of a sellout. Other venues reported similar stories: an afternoon show in Seattle was attended by 8,000, while nearly double that attended the evening show. At San Francisco's Candlestick Park, the site of the final public Beatle concert, 25,000 fans showed up in a venue that could have seated another 20,000.

All of the negative attention, added to the "butcher cover" controversy two months earlier, seemed to subdue the acclaim normally accorded a new Beatles album. Sales were strong enough: *Revolver* went gold quickly, reaching sales of $1 million by August 22. On the charts, it took just one month to ascend to the top of *Billboard*'s album chart, displacing its U.S. predecessor, *"Yesterday"* . . . *and Today*, and maintaining its position for six weeks until bumped by *Supremes a' Go-Go*. In Britain, where the Capitol product did not exist, *Revolver* took the top spot in *Record*

KRLA BEAT

Volume 2, Number 22 — August 27, 1966

'More Popular Than Jesus'

JOHN 8:4

What seemed to be a harmless interview at the time has touched off one of the most heated controversies of the modern generation. The following is an exert from the explosive text of Maureen Cleave's article on John Lennon that has caused the heated blasts against the Beatles.

Miss Cleave quoted Lennon as saying:

"Christianity will go. It will vanish and shrink. I needn't argue about that. I am right and will be proved right.

"We're more popular than Jesus. I don't know which will go first—rock 'n roll or Christianity. Jesus was all right, but his disciples were thick and ordinary. It's them twisting it that ruins it for me."

In the article, Miss Cleave said of Lennon, "Not that his mind is closed, but it's closed round whatever he's thinking at the time." She said Lennon had been conducting a thorough religious investigation for some time.

Beatles 'Ban-Wagon' Rolls!

John Goes Solo For New Film

With the Beatles stymied at the stormiest, most closely watched point in their careers, John Lennon quietly announced he is going on his own—at least temporarily.

The BEAT has learned that John, the brash focal point of the Beatles, plans to act in a movie—without the other Beatles—for the first time since the origin of the group.

A spokesman insists, however, that Lennon's single act will not involve a permanent split among the group. Lennon will be back with the other Beatles for the next group movie in January.

And, of course, it does not affect recording sessions or the Beatles' U.S. tour in August.

The Beatles are believed to have been disenchanted with the rigors of their singing routine for some time. Those close to the Beatles say the boys want to start doing more things individually.

Two Animals Leave Group

The BEAT has learned that at least two and maybe three members of the original Animals will be leaving the group. Both Hilton Valentine and Chas Chandler have said they will now concentrate on record production.

Drummer Barry Jenkins is expected to continue working with Eric Burdon, but the future of jazz organist Dave Rowberry is still unknown.

Inside the BEAT

BEAT MEDIATES
Eureka—a Solution!

The BEAT is proud to announce "The Great Compromise."

Acting as a voluntary mediator in the dispute which has strained relations with our closest ally and turned brother against brother and daughter against mother in America, The BEAT has successfully negotiated a reciprocal agreement with the Beatles.

After exhaustive negotiations they have agreed—in return for similar concessions on our part—that they will not attempt to interfere with our rights to freedom of speech or freedom of religion.

Nor will the Beatles try to force any Americans to praise England, provided we don't ask them to praise America. Most important of all, perhaps, the Beatles have unanimously agreed not to ban any American radio stations.

Thus, now that this really vital crisis has been settled, the world can return to less pressing problems such as Viet Nam, disarmament and starvation.

Epstein Fears Security Dangers During U.S. Tour

Embroiled in a controversy which produced more mass reaction than the Viet Nam war or big-city race riots, the Beatles launched their third American tour prepared for an uncertain reception.

Manager Brian Epstein, trying desperately to soothe ruffled feelings, openly expressed fears of security dangers while denying rumors that some of the 14 scheduled concerts might be cancelled.

Still unresolved was the intent of John Lennon's statement that the Beatles are "more popular than Jesus." The writer whose interview created the furore claimed the statement was taken out of context, and John quickly followed suit.

But many Americans were still dissatisfied and dozens of radio stations across the U.S. continued to ban Beatle records and organized mass burnings of Beatle records and photographs.

Subsequent statements by two other Beatles merely aggravated the situation.

Columnist Maureen Cleave appeared to ease hostile feelings when she stated that her article had been "completely misinterpreted and that Americans have the story entirely wrong."

Lennon Christian

Miss Cleave said that Lennon, whom she termed a "Christian with a young son who has also been Christened," deplored the lack of interest in the Christian Church.

Lennon, according to Miss Cleave, observed that the "power of Christianity was on the decline in the modern world and that things had reached such a ridiculous state that human beings (such as the Beatles) could be worshipped more religiously than religious figures.

She said that Lennon, far from approving this type of worship, was appalled by it.

But if Miss Cleave's explanation of the article eased feelings, ensuing statements by the other Beatles rekindled anti-Beatle sentiment.

Beatles Paul McCartney and George Harrison got in on the act while Manager Epstein was in New York City attempting to clarify Lennon's statements. McCartney said he found the American people's pursuit of money "sort of frightening," and Harrison said he wasn't really looking forward to the Beatles' current U.S. tour.

Doesn't Like U.S.

McCartney said he liked England better than the United States chiefly because of "the attitude of the people in America." He said, "They seem to think that money is everything.

"And this applies especially to the kind of people we meet — agents and corporation people. You get the feeling everybody's after it—money—and it's sort of frightening," Paul declared in a BBC radio interview.

Harrison, who earlier said the Beatles were "coming to America to get beaten up," eased his blast against the United States only where he spoke of California—where the Beatles finish their tour in late August.

"At least there," he said, "we *(Turn to Page 16)*"

READERS REACT TO BEATLE BAN PAGE 2

(Turn to Page 16)

JOHN—Storm Center

GEORGE—Dreads Tour

PAUL—dislikes U.S.

The KRLA Beat was a locally produced rock-music journal, running from 1964 through the spring of 1968. Their Beatle coverage was stellar, due in no small part to Tony Barrow's regular updates on the band's doings. It was also refreshingly honest in its reporting, as seen here.

Retailer's survey just one week after its issue, reigning supreme for seven weeks—a better performance than here; but then, in the U.K., it *was* a better album. The fact that Brits had to wait eight months between long-players—the longest gap so far—couldn't have hurt sales.

(*Revolver*'s chart-topping run was bookended in England by the soundtrack of the film *The Sound of Music*. As impressive as any rock album of the era performed chart-wise, the English seemingly couldn't get enough of "Do-Re-Mi" and other such songs, keeping the long-player at the top for a total of *sixty-nine weeks* between 1965 and 1968. Only releases by the Beatles, the Rolling Stones, the Monkees, and Val Doonican interrupted its remarkable performance. What was different in the U.K.? Tightly controlled airwaves, for one thing, which kept pop marginalized for many years—a situation that bred the rise of pirate radio. The heavy commercialization of youth culture in the states, in comparison, facilitated sales of all things that teens would buy—records being at the top of the food chain.)

But few wanted to discuss the artistic breakthroughs evident on *Revolver*, not when there were far sexier things to talk about. A survey of the press conferences the group gave at each stop on their final tour shows far more interest in their religious views than musical matters. On the rare occasion when they were asked something about their music, the group almost couldn't help but be flip in their response.

In Los Angeles, the Beatles' news conference was held at the Capitol Records Tower, where they were awarded gold records for recent sales. Though photographed before a large blowup of the *Revolver* cover art, their questioners otherwise tended to ignore their new release explicitly. One question that did elicit a memorable response came from a journalist who cited a recent *Time* magazine article, which asserted that "Day Tripper" was written about a prostitute, while "Norwegian Wood" was about a lesbian. "I just wanted to know what your intent was when you wrote it, and what your feeling is about the *Time* magazine criticism of the music that is being written today."

Before John could get a word out, Paul answered, "We were just trying to write songs about prostitutes and lesbians, that's all." ("'Quipped Ringo,'" John joined in.) The ensuing laughter helped keep things light at a time when relationships between the press and the group were more adversarial than they'd ever been before.

Rock journalism as we know it today didn't really exist in 1966, though it might be argued that the Beatles, with *Revolver*, underscored the need for its inception. Theirs was a serious effort to produce lasting art while expanding the boundaries of a genre largely regarded by the Establishment as a transient rite of passage for the young. Though an occasional acknowledgement of their music might turn up in adult publications like *Time*, *Newsweek*, or *Life*, youth-oriented publications tended to focus on everything *but* their music. (BEATLES [sic] WEIRD WISHES shouted a headline on the August 1966 issue of *16* magazine.)

Rolling Stone was over a year away from their first issue (which would feature John on its cover when it did appear); *Creem*, three years. *Crawdaddy*, one of the more literate rock journals of the 1960s and 1970s, did begin publication in early 1966, but only as a fanzine. Still, it covered *Revolver* in its fifth issue, giving the abridged U.S. issue a mixed review: criticizing the lack of holistic integration and balance (while acknowledging the U.S. version wasn't really by the group's design), praising it for the array of material. The reviewer, publisher Paul Williams, heaped praise on George's "Love You To" and Paul's "Eleanor Rigby" while disrespecting "Tomorrow Never Knows" ("A good artist doesn't publish first drafts") and "Yellow Submarine" (comparing it to Sgt. Barry Sadler's "Ballad of the Green Berets" as an unworthy novelty: "blah").

Ahead of the curve in recognizing *Revolver* as something special was critic Richard Goldstein, writing for New York's *Village Voice*. Just out of college, Goldstein was on his way to a

The VIPs salute The Beatles! Beginning their fabulous 1966 tour in Chicago, they'll perform across the country . . . . .

August:
Friday/12 . . . . Chicago
Saturday/13 . . . . Detroit
Sunday/14 . . . . Cleveland
Monday/15 . . . . Washington D. C.
Tuesday/16 . . . . Philadelphia
Wednesday/17 . . . . Toronto
Thursday/18 . . . . Boston
Friday/19 . . . . Memphis
Saturday/20 . . . . Cincinnati
Sunday/21 . . . . St. Louis
Tuesday/23 . . . . New York
Thursday/25 . . . . Seattle
Sunday/28 . . . . Los Angeles
Monday/29 . . . . San Francisco

Hear Jim Stagg's exclusive reports on WCFL/Radio 10.

The decision to quit the road for good was made official at some point during the Beatles' final jaunt across North America.

long and distinguished career when he sang the praises of this new Beatles release. "Hear it once and you know it's important. Hear it twice, it makes sense. Third time around, it's fun. Fourth time, it's subtle. On the fifth hearing, *Revolver* becomes sublime." Though his review overall gave the Beatles much credit for doing something distinctly new as they explored the possibilities of what a rock album could be, Goldstein would distinguish himself the following year as one of the few professional critics that did not fall all over himself to exalt *Sgt. Pepper*.

In Britain, the response to *Revolver* was equally positive, if less expository. A reviewer in *New Musical Express* wrote that *Revolver* ". . . certainly has new sounds and new ideas, and should cause plenty of argument among fans as to whether it is as good as or better than previous efforts." *Melody Maker*, who'd previewed the album, merely stated what would become a near-universal reaction, reporting to readers that "their new LP [will] change the direction of pop music." *Disc and Music Echo* tapped the Kinks' Ray Davies to act as celebrity reviewer, and ran his song-by-song take in the July 30 issue. He was predictably frank with his appraisal, calling BS where he saw it ("Yellow Submarine"—"a load of rubbish, really" and "Doctor Robert"—"not my sort of thing") while dispensing praise where he felt it was earned: "The best thing on the album," he declared "I'm Only Sleeping" (an unsurprising judgment, given how closely Davies's work resembles it). Their experimentation on "Tomorrow Never Knows" didn't particularly impress him ("I can imagine they had George Martin tied to a totem pole when they did this").

The Beatles found themselves in the unfair position of not being allowed to savor any praise coming their way over *Revolver*, given how it had become overshadowed by the Christianity controversy. But the satisfaction they clearly felt with it simply confirmed that touring was impeding their progress as artists, despite what they might be saying publicly. When asked point blank in July whether the group could survive without playing live, sustaining themselves only with recordings, John was dismissive, but with traces of resentment escaping his lips. "Not the way the fans keep moaning about not seeing us all the time."

Brian Epstein, for one, was not about to let their achievement be overshadowed by transient issues, further suggesting that anyone preferring live appearances over artistic progress was missing the point. "I doubt whether (the public) realize what an explosive LP *Revolver* really is. They've covered such new and important territory. While they are creating albums like *Revolver*, how can the public expect much more of them?" As for the band, they'd already reached their tipping point. Between "bigger than Jesus," the "butcher cover," and the debacle in the Philippines in July (wherein a perceived snub of dictator Ferdinand Marcos's wife Imelda resulted in the entourage being forced from the country under threat of violence), the end of their road show had come.

If there had arisen a gap in the space occupied by the Beatles during the last few years as the primary personality-driven musical entity in the lives of adolescents, it was about to be filled. Whether by design based on a close observation of the Beatles' continued growth outstripping their audience's attention, or simply pure copyist instincts, a pair of American television producers saw the opening created by the group's artistic development that left some longing for the Fabs' *A Hard Day's Night*–era immediacy.

Bert Schneider and Bob Rafelson had, even before the release of *Revolver*, been at work developing a weekly series featuring a fictitious, struggling rock band. Visually and comedy-wise, it would take its cues straight out of the two Dick Lester Beatle films, with *non sequitur* musical sequences thrown in. (The music was always envisioned as a component of the show, but records were viewed as little more than a promotional afterthought.)

The Monkees was created with no superficial Beatle-ism left unexplored. To begin with, the four musician-actors cast had distinct personalities that more or less followed the Beatle template: guitarist Michael Nesmith was the self-assured spokesman— the serious "John" character. (In fact, the outspoken "bad cop" Monkee would very quickly take on the role of ringleader, leading the rebellion against their handlers that gave the group the autonomy with their musical product in early 1967.)

Micky Dolenz, forced to play the role of drummer (though in real life he'd played guitar in a local Los Angeles band, the Miss-

The timing for the Monkees' arrival couldn't have been better, coming as the Beatles vacated their previously held role as the mop-tops of the day.

ing Links), represented Lennon's other side: the outgoing clown with the great voice. Hailing from Manchester, Davy Jones was the cute heartthrob, appealing to the "Paul" fans (while possessing not a whit of his archetype's musical gifts). In real life, Peter Tork—an accomplished multi-instrumentalist with a deep interest in Eastern philosophy—most closely resembled "George," but instead, he was cast as the "Ringo": an amiable dunce that begged to be mothered.

Any Beatles fans that might have been left feeling alienated by their musical direction or offended by the controversies dogging them that year didn't have to look very far to find another act to whom to attach their allegiance. *The Monkees* premiered on September 12, two weeks to the day after the Beatles took their final bows in San Francisco. "Last Train to Clarksville," the group's first single, had been issued a month before the show began airing. Composed by the professional songwriting team of Tommy Boyce and Bobby Hart, the song had been deliberately styled after "Paperback Writer," as the composers freely admitted. With a wave of grandiose hype not seen since 1964's "The Beatles are coming!" campaign, the song took off once the show began airing, while teen magazines quickly became glutted with Monkee images the same way they had been with Fab ones two years earlier. In November, "Last Train to Clarkesville" hit number one on the *Billboard* charts—not bad for a group that hadn't yet played a note in public.

As for the Monkees' role models, the four Beatles spent the next several months enjoying something they had not had since their first hit: time off to pursue individual interests. Thought the Beatles had not found a film script earlier in the year upon which that they all agreed, John did accept Dick Lester's invitation to take a minor role in Patrick Ryan's antiwar black comedy *How I Won the War*. The shoot would take him out of England for what must have seemed like the certain calm and tranquility of Almeria, located on the Mediterranean in southern Spain, beginning in September.

Paul likewise took on film work, though (predictably) it took the form of composing a score. *The Family Way*, a Boulting Brothers film that marked actress Hayley Mills's transition into adult roles, gave Paul the opportunity to work with George Martin outside the Beatles. As he would when composing in the classical idiom in later years, Paul relied on a knowledgeable, experienced professional to put his ideas on paper and translate them into a language that an orchestra could play. The work itself relied less on his composing skills than it did his powers as an arranger (there were, after all, only two themes, fleshed out into numerous variations).

While the two "senior" Beatles thus took on tasks that amounted to little more than busy work, George was on a personal quest

When the third Beatles movie failed to materialize, John accepted Dick Lester's offer to appear in a supporting role in this antiwar black comedy. The experience confirmed for John that he was not cut out to be an actor.

of self-discovery. He and Pattie headed out to India, where he met Ravi Shankar on his own turf. It was Ravi that steered the questioning young man onto the paths that set him on his way as he sought tranquility and order within a world thrown into chaos by life as a Beatle. Rock 'n' roll suddenly became very small, and as George began a serious study of the sitar, he all but abandoned the guitar.

For Ringo, life was much simpler. He had work done on his home; enjoyed his one-year-old son, Zak; and stayed out of the public eye. When John, with whom he'd kept contact long distance, intimated that he was getting lonely on location, Ringo flew out to keep John company in time for the latter's birthday. Implicit in all of the Beatles' off-duty pursuits was the realization, for fans and EMI alike, that for the first time in three years, there would be no new Beatle long-player at Christmastime. Parlophone saved the day (in the U.K., at least) by pulling together singles old and new (augmented by the previously U.S.-only cover "Bad Boy") for a compilation called *A Collection of Beatles Oldies (But Goldies!)*. It must have been obvious to anyone paying attention that, given the low-rent design and their own oft-stated aversion to compilations, the Beatles had nothing to do with this project.

Gauging *Revolver*'s influence on the music that came in its immediate wake is not easy. The Beatles were quite conscious of the fact that its very diversity would make it a challenge to emulate. ("They'll never be able to copy this," Paul crowed in the pages of *Melody Maker*.) He was, as it happened, correct, though it could be argued that of those capable, few were interested. To even compete on the same level of studio craft would've required considerable support from the label, a visionary producer and engineering staff, and the financial wherewithal to foot the bill for the use of outside musicians and studio hours. Few artists came close to possessing the resources available to the Beatles; and even if they had, success at that level was predicated on following your own muse, not hitching your wagon to the Big Thing of the moment.

The Rolling Stones would not release a full-length follow-up to *Aftermath* until early 1967, but they did crank out a series of increasingly accomplished singles in the meantime: "19th Nervous Breakdown"; "Paint It Black"; and "Have You Seen Your Mother, Baby, Standing in the Shadow?" As friends of the highly social Beatles, Jagger, Richards, and Jones were well placed to observe the group's work in progress; Mick even popped in to visit during the *Revolver* sessions. While pursuing their own artistic destiny, the Stones certainly were as susceptible to the Beatles' influence as anyone; and when work began in August on what was issued the following year as *Between the Buttons*, it was clear that they too were now following the Liverpudlians' lead by attempting to create a sustained listening experience.

Bill Wyman conceded as much, writing in his memoirs that what they produced was ". . . the result of the first studio session at which we concentrated on an album as a finished product," meaning the resulting long-player wasn't going to be a random series of potential singles. (As with the Beatles, their U.S. label, London, sliced and diced the group's LPs according to what they felt would sell in the states; thus, the U.S. iteration of the record was augmented with the hits "Ruby Tuesday" and "Let's Spend the Night Together," songs absent from the U.K. release.)

This put the Stones' thinking squarely on the same page as the Beatles'. Overt Fab influence on their lackluster *Between the Buttons* ran minor, more along the lines of stylistic variation than any obvious technical innovation. (The array of sounds was more than heard previously on a Rolling Stones long-player, but well short of outright Beatle mimicry.) As usual, Brian Jones's tendency to take on exotic instrumentation deepened with this record. In the past, he'd used marimbas, dulcimers, sitar, and a Japanese *koto*; here, he extended his explorations to include accordion ("Back Street Girl"); recorder ("Ruby Tuesday"); saxophone ("Something Happened to Me Yesterday"); and kazoo ("Cool, Calm & Collected").

The Stones, at this juncture, weren't prepared to follow the Beatles' path of experimentation. To begin with, they had a three-week window to get it done, as opposed to three months. (This approach would change drastically upon their return to the studio the following year with *Their Satanic Majesties Request*, an album roundly condemned as a weak attempt to steal *Sgt. Pepper*'s thun-

HAVE YOU SEEN YOUR MOTHER, BABY, STANDING IN THE SHADOW?

The Stones' continued efforts at stirring outrage could be seen and heard with their September 1966 single. "Have You Seen Your Mother, Baby, Standing in the Shadow?" featured their "drug" look (as seen in the ads and the promo films); sonically though, the feedback-laden track, featuring buzz-saw guitars and a horn section, didn't come off to their satisfaction, suffering from a rushed mix.

der.) If anything, *Between the Buttons'* focus on songcraft seemed to simultaneously channel Bob Dylan (displaying a distinct *Blonde on Blonde* preoccupation with observational lyricism) and the Kinks, with tart British music-hall settings evident in places. Contemporary reviewers noted the latter fixation, with one expressing disappointment that the Stones' follow up to *Aftermath* sounded "more like a bunch of vaudevillian Kinks' outtakes than a bona fide Stones" release.

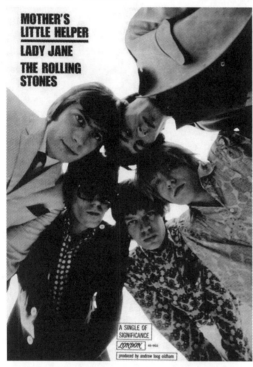

"Significance," the ad copy read. "Mother's Little Helper" was indeed a bold statement, being a stark commentary on the Establishment's hypocrisy toward self-medication: bad among youth, but perfectly acceptable among straights.

Indeed, with so many peers in rock reaching the height of their creativity in 1966, it was impossible for all of them to not listen closely to what everyone else was doing. (Ray Davies grandly suggested that the Beatles were waiting for the next Kinks album to arrive; perhaps to provide an early clue to the new direction.) No one was listening more closely to the Beatles' latest than Brian Wilson. He felt that with *Revolver*, *Pet Sounds* had been effectively one-upped, taxing his creativity to the limit. (It had not been a robust seller in the U.S., peaking at number ten and then only briefly, prompting Capitol to issue a *Best of the Beach Boys* compilation two months later as if to erase the taint of such an unrepresentative work.)

Pet Sounds did much better across the Atlantic, peaking at number two and garnering rapturous reviews from people not steeped in surfing and hot-rod culture. Indeed, for the only time during their recording career, the Beatles were bumped from the top position in the year's end *NME* poll, second to the Beach Boys as

Top Pop Group for 1966. Also for the first time, *NME* announced a tie for Album of the Year between—naturally—*Pet Sounds* and *Revolver*. Luckily, Wilson had a potent arrow in his quiver, one originally intended for inclusion on *Pet Sounds*. "Good Vibrations" was judged not to fit the album's overall arc and was held back. The product of seventeen sessions, four studios, and a reported $50,000, it was released as a single two months after *Revolver*.

The ambitious 3:35 recording, featuring stacked vocals, cellos, and, most distinctively, the Electro-Theremin—an eerie-sounding electronic instrument heretofore heard mostly in science-fiction TV shows such as *My Favorite Martian*—quickly shot up the charts, reaching number one in the U.S. in December for one week only (briefly displacing the idiotic "Winchester Cathedral" by the New Vaudeville Band for the top slot during its two-week run) as well as the U.K., where it reigned for two weeks.

Revolver's blend of musical variety and stunningly effective use of studio wizardry impelled Brian to go all out. The Beach Boys' new project, dubbed *Dumb Angel*, would be "a teenage symphony to God," Wilson told the press, therein putting his finger on the direction toward which he believed pop music was headed: a divine one. Though spiritual themes did indeed surface in rock albums recorded during the years that followed (notably the Who's *Tommy*, but also Van Morrison's *Astral Weeks*, among others), it was a trend that went wholly ignored by the Beatles, save George, who conspicuously devoted nearly the whole of his post-Beatles career to this particular path.

To fulfill his stratospheric ambitions, Wilson enlisted a new songwriting partner, the singular Van Dyke Parks. Though Tony Asher, *Pet Sounds'* lyricist, was none too pleased to see his tenure come to an end, Brian was certain that Parks possessed the "intellectual passion and esoteric way with words (that) seemed to mesh with the way I was feeling." Parks had recently worked with the Byrds on *Fifth Dimension*—though as an organist, not a songwriter. (He'd also been a child actor, most notably playing Tommy Manicotti on "lost episodes" of *The Honeymooners* at age twelve.) Given the difficulty Wilson had in getting his bandmates behind him on *Pet Sounds*, he was courting disaster by partnering

It took over four months and four studios to achieve perfection with "Good Vibrations," but the time and expense was judged worth it, even by Capitol. In the end, however, it represented the beginning of the end—not the end of the beginning—of Brian Wilson's creative renaissance.

with a man that Mike Love had dismissed as a purveyor of "acid alliteration."

With the goal of simultaneously besting *Revolver* and getting down on tape the sounds he was hearing in his head, Wilson set out to give listeners a true "concept album" with *Smile* (as the project was re-titled), featuring thematically linked songs and a mini-suite based on the four elements. Beginning with "Heroes and Villains," one of only a handful of viable recordings to emerge from the sessions, *Smile* was crafted as a sort of Americana tale, designed as a response to the inescapable influence of British artists that the Beatles, of course, had spearheaded.

The work began in August 1966—just after *Revolver* emerged,

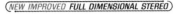

The legendary status built up around Smile *as a lost masterpiece would have surely been impossible for* any *album to fulfill. Indeed, the 2011 issue at long last revealed, at best, an* unfinished *masterpiece. Here's Frank Holmes's original artwork.*

but only three months before the *Sgt. Pepper* sessions commenced with "Strawberry Fields Forever." Wilson's methods differed considerably from the Beatles': he used platoons of studio pros (the other Beach Boys weren't considered essential to the work bearing their name, beyond the vocals), several recording facilities, and by this time was recording *components* of songs rather than complete takes; these were intended to be spliced together later. Also, he produced himself, and didn't have (or need) the benefit of George Martin's knowhow to make things happen.

But putting so much pressure on himself was, again, inviting trouble. The album was scheduled to be completed and issued by January 1967. But by then, violent arguments had erupted between Wilson and his band, notably Mike Love, who again took issue with what he saw as general self-indulgence; Parks's impenetrable lyrics (which were beyond his comprehension as well as—he felt—their fans'); and Brian's ongoing shift away from the formula that had brought them this far. Added to this was Brian's copious drug use, especially of LSD; his latent paranoia; and his own personal demons and delicate psyche. The stage was thus set for a spectacular collapse.

It has been said that Brian was in his car with the radio on when he first heard "Strawberry Fields Forever." He pulled over to listen to the entire recording, and when it was over, he wept, saying, "They got there first." This must have been in February; and when the now past-due project suffered the defection of Van Dyke Parks the following month, *Smile*—the masterpiece that never was, intended to show the world as well as the Beatles who rock's biggest genius was—became irretrievably derailed. Capitol announced its shelving in May, just before *Sgt. Pepper* was released.

Among the giants of rock in early 1967, Brian Wilson had self-destructed; Bob Dylan was recuperating from his motorcycle accident, and the Rolling Stones were still playing catch-up before a series of drug busts sidelined them for most of the year. The Beatles' path to artistic supremacy—with their first post-touring album—could not have been clearer.

7

TAKING MY TIME: "STRAWBERRY FIELDS FOREVER" AND *SGT. PEPPER*

"We have always changed our style as we went along, and we've never been frightened to develop and change."
—PAUL MCCARTNEY, 1967

The bridge between *Revolver* and its follow-up, *Sgt. Pepper's Lonely Hearts Club Band*, was their February 1967 single release, "Strawberry Fields Forever" / "Penny Lane." Informed by the decision to quit the road, the single represented all the possibilities of what it meant to be a recording band, or as Paul pointed out, "the record *was* the performance." The string of media controversies running through the 1966 tour codified the decision to quit the road. *Revolver* showed the band what working in the studio at their relative leisure could produce. "Strawberry Fields Forever" consolidated their successes to this point, thus becoming the signpost pointing to their future. As George Martin would later observe, though the single was not included on *Sgt. Pepper*, "it set the agenda for the whole album."

November 1966 had been a richly portentous month for the Beatles. John, sporting newly shorn locks and National Health glasses, returned home after completing work on *How I Won the War*, carrying with him a song composed in Spain that would occupy one side of the group's next single. (Days later, he'd meet his future partner, Yoko Ono, at Indica Gallery.) Paul, after traveling throughout Europe and Africa with Beatles roadie Mal Evans, also arrived home that month. The notion that the Beatles' next album should be credited to a fictitious act—"Sgt. Pepper's Lonely Hearts Club Band" (in the *au courant* tradition of America's West Coast rock acts)—as a means of freeing themselves from the limitations imposed by the expectations that came with being "Beatles," popped into his head during the long flight home. Soon after landing, he at last succumbed to the inevitable, taking his first acid trip with Tara Browne midmonth.

A week earlier, *Melody Maker* had reported that the next Beatles single would be out before Christmas. This was not to be: *A Collection of Beatles Oldies (But Goldies!)* and their annual holiday fan-club release would be the only new product released before the end of 1966. On November 13, Brian Epstein's home was picketed by a small group of protesters, demanding that the Beatles schedule some concert dates—in Britain, at least. Word that the Beatles were not planning to perform the usual Christmas shows was filtering out, disappointing not only those who weren't yet ready to give up the experience of seeing them perform live, but also alarming those that believed that they were subtly signaling their retirement. (Further confusing things was a report issued that same day in the *Sunday Telegraph* that said that two of the Beatles, through a third party, had approached Allen Klein, the Rolling Stones' manager—who happened to be in London at the time— in the apparent hopes of discussing a management deal. Brian dismissed the assertion as ridiculous.)

But change lay heavy in the air within their world. Nowhere was it felt more strongly than at their workplace: on Thursday the twenty-fourth, the four Beatles and George Martin convened at EMI's Abbey Road facility for the first time in five months. On this evening, John stood before George Martin and the others, playing "Strawberry Fields Forever," a composition quite unlike anything he'd ever before written. As presented on this evening, it was a wistful acoustic ballad. If their producer had had his way, the song would not have been embellished much beyond this. But having freed themselves from the self-imposed limitation of recording only what they or George Martin could perform in the studio without outside help, and having acquired an entirely new set of tools during the recording of *Revolver*, it would have taken almost superhuman restraint *not* to explore all the available options.

STRAWBERRY FIELDS FOREVER

Words and Music by JOHN LENNON and PAUL McCARTNEY

northern songs france
67, rue de Provence - PARIS 9ᵉ - ☎ 874.26.36 874.19.41

The Beatles, 1967.

Though John initially asked for the studio craft to stay light, fully in evidence on the first take (released on *Anthology 2* in 1996 with the harmonies mixed out) were double-tracked vocals, vari-speed, and Mellotron, beginning with Paul's intro (using the "flute" voice) beneath the vocal, as well as the apparent slide guitar from George (actually achieved by manipulation of the pitch control on the Mellotron, set to the "slide guitar" voice). Heavy with "Because"-like backing harmonies and without the verse / chorus structure fully worked out, it was a departure from the sound of *Revolver*, but not yet the psychedelic *tour de force* it eventually became. This melancholy, delicate arrangement sustained the fragility inherent in John's demos. As is, it would have been a fine recording by the standards of the day, but the Beatles were not satisfied, feeling this one take was merely a good start.

The unprecedented three months spent crafting *Revolver* showed the group the possibilities that unfettered studio time (more or less) to get things just so offered. Tapping the virtual carte blanche being given them by their record label (or as Ringo bluntly expressed it: "We're big with EMI at the moment. They don't argue if we take the time we want") instead of simply settling for what they could put together in a reasonable amount of time became the rule. Not everyone had this luxury: the Beatles' success set them apart from virtually all their peers (only Brian Wilson toiled longer) by affording them the platform to continue the sonic experimentation needed to perfect their recordings.

"Strawberry Fields Forever" would take fifty-five hours and three recordings built from the ground up to fully realize (or at least to produce a releasable recording; to his dying day, John *insisted* that it fell short and could be bettered). George Martin's unique studio alchemy was never shown more explicitly than on this production, wherein he masterfully deciphered John's vague clues as to how to capture his vision while leaping past the outer limits of what (until then) was believed to be achievable.

After taking time out to record their most ambitious Christmas message to date (*Pantomime: Everywhere It's Christmas* was a scripted, episodic undertaking, complete with numerous skits, characterizations, and a theme song), a second attempt at "Strawberry Fields Forever" commenced on November 28, resulting in only two complete—and unsatisfactory—takes to show for their evening's work. Still, for all their efforts, the group and their producer were getting closer to getting a handle on what would become their most complex recording to date. The sole complete take nailed the following day (dubbed "take six") became the keeper for the moment, and was mixed down to free track space for overdubs. As "take seven," it featured bass and additional

Mellotron from Paul, drums, two guitars, and vocals (the last element treated with ADT).

The group then took more than a week off, each receiving an acetate of the work completed thus far to study. Two days after they reassembled with the intent of working on Paul's "When I'm Sixty-Four," a lighthearted music hall–type of number they'd started on December 6, John approached George Martin with a request. What he'd intended as a dreamy song had become too strident; perhaps a softening blanket of outside instrumentation would mask this approach. As noted in Martin's autobiography, John said, "I'd like you to score something for it. Maybe we should have strings, or brass or something." Martin acquiesced;

The fourth annual Beatles Christmas message was an ambitious affair, but due to its completion so close to the holiday season, neither this one (nor the ones that preceded it and followed it) were sent to American fan-club members. Instead, they received a postcard featuring a photo and holiday greetings.

and after discussing the matter, concluded that three cellos and four trumpets would provide the right touch. All agreed that they would have to cut a new rhythm track as well.

Though remakes were not unknown within the Beatles' recording history, their third try at laying down a song of which they'd already secured at least one perfectly releasable take—at considerable time, effort, and expense—may be seen by some as an unneeded indulgence. But implicit with the decision of the group and their producer to go forward was the understanding that they'd fallen short. Fifteen attempts were made, nine of them complete, with the song's key changed from A major to B major, and a more brisk tempo imposed. Take twenty-five—an edit piece of take fifteen and take twenty-four—was judged best and mixed down the next day, becoming "take twenty-six."

Onto this were dubbed lead guitar, played by Paul; the outro Mellotron sounds; and artifacts like backwards cymbal and timpani. (Also caught on this take were two of John's utterances, picked up by the drum mics at the end: "Calm down, Ringo!" as well as "cranberry sauce"—twice.) George's swarmandal, a second vocal track, piano, plus brass and strings were added to complete work on this remake, referred to as the "fast" version.

It's been taken as a matter of faith that John listened to both completed versions—slow and fast—and opined to the producer that he liked the beginning of the slow one and the second half of the faster one, forcing Martin and Emerick to figure out a way to conjoin the recordings and make a single, unified work. Researcher Joe Brennan of Columbia University has conducted considerable study into the Beatles' recordings, concluding that by the time of the brass and string overdubs, the decision had already been made to complete the song with "the big edit," as the fast version begins with the second verse, suggesting that the intention had been to create an edit piece all along rather than serendipitously combining two separate and complete performances into one.

Still, it took a certain amount of skill, luck, and happy coincidence to pull off this studio magic. Nowadays, with the recording process largely computerized and digitized, a splice like this would be routine, but not so in 1966. With painstaking care, the fast version was slowed and the slow version sped up, with the keys meeting near B-flat. As it happened, the tempos also meshed beautifully and *voila!*—the miracle occurred. To anyone interested—and consider this: once you know where the edit happens, you will never not hear it again—the splice joining takes seven and twenty-six occurs at roughly one minute in, between the lines "Let me take you down / 'Cause I'm" and "going to." (Worth noting: since take seven was arranged without a chorus between the first and second verses, a chorus occurring later in the performance was flown in and placed at 0:55, just before the *big* edit.)

Beyond the compositional advance and heightened studio craft, the Beatles' development as musicians at this juncture is worth noting. Oddly, it was Ringo—a man who practically boasted that he never practiced his instrument, and who had even less to do in the studio than the others—that showed a major leap forward with his approach. Though one can be certain that he wasn't spending his down time woodshedding before the group reentered the studio, his work on "Strawberry Fields Forever" represented a major breakthrough. Both the sound of his drums—abetted by Geoff Emerick's pioneering recording techniques, but also the drummer's own sense of how he wanted them to sound—and a sudden preoccupation with colorful, unpredictable tom-tom fills, makes his work on this track unlike anything else on a Beatles record.

Ringo alluded to the effect that their recreational use of illicit substances had on their instrumental abilities. "And because [John, Paul, and George] were writing different material, we were playing differently. We were expanding in all areas of our lives, opening up to a lot of different attitudes." Whether drugs influenced his stylistic evolution; or that it is simply Starr following the development of the group's music; or if he is undergoing the natural artistic growth of someone now in their twenty-sixth year who'd been drumming for well over a decade, is hard to pinpoint. A combination of all these factors is probably responsible. But it takes very conscious effort to recalibrate the approach one applies onstage, versus in the studio creating a record, just as filmmakers segueing from silent to sound pictures had to rethink their methodology.

In 1966, the Beatles were as one in making this transition, supported by the bedrock of Ringo's evolving drumming. Writer / drummer Hal Howland observed, "It is fascinating to trace [Ringo's] stylistic development from rock-steady club veteran to studio innovator." This assessment was seconded by Phil Collins years later—himself no slouch on the pagan skins. "I think (Ringo's) vastly underrated. The drum fills on 'A Day in the Life' are very complex things. You could take a great drummer today and say, 'I want it like that.' They wouldn't know what to do."

Had "Strawberry Fields Forever" been issued on *Sgt. Pepper*, perhaps much of the criticism through the years directed toward the album's (in places) lightweight content would have been blunted. But the world of recording-industry marketing was not keeping pace with the artistic side. Under pressure from EMI, Brian Epstein approached George Martin to check on the work in progress. Since a new album was clearly a long way off, what about a single? It had been nearly five months since "Yellow Submarine" / "Eleanor Rigby," and even longer since the last non-album one.

Martin volunteered that the group had two songs very near completion: "Strawberry Fields Forever" and "When I'm Sixty-Four." This very nearly became the pairing approved for release, but then Paul had brought in a new song, one that appeared to share some implied thematic unity with the obvious A-side. "Penny Lane," having been likewise sparked by a backward glance at childhood in Liverpool (though from a very different perspective), was deemed a worthy companion piece. Indeed, the composition was promising enough to promote as another double A-side; this was a practice that had commenced with "Day Tripper" / "We Can Work It Out" a year earlier.

Work on "Penny Lane" had begun on December 29, just as the two earlier recordings were undergoing final mixes. But before the new song was even finished, the decision was made to pair it with John's composition, so perfect a counterpart it was. George Martin empathized with Brian's entreaties concern-

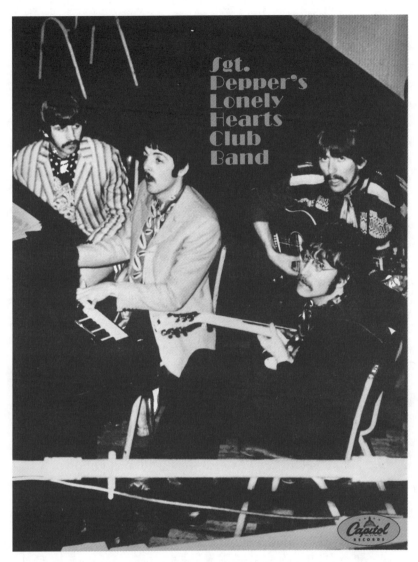

Some of the record-label ads for Sgt. Pepper *took the trouble to emphasize that the band in question really was the Beatles, lest fans become confused.*

ing the risk of sagging popularity with a widening gap between releases, and gave his approval. It was a decision made in the face of commercial pressures at the expense of aesthetic judgment, one that the producer rued the rest of his life. It meant, in his mind as well as the group's, that the two tunes were now off the table for inclusion on the new album.

"The biggest mistake of my professional life," Martin later lamented in his autobiography. Not only was *Sgt. Pepper* deprived of two of the strongest Lennon–McCartney songs of the era, but the strategy of issuing the two best recordings as a single misfired. Their streak of numbers ones ended in Britain when "Strawberry Fields Forever" / "Penny Lane" stalled at number two, blocked from the top by crooner Engelbert Humperdinck's middle-of-the-road ballad "Release Me." In the long run, such a transient indicator didn't matter much; but at the time, it prompted another round of "Have the Beatles finally peaked?" speculation. Ever the second-guesser, Martin concluded latter-day that the group would've been better off having issued the two songs separately. "We would have sold far more and got higher up in the charts if we had issued one of those with, say, 'When I'm Sixty-Four' on the back."

In the wake of this strong start, work on *Sgt. Pepper* proceeded at a leisurely pace, informed by the spectacular results they'd achieved thus far by crafting material until it was perfected, and tapping every technological resource at hand to layer sound upon sound onto tape, striving to capture sounds heard in their heads and / or previously unheard entirely. Meanwhile, with acclaim for *Revolver* dampened in the U.S. at the time of its release, some belated recognition came the Beatles' way in early 1967. On March 2, the 9th Annual Grammy Awards were held. In addition to Klaus Voormann's award for design, the group won for Best Rock & Roll Solo Performance for "Eleanor Rigby," credited to Paul.

For the second straight year, they lost out to Frank Sinatra ("Strangers in the Night," co-written by Bert Kaempfert, the producer of their Tony Sheridan recordings) for Best Male Vocal Performance, as well as to the New Vaudeville Band ("Winchester Cathedral," a novelty recording) for Best Rock & Roll Recording, with "Eleanor Rigby" nominated in each category. The Beatles did win Song of the Year that night, though, for *Rubber Soul's* "Michelle." All in all, a good evening for Paul.

The reception accorded the Beatles' newest single in early 1967 served as a pretty good measure of just how far the Beatles were getting ahead of the public. Though missing the number-one slot in the U.K., the "Penny Lane" side of the single topped the U.S. charts for one week (while "Strawberry Fields Forever" peaked at number eight). It sold in numbers as robust as any Beatle offering, yet a mood of disquiet seemed to greet its release. Britain's *New Musical Express* typified the view of most mainstream reviewers, expressing bewilderment at their new direction ("Certainly the most unusual and way-out single the Beatles have yet produced . . . I don't really know what to make of it").

This unsettled response was furthered by the twofold visual presentation accompanying the release. "Picture 45 sleeves" were common in the U.S.; but for the first time in Britain, a deluxe full-cover sleeve had been prepared for the issue. On one side was an arty studio picture of the Beatles as they now looked, with all four sporting mustaches and / or beards. The affectation seemed to age them; also gone were the days of matching suits for photo sessions. The other side of the sleeve displayed four individual photos of the group as pre-toddlers. To fans that might not have been following the Beatles' evolving images in the teen-oriented magazines, their departure from what had been a more or less youthful, dynamic (as well as uniform) look until now, coupled with their apparent retirement from live appearances, made many fans wonder what was going on with the group they'd known and loved for the past three years.

Second, promo films were prepared for both sides of the single. The Michael Lindsay-Hogg shorts for the "Paperback Writer" / "Rain" single had been groundbreaking enough when produced seven months before; but with such a profound musical departure from previously existing paradigms apparent, the Beatles were ready to raise their game for the video accompaniment. On the recommendation of Klaus Voormann, who not long after designing *Revolver* had joined Manfred Mann, the Beatles hired Swedish director Peter Goldman.

Goldman worked in Swedish television, mostly on children's shows and live musical events. On its face, he was an odd choice, but he did possess an avant-garde sensibility, making him the perfect fit for the assignment. While flying over to England for the assignment, he brainstormed concepts. One theme kept recurring to him: horses. After meeting with the group, they acqui-esced to the ideas Goldman presented, issuing only one order: "You are the director. Direct!"

Filming commenced on January 30 at Angel Lane, Stratford (which stood in for Liverpool's Penny Lane district) and a pasto-ral setting in Knole Park near Sevenoaks, Kent, located between Twickenham and Richmond, southwest of London. On the sec-ond day of the four-day shoot, John happened into an antiques shop near the hotel where they were staying. Before leaving, he had purchased a framed nineteenth-century circus broadside; one that, with little embellishment, became the basis of his lyrics for a *Sgt. Pepper* tune, "Being for the Benefit of Mr. Kite!"

Given the apparent complexity of the two promos, it is aston-ishing that they came together so quickly. The final mix of "Pen-ny Lane" had only been completed five days before the shoot for "Strawberry Fields Forever" began. Filming wrapped on the "Penny Lane" clip on February 7; the first television broadcast came five days later. With the single released in the U.S. and U.K. on February 13 and 17 respectively, this was a fairly whirlwind undertaking.

In 1966, the British Musicians' Union launched a *Keep Music Live* campaign, leading to a ban on mimed performances. This meant that rock bands plugging their latest release on television had to actually play it instead of lip-synching to a backing track. With recordings as clearly complex as these two Beatle tunes were, any visual pretense of performing them was chucked out the window—which suited them just fine. If the Chiswick House promos pointed the way to the future of conceptual rock videos as we know them, Peter Goldman's work codified it.

The "Penny Lane" clip was relatively straightforward, depict-ing the Beatles meeting up in the street before donning match-ing red riding jackets and adjourning to a field, on horseback. (Three of the animals are white; in an uncanny portent of things to come, George was assigned the "dark horse"). There, they take tea, served by bewigged attendants, before taking up their instru-ments just as the song ends. Oddly, a recurrent focus on one of the Beatles walking the busy city street is intercut throughout; not

Paul, as one would expect, but John, shown as if in a nostalgic reverie.

Goldman's "Strawberry Fields Forever" clip was described by writer Michael Shore in *The Rolling Stone Book of Rock Video* as, "Richard Lester meets Kenneth Anger in the *Twilight Zone*." It's hard to argue with that assessment, given Goldman's use of jump cuts, slow motion, fast motion, and reversed footage. (A particularly skillful edit provides the illusion of Paul leaping from the ground to the limb of a massive, dead oak tree, whose presence in the film serves as a sort of totem around which all the action revolves.) As comparatively light as the "Penny Lane" promo was, this one was dark, depicting the Beatles, particularly George, as stoop-shouldered and aging. (At one point, Paul literally changes day to night.) The group is also seen, amidst timpani and spotlights, pouring paint over a broken-down piano, evoking the sort of visual *non sequitur* milieu one usually finds in bad dreams.

For a lot of people, first exposure to the new songs came from these promo films. They premiered in Britain on *Top of the Pops* on February 16, just four days after first airing stateside on *The Ed Sullivan Show*. On February 25, the clips were aired again in America, this time on the old-school variety show *Hollywood Palace*, where old-school actor Van Johnson introduced them. Just three years after four so-called mop-tops had introduced themselves to the country on another stage by playing "All My Loving," their new personas were introduced to the world via celluloid.

Though not quite on the same level of Dean Martin's turning the Rolling Stones into a punch line back in 1964 on the same show, Johnson likewise exhibited a little difficulty wrapping his head around what youth entertainment had become. After "Penny Lane" finished, he told the audience, "And if you thought that one was far out, wait'll you see their next one, 'Strawberry Fields.' It's a musical romp through an open field with psychedelic overtones [rolls eyes] and a feeling of expanding consciousness. [Pause.] [If] you know what that means, let me know . . ."

Dick Clark ran the promos on *American Bandstand* on March 11. While one might have expected the audience at *Hollywood Palace* to respond with a mixture of headshaking bewilderment or bemusement, the teens populating Clark's set were likewise almost entirely confused or underwhelmed by what they saw. After running the films, which in this context seemed calculated to provoke while introducing fans to their new look (with multiple close-ups

THE "MONKEES" ●
PLAY GRETSCH
GUITARS & DRUMS.

The fabulous Monkees, stars of
their own TV show are with it!
Why don't you get with
"That Great Gretsch Sound!"

THE FRED. GRETSCH MFG. CO.
60 Broadway, Brooklyn, N.Y. 11211
Please send me
Free information in full color on:
☐ Gretsch Drums
☐ Gretsch Guitars
Name
Address
City
State   Zip Code

GRETSCH

© 1966 RAYBERT PRODUCTS, INC. T.M. OF SCREEN GEMS, INC.

The Monkees faced a "bigger than Jesus" backlash of their own in 1967 after the public discovered that they didn't support themselves instrumentally on their own records. Somehow, the use of studio pros didn't similarly boomerang against the Byrds, Beach Boys, the Mamas and the Papas, or any number of other chart acts.

of their eyes and facial hair in the "Strawberry Fields Forever" clip), Clark solicited opinion. While the first respondent offered an enthusiastic thumbs-up ("That was great!"), the rest of those asked looked betrayed. "I thought it was weird," one girl volunteered. "Weird," another quickly seconded. Sniped one male audience member, "They're as bad as the Monkees!"

As it happens, the Monkees arrived in England in February 1967, making the promotional rounds on behalf of their television show. There were some observers that believed that this group, comprised of four strangers of varying musical backgrounds, cast in a sitcom without first being allowed the benefit of the usual organic development that bands undergo prior to making a record, would be viewed with disdain—if not outright hostility—from their very antithesis, the self-made Beatles.

But the Fabs got the joke (in fact, they were fans of the show). Perhaps they recognized that the two ensembles were mirror images of each other: the Monkees were a pretend band that became real (on their third album), while the Beatles were a real band preparing to assume the identity of a false one with their latest undertaking. Furthermore, the Monkees' success liberated their counterparts, as the "pre-Fab Four" slipped into the void left by the original Fab Four's musical adventuring. It gave fans a pleasant substitute to which to attach their adoration while buying the Beatles time to work their magic—by which time, hopefully, their audience would have caught up.

(It probably helped that the two groups got along well as people. The day that shooting ended on the "Penny Lane" video, Paul hosted Micky Dolenz at his home for a night of socializing, while the Lennons invited the Nesmiths to stay at Kenwood as their guests. On February 10—the evening that the orchestral buildups for "A Day in the Life" were recorded—Mike Nesmith was on hand and captured in the promo film.)

If fans couldn't fully grasp the implications of "Strawberry Fields Forever" / "Penny Lane" upon its release, by late spring they'd surely come to realize that if those two songs were any indication, the long-player to follow was going to be mind-blowing. And so it was that the anticipation began to build. The band's labors continued on for another two months, running up a total of 700 hours at a cost of £25,000 to produce. (*Sgt. Pepper*'s elaborate cover artwork cost an additional £1,500, plus touch-up and copyrighting fees.) But like a neighbor's mysterious hammering at all hours in the garage, the group's prolonged work served to stir curiosity about exactly what they could be working on that was taking so much time.

In the meantime, their place in the singles charts was filled by offerings from acts old and new. Frank Sinatra, paired with daughter Nancy, offered "Something Stupid," while newcomers like Buffalo Springfield, Jefferson Airplane, and the Doors charted with the singles "For What It's Worth," "Somebody to Love," and "Light My Fire," respectively. Acts sometimes lumped in with the Beatles going back a few years were, for the most part, crafting releases in the face of shifting paradigms. The Dave Clark 5, once regarded (at least briefly in 1964) as a threat to Beatle supremacy, charted their final Top Ten U.S. single in early 1967 with "You

Though starting out as earnest folk-rockers in 1965 with a cover of Bob Dylan's "It Ain't Me, Babe," the Turtles eventually found their groove as pop purists.

Got What It Takes," while Herman's Hermits—a group from Manchester that managed to become far more successful on American charts than their native British ones—hit the U.S. Top Ten one last time with "There's a Kind of Hush."

Petula Clark was an English songbird whose chart career started long before the Beatles' had, but not until the "British Invasion" began did she get a foothold in the states. Starting in 1964, she'd charted eight Top Ten singles here, but "Don't Sleep in the Subway," released in the spring of 1967, ended her streak. Those unable to adapt to changing tastes fell by the wayside, while those who managed to keep step with the example set by England's finest managed to thrive within rock's ever-evolving parameters.

The Rolling Stones were one example. They'd managed to hold their own in early 1967 with a double-A-sided single, "Ruby Tuesday" / "Let's Spend the Night Together." The first tune, a

Replete with a Pop Art cover design, the Who's sophomore long-player also featured "A Quick One, While He's Away"—a "mini-opera" suite that signaled Pete Townshend's future ambitions.

"Baroque and roll" offering, certainly owed a little to the Beatles' influence, seeing the Stones move away from their R&B roots. The flip side was banned in some locales, owing to its "suggestive" lyrics. Meanwhile, the Who, in one year's time, had released seven singles in the states; some missed the national charts completely, and none rose higher than number seventy-four in the Hot 100. Relentless touring, notoriety from their offstage antics, and a highly combustible live presentation finally paid off when "Happy Jack," an out-of-leftfield recording if ever was, reached number twenty-four upon its March 1967 release.

Homegrown artists making their mark in America included the Turtles, who'd enjoyed a megahit with "Happy Together" in the spring of 1967. Tommy James had had a number-one hit in 1966 with "Hanky Panky," a two-year-old recording resurrected and given relentless airplay. Early 1967 saw "I Think We're Alone

Now" peak at number four; for the follow-up, he literally turned the chord sequence around from the previous hit and wrote "Mirage," which made it to number ten. The Byrds' days as a singles band were winding down, though they didn't yet realize it. Their latest Bob Dylan cover, "My Back Pages," peaked at number thirty in the spring of 1967, their last offering to chart so high. Just a year before, "Eight Miles High" had climbed to number fourteen.

A great number of bands managed to produce at least one song drawing upon the Beatles' boundary breaking to claim a moment of glory. The Left Banke, a New York quintet, produced the lush, enigmatic "Walk Away Renée" in 1966; early 1967's "Pretty Ballerina" extended the formula one last time with a similarly bittersweet romantic melody, arranged with strings and an oboe solo (a feature heard in early takes of "Penny Lane," issued around the same time).

The blatantly Beatlesque Bee Gees enjoyed their first U.S. hit around that time with "New York Mining Disaster 1941," a melodic, harmony-laden song that might've fit on a *Revolver* follow-up, had the Beatles recorded one in 1966. Speculation in the U.K. press that the song was actually written by the Fabs (under a pseudonym) prompted angry denials from Barry Gibb. "I've been writing since I was ten, before Lennon and McCartney were even onstage. . . . If they don't believe us, they can ask the Beatles themselves," Gibb told *Disc and Music Echo* in 1967.

But the latter group had bigger things on their mind. Back in November 1966, there were two certainties: first, touring was irrevocably a thing of the past, and second, maintaining the status quo as "Beatles" was untenable. They'd been put into a box both by fans and by the media. Attempting to step out of the roles in which they'd been cast carried the danger of boomeranging against them, yet following where their artistry took them might have alienated the fans beyond the point of return—something they were loath to do. Paul's notion of creating an alternate identity, one that everyone knew was them but that would buy them a little space to deviate from the existing paradigm, could enable the group to go forward. Maybe a "Lucy in the Sky with Diamonds" or "When I'm Sixty-Four" would seem strange on a

"Beatles" record, but coming from "Sgt. Pepper's Lonely Hearts Club Band," songs like this would be perfectly acceptable.

Lacking a better alternative, John, George, and Ringo went along with the concept with varying degrees of enthusiasm. If accepting that being fronted by a hand puppet gave them license to create a work that completely rewrote the rules of what a rock album was supposed to be, so be it. To be sure, the songs recorded thus far bore not the slightest thematic unity or underlying "concept," despite what others would later claim. But George Martin agreed that not being "Beatles" gave them wider latitude to explore than they might otherwise have been allowed. Furthermore, he was determined to use this tabula rasa to stitch together a "listening experience," rather than a mere succession of potential singles.

"The aim of *Sgt. Pepper* is to sound like a complete programme, ostensibly by the club band," he told readers of *Record Mirror*. He noted that they set the scene, a concert hall, at the onset, and later returned to it by the album's end. Indeed, it was this contrived unity that gave the record its power as a singular piece. The title song would more or less bookend the album, while "A Day in the Life," a recording that would be a hard act to follow on any LP, served as the encore. Beyond this, any evident undercurrent tying the songs together was in the ear of the beholder.

By the end of April, the album was finished. Mono and stereo masters were cut, and the BBC was sent copies in preparation for airplay in advance of the June 1 British release date. The Beatles may have been startled on May 19 to learn that the Beeb was banning "A Day in the Life" from the airwaves on the grounds that it encouraged a permissive attitude toward drug use. (Somehow, "I get high with a little help from my friends" got a pass.) In the past, a decision like this might very well have stirred a huge controversy and knocked the group back on their heels. But in 1967, anyone caring enough might have seen a ban like this coming from the authoritarian broadcasters as a feather in the cap. Paul merely pointed out the obvious when he said of the action, "It just draws attention to the subject when all the time their aim is to force attention away from it."

That same evening, Brian Epstein, breaking with precedent, hosted a *Sgt. Pepper* listening party for the press at his home. To turn the unveiling into an event, he handpicked ten journalists, allowing them to rub elbows with all four Beatles as the record spun and food and drinks were served. (Also present was New York rock photographer Linda Eastman, who managed to deftly score herself entry to the exclusive shindig by presenting her portfolio to personal assistant Peter Brown. Epstein like what he saw, and so she gained admittance; that she'd met Paul four days earlier at the Bag O'Nails Club and partied with him doesn't seem to have influenced the decision, beyond strengthening her resolve to get herself in.)

If Epstein's intent was to curry favor in advance of the album's official June 1 release date, the ploy worked; though on its own merits, *Pepper* would've surely prompted the same positive outcome. Deejay Kenny Everett played the album in its entirety on his BBC radio show the following day [1], save the banned "A Day in the Life." That same day, *Disc and Music Echo* ran commentary on the record, calling *Sgt. Pepper* "a beautiful and potent record, unique, clever, and stunning." *Record Mirror* waxed likewise a week later: "A truly fine album," Peter Jones assured readers. *Sgt. Pepper* was ". . . clever and brilliant, from raucous to poignant and back again."

It was probably for the better good that the Beatles had paved the way for the arrival of *Sgt. Pepper* with a single as outré as "Strawberry Fields Forever." The very departure from what was expected from them undoubtedly heightened expectations of just how far they'd go with the long-player that came in its wake. When *Sgt. Pepper* arrived bearing nothing as outlandish or overtly experimental as even "Tomorrow Never Knows," it probably came as a relief to some fans, signifying that they weren't being left behind after all. Indeed, the most radical element of the new album was the elaborate packaging, a gatefold bearing

1. It had actually hit the U.K. airwaves for the first time on May 12, when pirate station Radio London played the entire *Sgt. Pepper* album from a pressing extorted from Beatles music publisher Dick James. James had purportedly been conned into providing the album after a Radio London deejay threatened to air a poorly recorded tape spirited out of EMI. Rather than let the public get its first exposure via a bootleg, James provided a fresh copy.

Though their concert days were behind them by 1967, the Beatles still figured prominently in Vox's advertising plans.

a full-color collage that was as visually extravagant as *Revolver*'s cover had been austere.

For the second time in a row, the album's artwork revealed a self-conscious look back at where they'd been: in 1966, it had come in the subtle form of a collage of past images, but a year later, it was manifest much more directly with their former selves (in wax) standing alongside their "Sgt. Pepper's Lonely Hearts Club Band" alter egos. To some, the bit of real estate lying before them, bedecked with decorative plants, resembled a grave, as though the "new" Beatles were bidding farewell to their old selves; this was not too far off the mark, as it happened.

Sgt. Pepper also featured, for the first time by a major rock act, a complete set of lyrics. And not just tucked away on the inner sleeve, either: these were given prominent display on the back of the jacket, allowing *would-be* buyers to peruse them through the shrinkwrap before making their purchase. The decision to present them so inescapably speaks volumes about the importance the group attached to their words for the first time, and how unwilling they were to leave their audience's getting the point of what they were singing about to chance.

The Beatles offered their own assessment of what *Sgt. Pepper* meant in interviews given upon its release. Paul, particularly, seemed to relish the moment when critics and fans who had written the Beatles off would at last get an earful. For months while they were at work, ". . . the music papers had been saying, 'What are the Beatles up to? Drying up, I suppose.' That's right." George, while noting the risks of losing their audience by being too bold, was careful to emphasize their desire to bring the fans along. "We're not trying to outwit the public. The whole idea is to try a little bit to lead people into different tastes."

Ringo, addressing fans that mourned the end of touring, attempted to put a positive spin on things. "We found our best work comes in making records." John amplified this point: "*Sgt. Pepper* is one of the most important steps in our career. It had to be just right. We tried, and I think we succeeded, in achieving what we set out to do. If we hadn't, then it wouldn't be out now." (Within a year, true to form, he'd reverse himself, calling the album "the biggest load of shit we'd ever done.")

The Beatles were always quite deliberate with the sequencing and presentation of their work. *Sgt. Pepper*'s opening-crowd ambience was a statement unto itself, offering the simulation of a setting no one would ever see the Beatles in again. By leading off the album in this fashion, one might have read it as their deliberately picking at what was a sensitive issue with fans at the time. More likely, the intent was simply to show their audience that there was an alternative to personal appearances.

Also, the songs were stitched together in a way that contained very little dead space between them, emphasizing the seamless listening experience that George Martin had championed. Furthering this thinking, no tracks were pulled from the album (at least not in 1967)—unlike its predecessor. While nominally a return to their pre-*Revolver* values, this time there was no accompanying non-album single. This forced radio stations to play album tracks if they were to feature new Beatles music on their airwaves at all. By doing so, the era of album-oriented rock was ushered in, just as FM radio was starting to take off, populated by songs too lengthy or esoteric for the AM Top Forty.

The sheer volume of ubiquitous acclaim laid on *Sgt. Pepper* dwarfed anything said about *Revolver* when it was released. It seems obvious in hindsight how much the reception *Sgt. Pepper* was accorded upon its release was heightened by any number of conditions breaking the Beatles' way. Among them were the natural buildup of expectancy between releases, and the timing of its issue, just at the start of what became known as the "Summer of Love" (with *Sgt. Pepper* as its soundtrack). Then, too, there was its arrival just as rock was becoming accepted as a viable aesthetic worthy of critique; indeed, some have argued, author Tim Riley among them, that "*Pepper* was the record that made rock criticism worthy of its subject."

It's easy at this distance to forget how marginalized and derided rock 'n' roll was for most of its existence by arbiters of culture. Granted, not all of the disdain was unwarranted; but then again, the chart offerings of, say, the Hollies or Paul Revere & the Raiders were never intended to compete for artistic longevity alongside contemporary releases by Duke Ellington or Maurice Jarre's score to *Doctor Zhivago*. About the only non-Beatles artist of the day accorded plaudits and respect on a regular basis that we still care about now was Bob Dylan, but then he wasn't exactly aiming for the *16* magazine crowd.

The Beatles, on the other hand, were—from virtually the moment Brian Epstein signed them—wholly focused on building the widest audience possible. Every aesthetic compromise he foisted upon them (and they accepted) was calculated to enlarge their appeal beyond their existing demographic. He'd succeeded pretty well with stirring at least a bemused tolerance from most of their elders, and by 1966–1967, even mainstream periodicals like *Life* magazine were willing to hype their newest offering over the course of a full spread. (The June 16, 1967 issue ran an article titled "The New Far-Out Beatles" that trumpeted the scale of their ambitions as they worked on *Sgt. Pepper*.)

It's easier to see now than it was then how hyperbolic some of the praise directed toward *Sgt. Pepper* was, as if every critic was seeking to outdo the other for the most lavish embrace of the Beatles' new direction, burnishing their hip credentials in the process. In England, *Times* critic William Mann had distinguished himself in 1963 by stepping away from his usual articles on opera and classical music, penning a gushing review of *With the Beatles* that did much to give the group credibility with the intellectually inclined. His was the first prestigious review that looked past the haircuts and screaming girls to divine some lasting potential within the Lennon–McCartney songwriting partnership.

Three-and-a-half years later, he was just as effusive, hailing the songs on the album as "more genuinely creative than anything currently to be heard on pop radio stations" (while steering clear of further references to "Aeolian cadences").

Among other Serious Music Authorities, Pulitzer Prize–winning composer Ned Rorem called "She's Leaving Home" equal to anything written by Schubert; composer-conductor Leonard Bernstein cited Schumann. In England, theater critic Kenneth Tynan outdid everyone with his staggeringly extravagant praise, calling the release of the Beatles' eighth album "a decisive moment in the history of Western civilization."

But not everyone was prepared to wax ecstatic. Among the ink spilled in *Sgt. Pepper*'s wake was a review so notorious that, in the words of another critic, it nearly got its author lynched. Richard Goldstein, the *Village Voice* writer who'd been among the few to call *Revolver* "revolutionary" a year earlier, was less charmed by the follow-up and said so, igniting a firestorm that prompted a rebuttal and a defense, as well as countless angry letters to the editor—more than had ever been stirred by any previous article. The interesting part is how prescient Goldstein's points seem in light of reassessments made of *Sgt. Pepper* in the last decade or so.

The album's arrival on June 2 in the U.S. represented the second time that the Beatles had electrified an entire country; the first being the night of February 9, 1964, their *Ed Sullivan Show* debut. Ten months was an unheard-of span between albums. Though the release of "Strawberry Fields Forever" / "Penny Lane" and media reports issued steadily in the interim helped reassure fans that the group was still in business, no one could quite conceive what the Beatles could possibly be up to. What they did know was that the Beatles were the greatest group of the age; anything taking this long to produce had to be amazing, and it's doubtful that any among the legions of fans would accept anything less from them.

When *Sgt. Pepper* dropped, it was as if a massive path cleared within the collective awareness of an entire generation. The seas parted, and the Beatles' new album took up residency for at least the course of the ensuing summer, quite literally in the ether from one end of the country to the other. Writer and academic Langdon Winner's oft-quoted summary describing the sensation cannot be bettered: "The closest Western civilization has come to unity since the Congress of Vienna in 1815 was the week the *Sgt. Pepper* album was released. . . . At the time I happened to be driving across country on Interstate 80. In each city where I stopped for gas or food . . . the melodies wafted in from some far-off transistor radio or portable hi-fi. It was the most amazing thing I've ever heard. For a brief while the irreparably fragmented consciousness of the West was unified, at least in the minds of the young."

Jefferson Airplane's Paul Kantner had a similar recollection of what it was like when everyone he knew was hearing the Beatles' new album all at once: "Something enveloped the whole world at that time, and it just exploded into a renaissance." Johnny Rivers, a reliable American hit-maker who nonetheless was about to be left behind in the rush to embrace all things psychedelic, hit the Top Twenty one last time in the 1960s with "Summer Rain" in early 1968; the wistful tune recalled the previous summer's joy, when "everybody kept on playing *Sgt. Pepper's Lonely Hearts Club Band.*"

It was as though the Beatles had put a human face on the counterculture, simultaneously embracing it and leading it. By the sheer power of the group's considerable influence, an entire generation was on board, while their elders seemed to be swayed, at least in part, to accept the sweeping changes in youth culture, lulled by the benign power of the Beatles' melodic gifts.

So it was in the face of such near-universal adoration that Richard Goldstein stepped in. He was not, by temperament, a provocateur, or otherwise given to disagreement for contrarian's sake. At twenty-three, he was also youthful enough to be fully in touch with his generation's culture. His assessment was informed at least in part by the perception that the Beatles were being dishonest with *Sgt. Pepper*, offering "an album of special effects, dazzling but ultimately fraudulent." Goldstein felt that the group's immersion in sonic experimentation at the expense of basic songcraft tended to mask a lack of heart within the material. "The obsession with production, coupled with a surprising shoddiness in composition, permeates the entire album."

Elsewhere, he likened *Sgt. Pepper* to ". . . an over-attended child." (In a word, "spoiled.") The album's cover, Goldstein asserted, was an apt metaphor for the LP's contents: "busy, hip, and cluttered." Goldstein felt that in retiring from live performing, the group was doing their art a disservice, for it put them in thrall to technology at the expense of interaction with their audience: ". . . the change is what makes their new album a monologue." By withdrawing, they had produced their work from what journalist Mikal Gilmore called "an insular vision," the very antithesis of the communal spirit of which flower power was the embodiment. Only one song, "A Day in the Life," escaped Goldstein's profound disappointment with their work. "It is a deadly earnest excursion in emotive music with a chilling lyric . . . its mood is not whimsical nostalgia, but irony."

Mostly, Goldstein asserts that by their own standards, the Beatles had failed. "When the Beatles' work as a whole is viewed in retrospect, *Rubber Soul* and *Revolver* will stand as major contributions. When the slicks and tricks of production on this album no longer seem unusual, and the compositions are stripped to their musical and lyrical essentials, *Sgt. Pepper* will be Beatles baroque— an elaboration without improvement."

Nowadays, for an otherwise popular work to be panned in a review is not unheard of. Less common is a rebuttal run in Goldstein's publication, essentially telling readers not to pay attention to the first review its writer published elsewhere (the *New York Times*). Writer Tom Phillips, backpedaling on behalf of the *Voice* in the face of the hornet's nest stirred by Goldstein's review, assured readers that *Sgt. Pepper* was in fact "the most ambitious and successful record album ever issued, and the most significant artistic event of 1967." While a commonplace assertion among many hardcore Beatlemaniacs, fans of the Doors, Jimi Hendrix, the Who, and Pink Floyd might beg to differ.

Goldstein, whose only sin was to offer some clear-eyed honesty amidst a sea of platitudes, was granted the opportunity to rebut the rebuttal, wherein he doubled down on his original points. While conceding that the album had its merits (". . . better than eighty percent of the music around today . . ."), he also expanded on his comparisons to the Beatles' earlier work. "In *Revolver*, I found a complexity that was staggering in its poignancy, its innovation, and its empathy. I call it a complicated masterpiece. But in *Sgt. Pepper*, I sense a new distance, a sarcasm masqueraded as hip, a dangerously dominant sense of what is stylish." The album was too intent on plugging into the *au courant*, and as a result, the timelessness usually associated with their work was lacking. (Goldstein cited "In My Life" as an example destined to stand the test of time.)

Lest anyone think he was in any way soft-pedaling his earlier remarks, Goldstein further fueled the fire: "'She's Leaving Home' is unlikely to influence anyone except the Monkees," he opined. Compared to earlier innovations, where "production follows, never determines, function," here "harps and strings dominate what are essentially a weak melody and shallow lyrics." It may be on this point where Goldstein's criticism rings the truest. Had the Beatles, in their fervor to pursue what Paul described as the goal of altering sound, of taking a note of music and changing it in order to "see the potential in it . . . (and) what else there is in it," outsmarted themselves?

While very much in the minority, Goldstein wasn't completely alone in his disappointment with the new album. John Gabree, writing in *Down Beat*, opined that the overkill of praise was coming from people to whom rock music was still a novelty. With such cutting-edge work as *Freak Out!* (by the Mothers of Invention) and *A Quick One* (by the Who) showing what could done by rock artists not burdened by commercial expectations, the Beatles, he asserted, were merely absorbing creative elements from others and re-presenting them—essentially what they'd been doing since Day One with rockabilly, R&B, and early American rock 'n' roll. "The Beatles," Gabree said, "are merely the populizers, not the creators."

It was only a matter of time, once the smell of incense and flower power had cleared and the Summer of Love passed into autumn, then winter, until the pendulum of adoration began to swing the other way. Fans and critics not of age during 1967 (and therefore not susceptible to nostalgia's clouding haze) tended to concur with Goldstein. "Eggheads and professors who'd proclaimed Beatlemania 'won't last six months,'" summed up Juan Rodriguez (no author relation) in the *Montreal Gazette* in 2011, "went gaga over *Sgt. Pepper*, the Beatles transformation of British music hall into stoned art songs . . . comparing them to T. S. Eliot, Schubert, and so on."

In the early years of the twenty-first century, a blogger by the name of "Cittorah" launched into cyberspace a devastatingly unsentimental summary, expressing what many knowledgeable music fans not beholden to received myth felt: "This album sounded dated by 1969 . . . because it had nothing at all to do with the direction that rock music took." To that, one could add: those acts that did take their cues directly from *Sgt. Pepper* (and that weren't Beatles) left behind curios that are equally of the time in which they had been created, and lack any contemporary value beyond simple nostalgia.

In the space of very few words, Cittorah spoke volumes about the superficiality of the reverence attached to *Sgt. Pepper*. This doesn't mean that some (or all) of the songs contained within aren't enjoyable. But it does say that a lot of the appeal that the album possesses, beyond the requisite surface-level tunefulness, may stem from the same attraction certain people feel for that mythic '60s vibe: all flowers, tie-dye, beads, and bell bottoms. Viewed critically, *Sgt. Pepper* can be seen as the musical equivalent of the *Yellow Submarine* film: both were arguably groundbreaking in their day in terms of presentation; but content-wise, just strip away the hyper-color. You'll find nothing new happening; yet each is now cultural shorthand for "the '60s."

Indeed, much that was lasting in popular music over the following year seemed to be created in reaction to *Sgt. Pepper*. A rootsy, back-to-basics approach (exemplified by the Band) that the Beatles themselves would emulate in 1968 took hold. Only progressive rock—an outgrowth of the art-rock ethos *Sgt. Pepper* embodied—took up the blueprint they had created, used, and then abandoned by years' end. As a genre, it never rose beyond a select appeal.

The period of 1966–1967 was rife with albums that inspired and influenced those which came after. There was *Pet Sounds*, the gold standard of every studio-as-instrument artist that followed. Dylan's *Blonde on Blonde* held sway over every songwriter with literary aspirations that came in its wake, as well as musicians building upon a sound crafted from pulling elements of folk, rock, country, and blues together into a seamless whole. March 1967 saw the issue of Velvet Underground's debut: a tremendously influential album whose echoes reverberated into the 1980s and 1990s with the rise of alternative bands and indie artists eschewing traditional elements of melody. Also pre-*Pepper*, traces of the Doors' debut album could be heard in the ensuing years, particularly with some of the darker bands emerging in the 1970s and '80s like the Cult and Joy Division.

Bands emulating *Sgt. Pepper* directly did so at their own risk. Personal friendship aside, John Lennon had a bee in his bonnet about the "revolutionary" tag being applied to the Rolling Stones, a band that in his estimation, simply did everything the Beatles did, six months later. Superficial examples abounded:

the use of sitar on "Paint It Black" as an echo of "Norwegian Wood"; strings on "As Tears Go By" being simply "Yesterday"-lite; and "We Love You" as an "All You Need Is Love" retread. His thoughts on the Rolling Stones album that followed *Sgt. Pepper* by six months are not recorded, but they would undoubtedly mesh with what one reviewer dismissed as "ersatz *Pepper*-oni."

While *Their Satanic Majesties Request* was comprised of a number of fine cuts ("She's a Rainbow" being the best known), the concept—that of an album simulating some sort of live event ("On with the Show")—mimicked that of the Beatles' so closely it would have been hard not to snicker before hearing a note of the music contained within. In fact, the cover artwork alone was enough to provoke derisive laughter. It showed rock's bad boys garbed in full psychedelic / medieval regalia, with Mick Jagger in the center, wearing a wizard's hat. A *papier-mâché* Saturn hung sullenly in the background above an equally arts-and-crafty-looking mountain and sparkly model of what appears to be a mosque.

The whole thing came off as a low-rent knockoff of *Sgt. Pepper* by a band far too talented to need to resort to such contrivances (they even took care to hire Michael Cooper—the same photographer who'd shot the Beatles' cover). Further evocation of the Fabs could be found with the four images of the Beatles' faces (the same ones seen inside *Sgt. Pepper*'s gatefold sleeve) subtly planted amongst the set's decorative shrubbery; they were perhaps returning the favor of the Beatles' WELCOME THE ROLLING STONES on their album jacket.

Like *Sgt. Pepper*, *Their Satanic Majesties Request* (the title was a play on the copy that appears inside British passports—"Her Britannic Majesty requests and requires . . ."—and had nothing whatsoever to do with any ungodly statement) was stylistically diverse. This truly was the band's finest hour when it came to experimentation, encompassing a few tools cribbed from the Beatles: vari-speed, ADT, Mellotron, and little space between tracks. It also contained, like its obvious model, little that could be performed onstage as-is; though unlike the Beatles, the Stones had not signaled any plan to quit the road.

There's much to commend on the album: the jagged, edgy

The original issues of **Their Satanic Majesties Request** *featured a lenticular design, giving purchasers a 3D effect that enhanced the album's trippy ambiance.*

rhythms of "Citadel"; the cosmically evocative orchestration of "2000 Light Years From Home"; the past-life reverie of "The Lantern." But coming at a time when there was a premium on originality, most people couldn't get past so obvious a Beatle influence. Had it been issued without so unmistakably Beatlesque packaging, it might have escaped the pillorying it received from fans and critics as mere copycatting. Instead, it was viewed by the band as a misstep, driving them into a full-blown retreat to their bluesy roots with their next outing.

On the other extreme, Frank Zappa took issue with what he perceived as the Beatles' co-opting of the counterculture for financial gain. In March 1968, the Mothers of Invention issued

We're Only in It for the Money, a scathing attack on flower power and hippiedom generally and *Sgt. Pepper* specifically. (The album's gatefold artwork brilliantly satirized the Beatles' packaging, even down to the "cutouts" enclosed in the original). Zappa apparently felt that the Beatles were jumping onto a popular bandwagon, as though they needed to resort to cheap gimmickry to move product. (In 1967, an album's worth of Gregorian chants by the Beatles would still have gone gold.) It's astonishing that a commentator normally as astute as Zappa could be so far off the mark.

If *Sgt. Pepper* did leave a lasting impression on what followed, it was this: up until then, rock's currency was the hit single. The Beatles had already raised the bar on what a long-player could be, transforming the medium from collections containing a hit or two (padded out with low-quality filler), to entire sets of a dozen (fourteen in Britain) cuts, each one of which could become a radio hit. This in itself was revolutionary, as few recording bands had the capacity for turning out so much top-drawer material. Not everyone assembling long-players saw it as a chore; the Who and the Kinks, for instance, each blessed with at least one strong songwriter, managed to put together solid collections of originals while striving to compete in the singles charts.

But acts like the Rolling Stones were more typical of the genre. Until 1966's *Aftermath*—recorded and released after *Rubber Soul*—the Stones had yet to issue a long-player without covers of other people's material on it. Most of the Stones' takes are eminently forgettable, especially alongside those of the original artists. (The group populated their first three U.K. albums with a generous helping of tunes from Chuck Berry, Motown, and Chess recording artists like Muddy Waters, Bo Diddley, and Solomon Burke.) Their capacity to sustain a full-length release came about only slowly, by which time the Beatles were recording *Revolver*, their 1966 tour de force. In its wake, the Stones responded with *Between the Buttons*, their first LP deliberately crafted as an album.

Sgt. Pepper showed the world that putting together a full-length collection of strong material did not have to be limited by the need to craft songs for AM airplay. Whether or not there was an underlying "concept" or not didn't matter: the notion that rock could indeed produce "art" comprised of a series of songs that added up to an explicit statement was novel. Though the Beatles weren't the first to recognize the album format as a large canvas upon which to create a sustained piece of work, the success of *Sgt. Pepper* underscored the idea. That is its lasting legacy.

Soon after, other acts took up the challenge of extending their musical ideas beyond a mere collection of self-contained tracks. This naturally encouraged pretension, with any number of albums emerging from less-evolved artists bursting at the seams with overblown themes. Few are regarded today as possessing any merit beyond that of period camp. Of the psychedelic era that coincided with the emphasis shifting to albums (as well as free-form FM programming), a handful of releases stand up today, transcending their era of origin.

Among them, none are viewed as particularly evocative of *Sgt. Pepper*: *Are You Experienced?* by the Jimi Hendrix Experience; *Days of Future Passed* by the Moody Blues (a true "concept album" if ever was); *Piper at the Gates of Dawn* by Pink Floyd; Cream's *Disraeli Gears*; and Love's *Forever Changes*, among others, are as memorable and, in their own way, influential, as *Sgt. Pepper*. All things being equal, their only lack was an overabundance of hype.

In an unintended bit of irony, one can see where *Sgt. Pepper*'s most powerful effect was felt: at its launch by those hearing it when it was new. It's comparable to the first time one sees a much-touted band perform live, and the way the impact diminishes with each repeat.

That's the experience that this album was intended to replace.

8

THERE'S SOMETHING THERE: *SGT. PEPPER* AND THE LEGACY OF *REVOLVER*

"As a musician, I preferred Revolver, and I preferred the 'White Album,' because we were back to being musicians. It was like everybody got the madness out on Sgt. Pepper, so it served that purpose."

—RINGO STARR, 2007

gt. Pepper's arrival in late spring 1967 came at a most opportune moment in Western cultural history: mainstream journalism had at last warmed to the idea of that the "rock" world (as distinct from "rock 'n' roll" or "pop") could produce a lasting masterpiece that transcended the genre's lowly origins, while a new and legitimate niche called "rock journalism" was working up its own head of steam, preparing to offer detailed analysis of some of the more worthy offerings emerging from top-drawer artists. As George astutely noted, "Suddenly, we find that all the people who thought they were beyond the Beatles are fans."

With the media's attention fully upon *Sgt. Pepper* (and legions of scribes poised to pronounce it a significant breakthrough), the only way that the Beatles could have failed was by unleashing a turkey of unprecedented magnitude. The closest they would ever come to this indeed arrived later that year with the *Magical Mystery Tour* film, giving their critics at long last something to pounce upon: evidence that they were human after all. It marked the proverbial pendulum's swing away from them, but for now, everyone wanted the Beatles to succeed—and to lead. The wind was at their back, and they knew it.

In retrospect, it's easy to see that what *Sgt. Pepper* really changed was perceptions. Journalists and critics were at last prepared to acknowledge the obvious: that the phrase "rock artist" was not an oxymoron. *Sgt. Pepper*, an overtly ambitious work created by the most successful act in rock history, provided a focal point that could not be ignored. As such, it sparked an orgy of praise. Said Christopher Porterfield in the pages of *Time*, "They are leading an evolution in which the best of current post-rock sounds are becoming something that pop music has never been before: an art form." Apparently, this was news to readers of *Time*, but to those doing the actual creating, such a proclamation was hardly revelatory.

Still, not everyone recognized the difference between art and artifice. One immediate and lasting result of the album's influence was the overt injection of pretension into rock (though, to be clear on this, not every pretentious concept was unlistenable; see the Moody Blues). Suddenly, anyone could be an auteur and put out their own Grand Statement following the Beatles' lead, presenting bundled assortments of half-baked motifs, cloaked in witless profundities, utilizing the fullest array of technology available to them and presenting it as a holistic package. (Thankfully, much of what *Sgt. Pepper* begat is forgotten today, but as examples, see *Clear Light* or *A Teenage Opera*.)

Once the hoopla died down and the Summer of Love passed into history, the substance of *Sgt. Pepper* became clearer to objective observers. What they found was a collection of songs that, at their best, summed up the spirit of '67 better than any equally accessible work this side of Donovan: the generation gap ("She's Leaving Home"); self-improvement ("Getting Better"); life in suburbia ("Good Morning Good Morning"); aging ("When I'm Sixty Four"); psychedelia ("Lucy in the Sky with Diamonds"); fighting ennui ("Fixing a Hole"); the sexual revolution ("Lovely Rita"); spectacle ("Being for the Benefit of Mr. Kite!"); and spirituality ("Within You Without You"). Implicit without being too overt was the unifying undercurrent of the drug culture, something that would've resonated with many listeners in 1967. (That legions of fans enhanced their *Pepper* experience through illicit means is the very definition of "a safe bet.")

Pretty much everything you need to know about who was in favor among America's youth in 1966 can be gleaned from this cover of **Teen World**.

The flip side of such a concerted effort to capture the moment was an inextricable linkage to its time. The very sounds that the Beatles pursued with such vigor in order to stay ahead of their contemporaries have, perversely, boomeranged against them, aging the album in a way that *Rubber Soul* and *Revolver* have withstood. The latter album was created with a spirit of exploration that betrayed no hint of self-consciousness. Not so *Sgt. Pepper*: it was, as critic Greil Marcus noted, ". . . that point at which the Beatles began to be formed more by the times than the other way around."

Closing the album, "A Day in the Life" was the one track that, by common agreement, lived up to the hype. While *Sgt. Pepper*'s other cuts made dazzling first impressions, the album's finale was a stunner, striking the ideal balance between songcraft and studio craft. (John frequently took the lead role for the final track on the group's albums. *Sgt. Pepper* marked the last time he did so, but at least he abdicated the position on a high note.) Less beholden to then-state-of-the-art studio effects or any contextual reference points other than material on the same album, it still packs a wallop today.

Mostly, though, the album's reliance on extravagant arrangements and electronic sleight-of-hand came at the cost of immediacy. While technological innovation itself is not an unworthy goal—*Revolver* was steeped in it—its effect of camouflaging the underlying lack of artistic advance, songwriting-wise, made it merely a deception, as Richard Goldstein had noted. It's no coincidence that every important player in rock moved away from *Sgt. Pepper*'s direction after 1967; only the wannabes embraced it directly, to varying degrees of failure.

Such ostentatious ornamentation distanced the group from their audience. The most communally engaging song on *Sgt. Pepper* was "With a Little Help from My Friends," which—no coincidence—was probably the most straightforward arrangement on the entire album. That Ringo—the group's decent Everyman—delivered it was a masterstroke. But the song is an exception within a body of work dressed up with cellos, vari-speed, flanging, orchestration, Indian instrumentation, tape manipulation, brass flourishes, Leslie speaker–amplified guitar, harps, animal effects, and a dog whistle. All but the last three touches were present on *Revolver*, but utilized in ways that seemed to enhance the songs, not disguise them. The latter album rocked as a matter of course; too much of *Sgt. Pepper* seems aimed squarely at the intellect: the antithesis of how the genre started in the first place.

While unmatched as a technical achievement, and stellar with regard to presentation, *Sgt. Pepper* comes off as the end result of too much calculation. It was hailed in its day as the wave of the future; but instead, it proved to be the exact opposite: a last

Thoroughly ahead of the curve with this psychedelic-flavored single, the Yardbirds, featuring Jeff Beck and Jimmy Page at this time, could not sustain their momentum, imploding before they were able to further their groundbreaking efforts.

triumphant burst of sunny escapist optimism before things got very dark. The Beatles had always been quite sensitive to prevailing cultural currents, anticipating what lay beyond the horizon and taking what they could use, repurposing the aspects that suited their creative goals. It's what they had always done, and was a key ingredient to their success. They rarely took credit as *originators* of trends, but would cop to being up in the crow's nest, perhaps sighting what lay ahead just before the rest of the passengers traveling on the same ship did. In the instance of *Sgt. Pepper*, what looked like the shape of things to come was a mirage. Once the tide receded, *Sgt. Pepper*'s band became marooned out of time.

Pop-culture historians tell us that the prevailing gestalt that summer was of "we are one" solidarity between performers and listeners—a flower-power ethos that echoed the folk movement earlier in the decade (as well as forecast the punk movement that would follow). In a visit to Haight-Ashbury that summer, George and Pattie walked among the people—and were repulsed by what they saw. *Sgt. Pepper* signaled the group's intent to hide themselves away—first behind a contrived identity, and thereafter from any meaningful interaction with the public whatsoever, at least as "Beatles." It wasn't entirely their fault, as withdrawing seemed the only reasonable course to pursue in light of the assault that their fame had brought down upon them, literally as well as metaphorically.

But distance and withdrawal had eroded their cultural relevancy. By the time the echoes from the final chord of "A Day in the Life" had faded, the Beatles' days as spokesmen of their generation were numbered—just as members of the Establishment media were getting around to anointing them. Though their popularity as entertainers was as broad as ever when they finally called it a day as a collective recording act in 1970, other artists had long since moved on from looking to the Beatles for establishing rock's future path, instead taking their cues from Bob Dylan's admonition: "Don't follow leaders."

Some of their waning influence can be laid at the door of pushback against *Sgt. Pepper*'s excesses and aesthetic dead end; but in a real sense, the group's creativity had reached its outer limit. Henceforth, while still producing fine music, the Beatles' capacity for innovation had become largely a thing of the past, as each new record represented a refinement of something they'd already done. As craftsmen, they were untouchable, but without a sense of purpose to unite them as artists, little reason to continue as a band remained. As John told Kim Fowley in 1969, "We stopped being a group when we stopped trying to improve on the records that we liked."

Viewed in this light, *Sgt. Pepper* was the afternoon following *Revolver*'s twelve o'clock high, with each subsequent release bringing them closer to the sunset. As David Quantick said in *Q* magazine in 2000, "There's a case to be made that the Beatles went on to do *Sgt. Pepper*'s because there was nowhere else to go but too far. With *Revolver*, they had mapped out the pop universe so perfectly that all they could do next was tear it up and start again."

By appearances, one could conclude that the group went beyond what was necessary in their approach to *Sgt. Pepper* because they felt that the richness of *Revolver* had been overlooked upon its release, overshadowed by controversies having nothing to do with music. Their first post-touring long-player would be impossible to ignore. Not mincing words, Paul said of their ambitious undertaking, "To me, there was an absolute inevitability to something like *Pepper*. . . . When it finally happened, it was apocalyptic." It's a curious choice of words about a work that, "A Day in the Life" notwithstanding, is commonly viewed as positive overall. Independent of one's feelings about *Pepper*, Paul's line of thought—that the album represented a turning point in rock—is hard to contest. Whether this was for good or ill in the long run is another matter entirely.

We have seen throughout the course of this chapter and the last the forces and circumstances that marked the different receptions accorded *Revolver* and *Sgt. Pepper*. The latter album became iconic in popular imagination in a way that *Revolver* never did; people that know little of rock or its history are aware that the Beatles created an album called *Sgt. Pepper* that is widely regarded as their finest hour. It took time for fans and critics to take a second look at both albums; and when they did, *Revolver* is the one almost universally judged to be the superior work. It possesses an immediacy and bite that the other album does not, and is less reliant on the listener's willingness to suspend critical judgment to accept a "concept" that peters out after the first two cuts.

The belief that *Sgt. Pepper* was a "concept album" (or more egregiously, the "*first* concept album"—it wasn't: see Frank Sinatra's fifties output, including 1955's *In the Wee Small Hours*, or, for a rock example, 1966's *Freak Out!* from the Mothers of Invention) has, for some, given the latter album the edge as the superior (or more "serious") work between the two. This stems from the common notion that the record was intended to depict a concert-hall performance by the Edwardian brass band of the album's title. It wouldn't

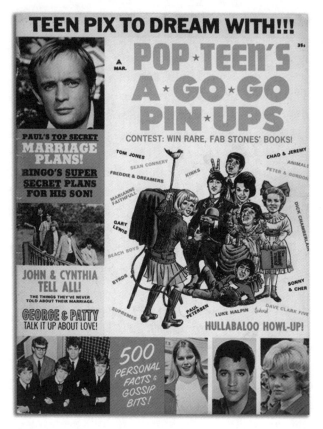

Typical of the era was the type of coverage the Beatles received in publications like this, aimed squarely at adolescent girls.

have taken much for the Beatles to follow through on the simulated concert idea; they nearly did by reprising the title track, at Neil Aspinall's suggestion. But they lost interest in maintaining the deception or portraying characters beyond Billy Shears. As Lennon explained later, "All of my contributions have absolutely nothing to do with this idea of Sergeant Pepper and his band. . . . It works because we *said* it works, and that's how it appeared."

Perhaps it would be more accurate to say it was a "meta-concept album"; and through sheer force of the Beatles' star power, along with the public's need to believe, its capture of so many imaginations gave it legs. If one looked closely, *Revolver* too had unifying themes, but not the types that were likely to draw adoration. Also, it was in all likelihood not a deliberate design, but there it is nonetheless. If *Sgt. Pepper*'s unifying theme can be read as "escapism," *Revolver*'s can be seen as something far more immediate: isolation and death.

We are told at an early age to expect only two certainties in life: the proverbial death and taxes. Thus does *Revolver* kick off with an evocation of that most fundamental of material-world assurances. Still, the two-and-one-half minutes do not slide by without a reminder of life's other certainty: "Now my advice to those who die / Declare the pennies on your eyes." Right from the jump, George has put listeners on notice that what's to follow will not be the usual good-time froth that the Beatles had heretofore dispensed so effortlessly. While offering up ear-pleasing entertainment, *Revolver* was also going to take its audience on a journey, one designed to provoke thought as much as toe-tapping.

No sooner had the last notes of Paul's alien-sounding lead decayed away than a rush of strings and urgent *vocalese* arrived to further along the forward momentum. "Eleanor Rigby" spoke directly and frankly to the sad specter awaiting those passing through the world alone. Without offering any solutions, the song reported with stark clarity on a pair of true "lonely hearts" whose earthly existence would be erased upon their departure. In an ironic twist worthy of Rod Serling's *Twilight Zone*, we are told that these two solitary individuals, who might have been able to ease each other's loneliness, only crossed paths when it was too late. Paul was sometimes derided for his storyteller bent, contriving personas and plotlines that depicted, in John's words, "boring people doing boring things." But "Eleanor Rigby" shows him at the height of his narrative powers, using fictitious characters to address greater truths.

John weighed in next with "I'm Only Sleeping," which described his desire to detach from the world's demands. Lyrically, that he doesn't even attempt to evoke "dreams" or visions in an apparent ode to sleep is telling; he instead extols the virtues of letting go ("float upstream") as the alternative to engaging. To pursue what society declared to be important and necessary was a waste of time as far as he was concerned ("Just a state of mind," he sang elsewhere). Implicit within the dreamlike setting of acoustic guitar, awash in ride cymbal, and colored with exotic backwards guitar lines was the all-but-explicit suggestion that one might find their liberation in a higher state of consciousness. It was the opening act of a thematic thread that ran through all of John's recent compositions.

"Love You To," George's next turn at center stage, amplified the latent exotica of the previous track. Within the driving rhythms and evocations of something at once ancient and cutting-edge, he delivered a reminder that time on Earth was finite ("A lifetime is so short / A new one can't be bought") and hectic. But instead of seconding John's advice to disengage, George's seems to be more along the lines of seizing the day. That said, he also threw in a warning that echoed Paul's implied point (in "Eleanor Rigby") that the traditional church had failed to bring serenity to the masses, not when "There's people standing 'round / Who'll screw you in the ground / "They'll fill you in / With all their sins / You'll see."

It should be observed here that there was a very deliberate plotting to the sequencing on the album. No two songs sharing the same sound appear back to back, as if to call out the collection's stylistic scope. Some observers have suggested that each track inspired its own subgenre in rock; this may be an exaggeration, but only a slight one. Mostly, *Revolver*'s diversity served as its own "concept."

Paul's "Here, There and Everywhere" followed George's raga workout; even though on the surface the two tracks bore no commonality, there too could be found the implication that constructs in which we wish to believe may not be as assured and everlasting as we want them to be. A perfectly satisfying romantic ballad—as fine as Paul would ever craft—it contains the implicit observation that though love seems eternal now, it may not be forever. "And *hoping* I'm always here" (emphasis added), he sings, as though aware that nothing is a sure thing, so he needs to reassure himself. There is also the suggestion that those in the throes of romance are isolated from the reality everyone else lives in; there is somebody speaking, but "she doesn't know he's there."

Nothing the Beatles ever recorded again (with the possible

For real.
Simon and Garfunkel have another hit.
"Fakin' It"

Where the authentic single action is. On COLUMBIA RECORDS

The literary qualities of Paul Simon's compositions drew attention from more academic and art-oriented reviewers, setting the table for the emerging class of rock critics that greeted **Sgt. Pepper's** *arrival in 1967.*

exception of "Octopus's Garden") was ever as purely escapist as "Yellow Submarine." While cloaked in the trappings of children's entertainment—a genre that plenty of serious rock artists dabbled in (or would in the future)—the song also offered something for idealists: a vision of an underwater utopia, populated by friends (and a band), taking those unwilling to accept the status quo off to a better world (one apparently free of any issues of claustrophobia).

There were many that thought the world of *Revolver*, but for this one song. While perhaps not to everyone's taste, it projected childlike innocence without being childish. It also bore the strengths common to every acclaimed Beatle recording: it was catchy, groundbreaking, a genuine group effort, and made creative use of the studio. "Yellow Submarine" pulled off what it set out to achieve and did it with style; it is by no means a misstep or an embarrassment.

The acid-drenched side closer, "She Said She Said," brought us directly back to mortality. As recounted elsewhere in this book, the showdown between actor Peter Fonda and John left the latter unsettled. But as a recording artist, he had the last word; his takeaway from the encounter was to reject the fear-mongering and darkness ("I know that I'm ready to leave") in favor of the life-affirming sunshine of childhood's ideal ("When I was a boy, everything was right").

That was driven home with the next track (requiring turning the record over in 1966, though not anymore), Paul's "Good Day Sunshine." In its way, the song takes John's sentiments in "Rain"

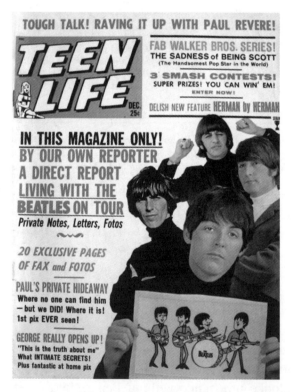

Paul was not really holding up a picture of the group's cartoon likeness as seen on this cover of Teen Life, *though if he had been, his expression would likely have been the same.*

and turns them on their head: in the latter song, people fall into the trap of letting external conditions—illusory ones, if you follow John's line of thought—determine one's outlook; but with Paul, his romantic idealism and sheer force of positive thinking *produce* the external conditions: "I'm in love, and it's a sunny day."

"And Your Bird Can Sing" amplified the anti-pretension bent of "She Said She Said." The person John is attempting to reach is full of himself, equating acquisition of material things and external experiences with the accumulation of insight and wisdom; these were attributes that John (assuming the first-person narrator is himself) already possessed. He "gets" it, and offers that, once his friend reaches an epiphany revealing the emptiness of his or her lifestyle, he'll be there for them.

Except for the first one, each "Paul" song on *Revolver* was, unsurprisingly, steeped in romanticism to this point in the album sequence. But "For No One" took the darkness of "Eleanor Rigby" and imposed it upon a romantic scenario, or more specifically, the end of a romantic relationship. The song's narrative was provided by someone operating outside of the world's reality: his partner had moved on from "a love that should have lasted years," leaving him at a loss to comprehend and accept the decision, much less where it had gone wrong. Indeed, as much as Eleanor, the narrator in this song also "lives in a dream."

Ten cuts in and apart from the novelty of "Yellow Submarine," the dark humor of "Taxman," and the gentle balladry of "Here, There and Everywhere," the majority of the material had been serious (or earnest) in tone. "Doctor Robert" was a chugging excursion into comic relief, asserting with great irony that all of one's emotional and psychological needs could be fulfilled through the wonders of science. The song echoed the sentiments of the Rolling Stones' "Mother's Little Helper," a track off of *Aftermath* from earlier that year which likewise pointed out that the so-called straights needed to be jacked up just as much as members of the counterculture in order to handle modern society. While not as explicit a death- or isolation-themed song as other *Revolver* tunes were, it does dovetail with the prevailing subtheme addressing the need for coping mechanisms.

George's "I Want to Tell You" expressed frustration with communication above the level of common discourse. His "head is filled with things to say"—something that comes with heightened consciousness—but the capacity for putting such nuanced thoughts into words is elusive. Again evoking the common thread of detachment running through the songs, he ultimately won't allow himself to be vexed by the situation indefinitely; if not in the subsequent life (". . . maybe next time around"), then eventually. After all, he has all of eternity for the problem to resolve itself, as he proclaims in the song's final line.

Even without knowing that "Got to Get You into My Life" was Paul's declaration of adoration for weed, one could easily read that there was more to it than a simple uptempo love song: "Another road where maybe I could see another kind of mind there." While asserting that the object of his ardor was a perfect fit, he cannot help but express a profound conflict—just as, in real life, Paul faced deep ambivalence toward joining the others in LSD experimentation: "If I'm true, I'll never leave, and if I do, I know the way there." He doesn't *think* he'll lose interest, but in case he does, he knows where his object can be found when he's ready to return.

If, as writer Chris Gregory postulated, "'Got To Get You Into My Life' hovers on the edge of the void, 'Tomorrow Never Knows' takes the plunge without any regrets." John's tour of what lay beyond the mortal coil assured listeners that despite the limitations of earthly being, corporal death was merely the end of the beginning. Relax, he told those that he would guide: "Turn off your mind." Existence was but a game (one prone to drag some down, as George had noted two tracks earlier) that led inevitably to a new start, thus fulfilling the "circle of life," as branded elsewhere. Thus was the circularity made plain over the course of a vehicle calling itself *Revolver*, as in "something that moves in a circular motion."

John's shamanic message would be refined over the next year, culminating with "I'd love to turn you on" (with "let me take you down" falling in between); though, despite what many were inclined to believe, viewed as a linear artistic development, what he seemed to want to turn listeners on to was not so much

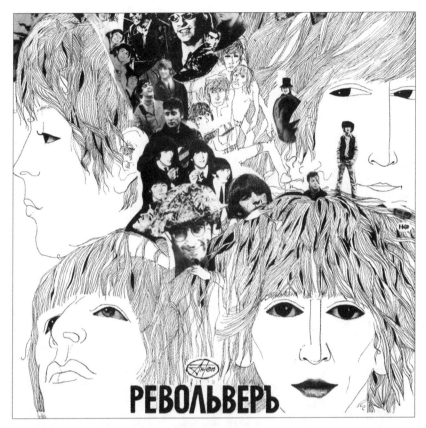

When issued officially in the former Soviet Union, Russian pressings of Revolver *featured an entirely different cover collage.*

psychedelics *per se*, but the revelation that material life is an illusion. The thread went back at least as far as "Rain," with a stop at Strawberry Fields along the way. George's artistic trajectory likewise meshed with what John was saying in these key songs; it is not surprising that the two Beatles that had shared an eventful evening together back in March 1965 would be the ones that embraced this perspective.

For the Beatles to have loaded up a pop album with such weighty content, albeit mostly between the lines, was strikingly singular for such a mainstream act still competing for chart success in 1966. Though not the first to experiment with LSD (or to share their conclusions), they did possess enough awareness of their influence not to be explicit with it. If they saw the experience as a shortcut to achieving a philosophical breakthrough, they were, after going public, at least careful to explain quite plainly that while the drug helped them gain insights, it wasn't a necessary component of achieving clarity, merely an accelerant.

Looking for themes and underlying concepts within an artist's work is always a highly subjective undertaking, especially when in the ensuing decades the creators of said work have never claimed either (beyond John's remark that "*Revolver* [was] the acid [album]"). George famously likened it to *Rubber Soul*, saying they "could be volume[s] one and two." In fact, the pair of albums are more like mirror images of each other. The first possessed a much more organic acoustic vibe, with the songs falling all well within established pop / rock genres. *Rubber Soul*'s advance was to consolidate their artistic strengths as studio craftsmen while advancing the maturity of their content. "Experimental" isn't a word that comes to mind when describing this album.

The second album had a conspicuous electronic feel and transcended all styles that came before it. Just as *Rubber Soul* marked John's coming into his own as a writer, *Revolver* marked Paul's. Also, as noted by the band themselves, the first record had been conceived and recorded under the mellowing influence of marijuana, resulting in more self-reflective lyrics than ever before. *Revolver*, a psychedelic experience altogether, took the inward exploration to a far deeper level, encompassing the subconscious as well as the conscious mind, and a connection with the world at large. The results were spread out over the course of entirely new pop paradigms and were, in a word, revolutionary.

Hobbled in America by the loss of three Lennon cuts; issued at a time when no one with a big megaphone could proclaim its greatness; coming just as the media were fixating on far less important issues; and marking such a major artistic leap forward that not everyone was prepared to hear it, the reception accorded *Revolver* was as underplayed as *Sgt. Pepper*'s was overblown. Would *Revolver* have become the album toward which every superlative was hurled had it been released under the same conditions that *Sgt. Pepper* was?

Without a doubt.

TIMELINE

1966

As a way to best illustrate the context of what was happening in the Beatles' world just before and after *Revolver* was created, here is a timeline depicting the events in their lives, as well as general developments in music.

JANUARY

Topping the U.S. charts this month:
"Sounds of Silence"—Simon & Garfunkel
"We Can Work It Out"—The Beatles

Albums released this month include:
Sophomore efforts from Them and the Spencer Davis Group

Singles released this month include:
"Michelle" by David and Jonathan (peaks at 18 in the U.S.)
"Michelle" by the Overlanders (peaks at 1 in the U.K.)
"Elusive Butterfly" by Bob Lind (peaks at 5 in the U.S. and U.K.)

Monday 3—"We Can Work It Out" and "Day Tripper" promos air in the U.S. on *Hullabaloo*
Wednesday 5—The Beatles rerecord elements of the Shea Stadium concert film at CTS Studio in London
Saturday 8—Final episode of *Shindig!* airs in the U.S., featuring the Kinks and the Who
Monday 10—"Woman," written by Paul under the pseudonym "Bernard Webb," is released by Peter and Gordon in the U.S., peaks at 14

Wednesday 12—*Batman* series debuts on U.S. TV

Monday 17—*Sounds of Silence* released by Simon & Garfunkel

Thursday 20—"Keep On Running" by Spencer Davis Group hits number 1 in the U.K.

Friday 21—George marries Pattie Boyd

FEBRUARY

Topping the U.S. charts this month:

"My Love"—Petula Clark

"Lightning Strikes"—Lou Christie

"These Boots Are Made for Walkin'"—Nancy Sinatra

Albums released this month include:

The Sonny Side of Cher by Cher

Doctor Zhivago score by Maurice Jarre

Singles released this month include:

"Daydream" by the Lovin' Spoonful (peaks at 2 in the U.S.)

"I Can't Let Go" by the Hollies (peaks at 2 in the U.K.)

"Listen People" by Herman's Hermits (peaks at 3 in the U.S.)

"Sha La La La Lee" by Small Faces (peaks at 3 in the U.K.)

"Hold Tight!" by Dave Dee, Dozy, Beaky, Mick & Tich
    (peaks at 4 in the U.K.)

"Homeward Bound" by Simon & Garfunkel
    (peaks at 5 in the U.S.)

"You Baby" by the Turtles (peaks at 20 in the U.S.)

Saturday 8—George and Pattie fly to Barbados for their honeymoon

Wednesday 12—"19th Nervous Breakdown" is released by the Rolling Stones, peaks at 2 in the U.S.

Friday 18—"It Won't Be Wrong" is released by the Byrds, does not chart in the U.S.

Monday 21—"Nowhere Man"/"What Goes On" is issued in the U.S., peaks at 3

Friday 25—George turns 23; he and Pattie return to London from Barbados

MARCH

Topping the U.S. charts this month:
  "Ballad of the Green Berets"—Sgt. Barry Sadler

Albums released this month include:
  What Now My Love by Herb Alpert & the Tijuana Brass
  If You Can Believe Your Eyes and Ears by the Mamas and
    the Papas
  Daydream by the Lovin' Spoonful
  The Fugs' self-titled debut

Singles released this month include:
  "Bang Bang (My Baby Shot Me Down)" by Cher
    (peaks at 2 in the U.S.)
  "A Groovy Kind of Love" by Wayne Fontana and the
    Mindbenders (peaks at 2 in the U.S. and U.K.)
  "Secret Agent Man" by Johnny Rivers (peaks at 3 in the U.S.)
  "Kicks" by Paul Revere & the Raiders (peaks at 4 in the U.S.)
  "Sure Gonna Miss Her" by Gary Lewis & the Playboys
    (peaks at 9 in the U.S.)
  "Shapes of Things" by the Yardbirds (peaks at 11 in the U.S.)
  "(I Can't Get No) Satisfaction" by Otis Redding
    (peaks at 31 in the U.S.)

March—Sometime this month, Brian Epstein flies to
Memphis to inquire about recording at Stax Studios
Tuesday 1—The Beatles at Shea Stadium film is broadcast on
TV in Britain.
Tuesday 1—"Frankie and Johnny" is released by Elvis Presley,
peaks at 25 in the U.S.
Wednesday 2—"Till the End of the Day" is released by
the Kinks, peaks at 50 in the U.S.
Friday 4—"Yesterday" EP is released in the U.K.
Friday 4—Maureen Cleave's profile of John published in
the *London Evening Standard*
Monday 7—"Caroline, No," credited to Brian Wilson, peaks
at 32 in the U.S.

Friday 11—Maureen Cleave's profile of Ringo published in the *London Evening Standard*

Monday 14—"Substitute" is released by the Who, peaks at 5 in the U.K.

Monday 14—"Eight Miles High" is released by the Byrds, peaks at 14 in the U.S.

Thursday 17—"The Sun Ain't Gonna Shine Anymore" by the Walker Brothers hits number 1 in the U.K.

Friday 18—Maureen Cleave's profile of George published in the *London Evening Standard*

Monday 21—"Sloop John B" is released by the Beach Boys, peaks at 3 in the U.S.

Tuesday 22—"Rainy Day Women #12 & 35" is released by Bob Dylan, peaks at 2 in the U.S.

Thursday 24—The Beatles and Brian Epstein attend the London premiere of *Alfie*, starring Jane Asher

Friday 25—Maureen Cleave's profile of Paul published in the *London Evening Standard*

Friday 25—Robert Whitaker stages the "butcher cover" session

Monday 28—George and Ringo go to see Roy Orbison at the Walthamstow Granada Cinema

Monday 28—The Good Rascals' self-titled debut album is released in the U.S.

Wednesday 30—*The Kink Kontroversy* is released in the U.S.

APRIL

Topping the U.S. charts this month:
"(You're My) Soul and Inspiration"—The Righteous Brothers
"Good Lovin'"—The Young Rascals

Albums released this month include:
The Seeds' self-titled debut
Love's self-titled debut
The Who's U.S. debut, *The Who Sings My Generation*

Singles released this month include:
"The Pied Piper" by Crispian St. Peters (peaks at 4 in the U.S.)

"It's a Man's Man's Man's World" by James Brown
(peaks at 8 in the U.S.)
"Leaning on the Lamp Post" by Herman's Hermits
(peaks at 9 in the U.S.)
"My Little Red Book" by Love (peaks at 52 in the U.S.)
"Solitary Man" by Neil Diamond (peaks at 55 in the U.S.)

Friday 1—John and Paul visit Indica Bookstore
Saturday 2—*Big Hits (High Tides and Green Grass)* released
by the Rolling Stones in the U.S.
Monday 4—"Red Rubber Ball" is released by the Cyrkle,
peaks at 2 in the U.S.
Tuesday 5—"Substitute" is released by the Who in the U.S.,
does not chart
Wednesday 6—*Revolver* sessions begin with work on "Mark I"
("Tomorrow Never Knows")
Thursday 7—Work begins on "Got to Get You into My Life"
Monday 11—Work begins on "Granny Smith" ("Love You To")
Tuesday 12—Jan Berry of the duo Jan and Dean is involved
in a near-fatal car accident
Wednesday 13—Work begins on "Paperback Writer"
Thursday 14—Work begins on "Rain"
Thursday 14—"Somebody Help Me" by the Spencer Davis
Group hits number 1 in the U.K.
Friday 15—*Aftermath* released by the Rolling Stones in the
U.K.
Sunday 17—Work begins on "Doctor Robert"
Monday 18—John and George go to see the Lovin' Spoonful
at the Marquee Club
Wednesday 20—Work begins on "And Your Bird Can Sing"
and "Taxman"
Wednesday 27—Work begins on "I'm Only Sleeping"
Wednesday 27—"Dedicated Follower of Fashion" is released
by the Kinks, peaks at 36 in the U.S.
Thursday 28—Work begins on "Eleanor Rigby"
Thursday 28—"You Don't Have to Say You Love Me"
by Dusty Springfield hits number 1 in the U.K.

Saturday 30—Folksinger Richard Fariña is killed in a motorcycle accident

MAY

Topping the U.S. charts this month:
"Monday Monday"—The Mamas and the Papas
"When a Man Loves a Woman"—Percy Sledge

Albums released this month include:
The Small Faces' self-titled debut

Singles released this month include:
"Did You Ever Have to Make Up Your Mind?" by the
Lovin' Spoonful (peaks at 2 in the U.S.)
"I Am a Rock" by Simon & Garfunkel (peaks at 3 in the U.S.)

Sunday 1—The Beatles perform in Britain for the last time at the *NME* Poll- Winners concert
Monday 2—Paul goes clubbing with the Rolling Stones and Bob Dylan
Tuesday 3—"Ain't Too Proud to Beg" is released by the Temptations, peaks at 13 in the U.S.
Wednesday 4—*Uptight (Everything's Alright)* is released by Stevie Wonder in the U.S.
Thursday 5—"Pretty Flamingo" by Manfred Mann hits number 1 in the U.K.
Monday 9—Work begins on "For No One"
Friday 13—"Paint It Black" is released by the Rolling Stones, peaks at 1 in the U.K.
Monday 16—*Pet Sounds* is released by the Beach Boys in the U.S.
Tuesday 17—John and Paul attend a *Pet Sounds* listening party hosted by Bruce Johnston at London's Waldorf Hotel
Tuesday 17—Bob Dylan is called "Judas!" at a concert in Manchester
Tuesday 17—Capitol execs approve the "butcher photo" for *"Yesterday" . . . and Today* LP cover

Thursday 19—The Beatles film the studio promos for "Paperback Writer" and "Rain"

Friday 20—The Beatles film the Chiswick House promos for "Paperback Writer" and "Rain"

Saturday 21—"Don't Bring Me Down" is released by the Animals, peaks at 12 in the U.S.

Thursday 26—Work begins on "Yellow Submarine"

Thursday 26—Members of the Rolling Stones attend Bob Dylan's Royal Albert Hall concert

Friday 27—John is filmed riding in a limo with Bob Dylan

Friday 27—John and George attend Bob Dylan's Royal Albert Hall concert

Monday 30—"Paperback Writer"/"Rain" is released in the U.S.

Monday 30—The Irish band Them, playing at L.A.'s Whisky A Go-Go, is joined onstage by warm-up act the Doors' singer Jim Morrison for an impromptu rendition of "Gloria"

JUNE

Topping the U.S. charts this month:
  "Paint It Black"—The Rolling Stones
  "Paperback Writer"—The Beatles

Albums released this month include:
  Freak Out! by the Mothers of Invention

Singles released this month include:
  "Sunny" by Bobby Hebb (peaks at 2 in the U.S.)
  "I Saw Her Again" by the Mamas and the Papas
    (peaks at 5 in the U.S.)
  "Bus Stop" by the Hollies (peaks at 5 in the U.S. and U.K.)
  "Along Comes Mary" by the Association
    (peaks at 7 in the U.S.)
  "Hideaway" by Dave Dee, Dozy, Beaky, Mick & Tich
    (peaks at 10 in the U.K.)
  "This Door Swings Both Ways" by Herman's Hermits
    (peaks at 12 in the U.S.)

"Over, Under, Sideways, Down" by the Yardbirds
(peaks at 13 in the U.S.)

Wednesday 1—The "party session" for "Yellow Submarine" is held

Wednesday 1—Following his London concert, attended by George and Pattie, Ravi Shankar is introduced to George at Peter Sellers's house

Thursday 2—Work begins on "Laxton's Superb" ("I Want to Tell You")

Saturday 4—Michelle Phillips is fired from the Mamas and the Papas

Sunday 5—The "Paperback Writer" and "Rain" promos are shown on *The Ed Sullivan Show* in the U.S.

Monday 6—Claudette Orbison, Roy's wife, is killed in a motorcycle accident

Wednesday 8—Work begins on "Good Day Sunshine"

Thursday 9—The "Paperback Writer" and "Rain" promos are shown on *Top of the Pops* in the U.K.

Friday 10—"Paperback Writer"/"Rain" is released in the U.K.

Friday 10—The decision is made by Capitol to recall the "butcher cover"

Friday 10—"I Want You" is released by Bob Dylan, peaks at 20 in the U.S.

Saturday / Sunday 11–12—"Operation Retrieve" put into effect by Capitol

Sunday 12—John and Paul visit the Mamas and the Papas, who are touring England

Monday 13—"5 D (Fifth Dimension)" is released by the Byrds, peaks at 44 in the U.S.

Tuesday 14—Work begins on "Here, There and Everywhere"

Wednesday 15—The official release date of *"Yesterday" . . . and Today*

Thursday 16—The Beatles appear on *Top of the Pops*

Saturday 18—Paul turns 24

Monday 20—*"Yesterday" . . . and Today* hits stores in the U.S. with a new cover

Tuesday 21—"She Said She Said" recorded; Paul walks out of the session

Wednesday 22—Mixing session ends work on *Revolver*

Thursday 23—The Beatles fly to Munich

Friday 24—George Martin marries Judy Lockhart Smith

Friday 24—The Beatles perform at Circus-Krone-Bau in Munich

Friday 24—The Rolling Stones give a news conference aboard a boat in New York, where they're photographed by Linda Eastman

Saturday 25—The Beatles perform at Grugahalle in Essen

Sunday 26—The Beatles perform at Ernst Merck Hall in Hamburg

Monday 27—*Blonde on Blonde* is released by Bob Dylan in the U.S.

Tuesday 28—The Beatles arrive in Tokyo

Thursday 30—The Beatles perform their first concert at Budokan

JULY

Topping the U.S. charts this month:
   "Strangers in the Night"—Frank Sinatra
   "Paperback Writer"—The Beatles
   "Hanky Panky"—Tommy James and the Shondells

Albums released this month include:
   Blues Breakers with Eric Clapton by John Mayall

Singles released this month include:
   "See You in September" by the Happenings
      (peaks at 3 in the U.S.)
   "Black Is Black" by Los Bravos (peaks at 4 in the U.S.)
   "Walk Away Renée" by the Left Banke (peaks at 5 in the U.S.)
   "Psychotic Reaction" by the Count Five
      (peaks at 5 in the U.S.)
   "Land of 1,000 Dances" by Wilson Pickett
      (peaks at 6 in the U.S.)
   "Guantanamera" by the Sandpipers (peaks at 9 in the U.S.)
   "7 and 7 Is" by Love (peaks at 33 in the U.S.)

Friday 1—The Beatles perform their second concert at Budokan

Friday 1—"The Kids Are Alright" released by the Who, does not chart in the U.S.

Saturday 2—The Beatles perform their third and final concert at Budokan

Saturday 2—*Aftermath* is released by the Rolling Stones in the U.S.

Saturday 2—"Mother's Little Helper" is released by the Rolling Stones, peaks at 8 in the U.S.

Monday 4—The Beatles perform at Ritz Memorial Football Stadium in Manila

Tuesday 5—The Beatles and their entourage are roughed up while departing the Philippines

Wednesday 6—The Beatles arrive in New Delhi in the early-morning hours

Thursday 7—Ringo turns 26

Thursday 7—After a day of sightseeing and shopping in India, the Beatles fly back to London overnight

Friday 8—"Nowhere Man" EP released in the U.K.

Monday 11—"Wouldn't It Be Nice" is released by the Beach Boys, peaks at 8 in the U.S.

Wednesday 13—"Sunny Afternoon" released by the Kinks, peaks at 14 in the U.S.

Friday 15—The Beatles' visit to Japan is profiled in *Life* magazine

Friday 15—Klaus Voormann, under contract to NEMS as a member of Paddy, Klaus & Gibson, is released by Brian so that he can join Manfred Mann

Friday 15—The Yardbirds' self-titled album (a/k/a *Roger the Engineer*) is released in the U.K.

Monday 18—*Fifth Dimension* is released by the Byrds in the U.S.

Monday 18—Bobby Fuller, 23, is found dead in Los Angeles under mysterious circumstances

Thursday 22—"Getaway" by Georgie Fame hits number 1 in the U.K.

Saturday 23—The Cavern reopens in Liverpool under new ownership; the Beatles do not attend

Thursday 28—"Out of Time" by Chris Farlowe, written by Jagger–Richards, hits number 1 in the U.K.

Friday 29—Bob Dylan is severely injured in a motorcycle accident

Friday 29—*Datebook* republishes the Maureen Cleave interviews with John and Paul

AUGUST

Topping the U.S. charts this month:
"Wild Thing"—The Troggs
"Summer in the City"—The Lovin' Spoonful

Singles released this month include:
"Turn-Down Day" by the Cyrkle (peaks at 16 in the U.S.)
"I Can't Turn You Loose" by Otis Redding
 (peaks at 33 in the U.K.)

Thursday 4—"With a Girl Like You" by the Troggs hits number 1 in the U.K.

Friday 5—*Revolver* and "Yellow Submarine"/"Eleanor Rigby" released in the U.K.

Friday 5—Brian Epstein holds a news conference in New York defending John's Christianity remarks

Monday 8—*Revolver* and "Yellow Submarine"/"Eleanor Rigby" released in the U.S.

Monday 8—Brian Wilson visits the Rolling Stones in the studio in Los Angeles

Thursday 11—The Beatles arrive in Boston to begin their U.S. tour, fly on to Chicago

Friday 12—The Beatles perform at the International Amphitheatre in Chicago

Friday 12—"The Kids Are Alright" issued by the Who, peaks at 41 in the U.K.

Saturday 13—The Beatles perform at Olympia Stadium in Detroit

Saturday 13—A Beatles bonfire protesting John's Christianity remarks sponsored by radio station KLUE is held in Longview, Texas

Sunday 14—The Beatles perform at Municipal Stadium in Cleveland

Sunday 14—Longview, Texas, radio station KLUE is knocked off the air by a bolt of lightning

Monday 15—The Beatles perform at Washington Stadium in Washington, D.C.

Tuesday 16—The Beatles perform at Philadelphia Stadium in Philadelphia

Wednesday 17—The Beatles perform at Maple Leaf Gardens in Toronto

Thursday 18—The Beatles perform at Suffolk Downs Racecourse in Boston

Thursday 18—"Just Like a Woman" is released by Bob Dylan, peaks at 33 in the U.S.

Friday 19—The Beatles perform at Mid-South Coliseum in Memphis

Friday 19—During the evening show, a cherry bomb explodes during the Beatles' performance of "If I Needed Someone"

Saturday 20—The Beatles' Crosley Field concert canceled due to heavy rain

Sunday 21—The Beatles perform at Crosley Field in Cincinnati in the afternoon, then fly to St. Louis to perform at Busch Stadium in the evening

Tuesday 23—The Beatles tour resumes with a concert at Shea Stadium in New York

Wednesday 24—The Beatles perform their final Shea Stadium concert

Thursday 25—The Beatles perform at the Coliseum in Seattle

Friday 26—"I'm a Boy" released by the Who, peaks at 2 in the U.K.

Saturday 27—The Beatles are featured on the cover of the *Saturday Evening Post*

Sunday 28—The Beatles tour resumes with a concert at Dodger Stadium in Los Angeles

Monday 29—The Beatles perform their last concert, at Candlestick Park in San Francisco

SEPTEMBER

Topping the U.S. charts this month:

"Sunshine Superman"—Donovan

"You Can't Hurry Love"—The Supremes

Albums released this month include:

The Mamas and the Papas' self-titled second album

Sunshine Superman by Donovan

Singles released this month include:

"Bend It" by Dave Dee, Dozy, Beaky, Mick & Tich
(peaks at 2 in the U.K.)

"Dandy" by Herman's Hermits (peaks at 5 in the U.S.)

"If I Were a Carpenter" by Bobby Darin (peaks at 8 in the U.S.)

"See See Rider" by Eric Burdon and the Animals
(peaks at 10 in the U.S.)

"The Dangling Conversation" by Simon & Garfunkel
(peaks at 30 in the U.S.)

"River Deep—Mountain High" by Ike and Tina Turner
(peaks at 88 in the U.S.)

Monday 5—John flies to West Germany to begin work on
How I Won the War

Tuesday 6—"Mr. Spaceman" released by the Byrds,
peaks at 36 in the U.S.

Monday 12—*The Monkees* premieres in the U.S.

Tuesday 13—"Spinout" is released by Elvis Presley,
peaks at 40 in the U.S.

Wednesday 14—George and Pattie fly to India

Thursday 15—Jefferson Airplane's debut album, *Takes Off*,
is released

Thursday 15—"All or Nothing" by Small Faces hits number
1 in the U.K.

Friday 16—John takes a break from filming and joins Paul
and Brian Epstein in Paris

Sunday 18—John arrives in Almeria, Spain, to resume work on the film

Monday 19—Brian celebrates what will be his last birthday, turning 32

Saturday 24—"Have You Seen Your Mother, Baby, Standing in the Shadow?" is released by the Rolling Stones, peaks at 9 in the U.S.

Saturday 24—"Lady Godiva" is released by Peter and Gordon, peaks at 6 in the U.S.

Monday 26—Brian Epstein is hospitalized for a drug overdose

OCTOBER

Topping the U.S. charts this month:
"Cherish"—The Association
"Reach Out I'll Be There"—Four Tops
"96 Tears"—? and the Mysterians

Albums released this month include:
The Feel of Neil Diamond, his debut release

Singles released this month include:
"Devil with a Blue Dress / Good Golly Miss Molly" by Mitch Ryder (peaks at 4 in the U.S.)
"Stop! Stop! Stop!" by the Hollies (peaks at 7 in the U.S.)
"No Milk Today" by Herman's Hermits (peaks at 7 in the U.K.)
"Gimme Some Lovin'" by the Spencer Davis Group (peaks at 7 in the U.S.)
"Rain on the Roof" by the Lovin' Spoonful (peaks at 10 in the U.S.)
"Happenings Ten Years Time Ago" by the Yardbirds (peaks at 30 in the U.S.)
"Wrapping Paper," Cream's debut single (peaks at 34 in the U.K.)
"I Can Hear Music" by the Ronettes (peaks at 100 in the U.S.)

Wednesday 5—Ringo, Maureen, and Cynthia arrive in
Almeria, Spain to visit with John in time for his birthday
Friday 7—Johnny Kidd is killed in a car accident
Sunday 9—John turns 26
Sunday 9—The Rolling Stones perform in Southampton;
it is their last U.K. concert for four years
Monday 10—The Monkees' self-titled debut album is released
Monday 10—*Parsley, Sage, Rosemary and Thyme* is released by
Simon & Garfunkel
Monday 10—"Good Vibrations" is released by the Beach Boys
in the U.S.
Saturday 15—*Complete & Unbelievable: The Otis Redding Dictionary
of Soul* is released
Saturday 22—George and Pattie arrive home in London
Monday 24—Lucille Ball stars with the Dave Clark 5 in
the *Lucy in London* TV special
Monday 24—"Mellow Yellow" is released by Donovan,
peaks at 2 in the U.S.
Wednesday 26—Alma Cogan dies of cancer at 34
Friday 28—*Face to Face* is released by the Kinks in the U.K.
Monday 31—Donovan arrives at Kinfauns, George's Esher
home, and spends the week

NOVEMBER

Topping the U.S. charts this month:
"Last Train to Clarksville"—The Monkees
"Poor Side of Town"—Johnny Rivers
"You Keep Me Hangin' On"—The Supremes

Albums released this month include:
Hums of the Lovin' Spoonful
The Psychedelic Sounds of the 13th Floor Elevators, the band's
debut album

Singles released this month include:
"Words of Love" by the Mamas and the Papas
(peaks at 5 in the U.S.)

"A Hazy Shade of Winter" by Simon & Garfunkel
(peaks at 13 in the U.S.)
"It Takes Two" by Marvin Gaye and Kim Weston
(peaks at 14 in the U.S.)

November—Sometime this month, Paul takes LSD for the first time with Tara Browne

Sunday 6—Paul flies to France for an extended road trip

Monday 7—John arrives home in London after completing filming in Spain

Wednesday 9—John Lennon meets Yoko Ono at Indica Gallery

Wednesday 9—Paul is killed in a car accident (according to fictitious reports years later)

Friday 11—The Who's *Ready Steady Who* EP is released in the U.K.

Saturday 12—Paul meets up with Mal Evans in Bordeaux, afterwards traveling to Spain and Rome; from there, they fly to Nairobi, where Jane Asher joins them

Sunday 13—A report in the *Sunday Telegraph* claims that two of the Beatles have approached Rolling Stones manager Allen Klein to discuss a deal

Tuesday 15—Brian Epstein issues a statement denying that the Beatles have split up

Saturday 19—Paul arrives home in London after his trip to Africa; on the flight, he comes up with the *Sgt. Pepper* idea

Thursday 24—The Beatles reconvene at EMI and begin work on "Strawberry Fields Forever"

Friday 25—The Beatles record their 1966 holiday message, *Pantomime: Everywhere It's Christmas*

Sunday 27—John films a cameo for *Not Only . . . But Also*

Monday 28—*George Martin Instrumentally Salutes the Beatle Girls* album is released in the U.S.

Wednesday 30—"Dead End Street" is released by the Kinks, peaks at 73 in the U.S.

DECEMBER

Topping the U.S. charts this month:

"Winchester Cathedral"—The New Vaudeville Band

"Good Vibrations"—Beach Boys

"I'm a Believer"—The Monkees

Albums released this month include:

Tim Buckley's self-titled debut album

Spirit of '67 by Paul Revere & the Raiders

Singles released this month include:

"Hey Joe," the debut single of the Jimi Hendrix Experience
(peaks at 6 in the U.K.)

Thursday 1—Paul goes to see the Young Rascals at Scotch
of St. James

Thursday 1—"Green, Green Grass of Home" by Tom Jones
hits number 1 in the U.K.

Monday 5—Buffalo Springfield's self-titled debut album is
released in the U.S.

Tuesday 6—Work begins on "When I'm Sixty-Four"

Friday 9—*A Collection of Beatles Oldies (But Goldies!)* is released
in the U.K.

Friday 9—Cream's debut album, *Fresh Cream*, is released
in the U.K.

Friday 9—The Who's second album, *A Quick One*, is released
in the U.K.

Friday 9—"Happy Jack" is released by the Who, peaks at 3
in the U.K.

Saturday 10—*Got Live If You Want It!* is released by the Rolling
Stones in the U.S.

Tuesday 13—John appears on the cover of *Look* magazine

Thursday 15—"Knight in Rusty Armor" is released by Peter
and Gordon, peaks at 15 in the U.S.

Friday 16—The Beatles' fourth annual Christmas message
is sent to fan club members

Sunday 18—Tara Browne killed in a car accident; a photo
of the scene appears in the next day's newspapers

Sunday 18—Paul and Jane Asher attend the London premiere of *The Family Way*

Friday 23—Paul's "Love in the Open Air" from *The Family Way* is released in the U.K.

Monday 26—John's cameo in *Not Only . . . But Also* is televised

Thursday 29—Work on "Penny Lane" begins

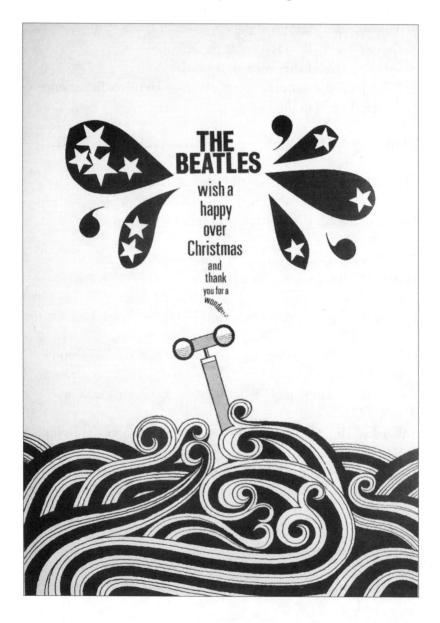

ACKNOWLEDGMENTS

Numerous folks were responsible for putting this project into motion or assisting along the way—wittingly or unwittingly. Then too were there people that influenced the book's trajectory—always a great help.

Thanks to Mike Edison at Backbeat for bringing it up in the first place, and—along with so many others—possessing the patience that enabled me to get it done. Also to the Hal Leonard crew: John Cerullo, Wes Seeley, Jaime Nelson, Joe Mareno, Bernadette Malavarca, Ross Plotkin, and the sales / marketing staff.

Numerous friends across the airwaves are also deeply appreciated. They are (in no particular order): Icon Fetch, Chachi Loprete, Casey Piotrowski, Howie Edelson, Mike Sweeney in the U.K., Fred Lindgren, Steve Sanders, Dennis Mitchell, Joe Johnson; and, of course, the local talent: Terri Hemmert, Nick Digilio, and Dan Sugrue, plus Mitch Michaels and Bart Shore. Rock on, Bob Stroud and Dick Biondi. Also, the guys at the Fab Fourum: Mitch Axelrod, Rob Leonard, Ken Michaels, Tony Traguardo.

Tom Repetny is a true master of all media—thanks for everything, as always. Also to Pete Pecoraro—music guru extraordinaire—and Jill Rodriguez, for getting the library ball rolling.

Image assistance came from Garry Day in the U.K. for *Beatles '66* as well as Pete Nash at *www.britishbeatlesfanclub.co.uk* (for the sheet music to "Got to Get You into My Life"). *Teen Life* courtesy of Guy Barbier of Ontario. Thanks also to Robert Brundish and to Heritage Auctions.

Lots of friends to thank, including Nancy Andrews, Belmo, Kris Engelhardt, Bill King and Beatlefan, Carol Lapidos, Mark Lapidos, GiGi and Clar Monaco, John Niems, Susan Ratisher Ryan, Woody Lifton, Stu Shea, Mark Caro, Keith James, Roger Stormo, Paula Brochu, and Allan Kozzin. Also: Doug Brooks for making it all possible.

A *great* big thanks to all my Facebook friends and visitors known and unknown—do visit *www.revolverbook.com* or *www.fabfourfaq2.com* to get hooked up.

I am indebted to my dear friends that answered the call: Blaine Bowman, Kim Kupisch Brondyke, Richard Buskin, Tom Frangione, Paul Griggs, Sarah Mourad, Kit O'Toole, Terry Ott, Tony Peters, Mike Sekulich, and Al Sussman.

Last, the loved ones: all of you Rodriguezes and Holcombs et al know who you are (and if you don't, see my previous titles). Zane and Zoe: I'm so proud to know that you are mine. Kati: if you're beside me, I know I need never care.

SELECTED BIBLIOGRAPHY

BOOKS

Babiuk, Andy. *Beatles Gear*. San Francisco: Backbeat Books, 2002.

Badman, Keith. *The Beatles Off the Record*. London: Omnibus, 2000.

The Beatles. *The Beatles Anthology*. New York: Chronicle Books, 2000.

Brackett, David. *The Pop, Rock, and Soul Reader*. New York: Oxford University Press, 2005.

Bramwell, Tony, and Rosemary Kingsland. *Magical Mystery Tours*. New York: Thomas Dunne Books, 2006.

Boyd, Pattie, and Penny Junor. *Wonderful Today: The Autobiography of Pattie Boyd*. London: Headline Review, 2007.

Carlin, Peter Ames. *Catch a Wave: The Rise, Fall & Redemption of the Beach Boys' Brian Wilson*. Emmaus, PA: Rodale, 2006.

Emerick, Geoff and Howard Massey. *Here, There and Everywhere: My Life Recording the Music of the Beatles*. New York: Gotham, 2006.

Gilmore, Mikal. *Stories Done: Writings on the 1960s and Its Discontents*. New York: Free Press, 2008.

Gould, Jonathan. *Can't Buy Me Love: The Beatles, Britain, and America*. New York: Harmony Books, 2007.

Granata, Charles L. *Wouldn't It Be Nice: Brian Wilson and the Making of Pet Sounds*. Chicago: A Cappella Books, 2003.

Harrison, George. *I, Me, Mine*. New York: Chronicle Books, 2007.

Hertsgaard, Mark. *A Day in the Life: The Music and Artistry of the Beatles*. Peaslake, Surrey, England: Delta Publishing, 1996.

Kozinn, Allan. *The Beatles* (20th Century Composers series). London: Phaidon Press Limited, 1995.

Lewisohn, Mark. *The Complete Beatles Recording Sessions*. London: EMI Records, 2006.

MacDonald, Ian. *Revolution in the Head*. London: Pimlico, 2005.

Marcus, Greil. *Bob Dylan by Greil Marcus: Writings 1968–2010*. New York: PublicAffairs, 2010.

Martin, George and Jeremy Hornsby. *All You Need Is Ears*. New York: St. Martin's Griffin, 1994.

McCartney, Paul, with Barry Miles. *Many Years from Now*. New York: Owl Books, 1998.

Riley, Tim. *Tell Me Why*. Cambridge, MA: Da Capo Press, 2002.

Sandercombe, W. Fraser. *The Beatles: The Press Reports*. Burlington, Ontario, Canada: Collector's Guide Publishing, 2007.

Sandford, Christopher. *McCartney*. New York: Carroll & Graf, 2006.

Sheff, David. *All We Are Saying*. London: Pan MacMillan, 2001.

Shotton, Pete, with Nicholas Schaffner. *John Lennon: In My Life*. New York: Stein & Day, 1987.

Spizer, Bruce. *The Beatles on Capitol Records (Parts 1 and 2)*. New Orleans, LA: 498 Productions, 2000.

Spitz, Bob. *Yeah! Yeah! Yeah!: The Beatles, Beatlemania, and the Music That Changed the World*. New York: Little, Brown and Company, 2007.

Stark, Steven D. *Meet the Beatles: A Cultural History of the Band That Shook Youth, Gender, and the World*. New York: Harper Collins, 2005.

Turner, Steve. *A Hard Day's Write*. New York: Carlton, 1994.

———. *The Gospel According to the Beatles*. Louisville: Westminster John Knox Press, 2006.

Unterberger, Richie. *The Unreleased Beatles*. San Francisco: Backbeat Books, 2006.

Wenner, Jann. *Lennon Remembers*. New York: W. W. Norton, 2001.

Whitaker, Robert. *The Unseen Beatles*. San Francisco: Collins Publishers, 1991.

Womack, Kenneth. *The Cambridge Companion to the Beatles*. Cambridge: Cambridge University Press, 2009.

MAGAZINES

The periodicals, vintage and contemporary, depicted in this book were all reviewed for their contemporaneous reporting. Here they are in list form:

Acoustic Guitar
Billboard (1965–1967)
Crawdaddy (1967)
Goldmine
Datebook (1966)
Disc and Record Review (1965–1967)
International Times
Melody Maker (1969–1980)
Mojo (July 2006)
New Musical Express (1966–1967)
New York Times
Playboy
Village Voice

WEBSITES

Far too many to list, but to suggest a great one-stop:
www.beatlesbible.com

Be sure to visit *www.revolverbook.com* for links and news.
Look for *Fab Four FAQ 2.0* on Facebook!

INDEX